DEATH RIDE AT EUCLID BEACH

Also by John Stark Bellamy II:

The Killer in the Attic
The Corpse in the Cellar
The Maniac in the Bushes
They Died Crawling

DEATH RIDE AT EUCLID BEACH

And More True Tales of Crime and Disaster from Cleveland's Past

John Stark Bellamy II

GRAY & COMPANY, PUBLISHERS
CLEVELAND

Chapter 17 was originally published in the Spring and
Summer 2003 issues of the Cleveland Police Historical
Society Hot Sheet.

Chapters 18 and 20 are adapted from the author's Internet-only publication By The Neck Until Dead: A History
of Hangings in Cuyahoga County (http://web.ulib.csu-
ohio.edu/speccoll/bellamy).

Gray & Company, Publishers
1588 E. 40th St.
Cleveland, OH 44103
(216) 431-2665

Library of Congress Cataloging-in-Publication Data
Bellamy, John Stark.
Death ride at Euclid Beach / by John Stark Bellamy II.
p. cm.
ISBN 1-886228-85-X
1. Crime--Ohio--Cleveland--History--Case studies.
2. Disasters--Ohio--Cleveland--History--Case studies.
3. Cleveland (Ohio)--History. I. Title.
HV6795.C5B444 2004
364.1'09771'32--dc22

This book is the fifth volume in a series of books on the
Cleveland of yesteryear. Narrative slide shows chroni-
cling some of the chapters are available for a fee, and
additional slideshows are under development. For
more information or bookings, contact John Stark Bellamy II via e-mail (jstarkbII@aol.com) or by mail via
the publisher of this book.

ISBN 1-886228-85-X

Printed in the United States of America

10 9 8 7 6 5 4 3 2

With all my heart to the love of my life,
Laura Ann Serafin

CONTENTS

Preface ix

1 **"He's Got a Gun!"**
   The Tina LaMont Story (1956) 3

2 **The Lion Sleeps (Forever) Tonight**
   Death at Public Hall (1934) 13

3 **Blind Murder**
   The Killing of Thomas Martin (1907) 17

4 **Seduced and Abandoned**
   Jennie, a Girl of the Cleveland Streets (1871) 21

5 **Death on the Hoof**
   The Cleveland Stockyards Fire (1944) 35

6 **Death on Derbyshire**
   The Newcomb Murder-Suicide (1934) 43

7 **The Vanishing Coed**
   The Disappearance of Ruth Baumgardner (1937) 49

8 **The Black Silk Handkerchief**
   The Murder of John Shipp (1900) 55

9 **The Man Who Led Two Lives**
   The Lawrence Bader Story (1957) 81

10 **Manhattan Beach Melee**
   The Bostock Animal Riots (1902) 89

11 **Death Ride at Euclid Beach**
   The Sad Fate of Joseph Senk (1943) 93

12 **Fractious Friday the Thirteenth**
   The Communist Relief Riots (1934) 97

13 **"She Made Me Sore . . ."**
   The Ida Deli Murder (1920) 111

CONTENTS, *continued*

14 **The Boy with Hitler's Face**
The John May Warren Photo Hoax (1938) 115

15 **Behind Every Successful Man**
The Glengary "Blue Book" Killing (1930) 117

16 **Alcohol to Burn**
The Russo Wine Company Fire (1948) 133

17 **"A Wretched Outcast From Society"**
The Murder of John Osborne (1853) 135

18 **"A Swing for a Swing"**
Slaughter on Cedar Avenue (1871) 145

19 **"I've Murdered My Mother!"**
The Krause Tragedy (1901) 159

20 **Bloody Doings at Olmsted**
The Lonesome Death of Rosa Colvin (1866) 165

21 **Don't Play Doctor**
Frenchy Balanescu's Little Love Pills (1926) 177

22 **Death of a Detective**
The Killing of William Foulks (1900) 197

23 **A Second Shot at Life**
The Gothic Tale of Eula Dortch (1965) 211

24 **"A Living Tomb"**
Ellen Hunt's Crusade (1897–1935) 223

25 **Black Monday at Garfield**
The Beverly Jarosz Tragedy (1964) 231

26 **"Straighten Them Out"**
The Celia Barger Horror (1953) 245

Photo Credits 265

PREFACE

Mother of mercy! Is this the end . . . of Forest City woe? Can it be that, after 10 years and some five score tales scoured from the depths of Forest City dismalia, I am finished with my annals of Northeast Ohio misery? Well . . . yes and no. When I first thought of writing about the dark side of Cleveland, I never dreamed that the project would so thoroughly overwhelm my life. Over the last decade I have explored literally thousands of dreadful events in Cleveland history and encountered some of the most terrible personalities ever known to these parts. During that same period of time, I have distilled the best (or perhaps the worst) of such happenings into five published books, one electronic volume, 15 slideshows, and a score of trolley tours of Cleveland murder and disaster sites.

It's all been tremendous and macabre fun, and I have enjoyed every second of it. But a number of factors now compel me to bring these narratives to at least a temporary close. Sometime in the near future, perhaps even before these words are published, I will be relocating to Vermont. Notwithstanding my intense feelings about Cleveland, I have long cherished the dream of retiring to the Green Mountain State's bucolic, montane pleasures, and I am fortunate in being able to do so, it is hoped, well before senescence overtakes me. But Cleveland is Cleveland and Vermont is Vermont, and it would be foolish for me to pretend that I could effectively pursue these Cleveland chronicles while living in New England. The first commandment of writing is to write about what you know—and I will know increasingly less with every day I am removed from Cleveland.

The other reason is simply lack of suitable material for more volumes of Cleveland woe. All murders and disasters are not created equal, and if I just kept recycling Cleveland murders and mishaps from the 1800s and 1900s (my index of same runs to over 1,000 pages), I would eventually be reduced to narrating mundane domestic killings, common grease fires, and unremarkable auto fatalities. Moreover, I'm not comfortable writing about tragic events still raw in the memories of those who lived through them. There are many amazing stories yet untold from Cleveland's 1960s, 1970s, and 1980s—and it will somebody else's job to tell them. I finally got around to the Beverly Jarosz murder in this book—40 years after it occurred—and that seems like a good place to stop, at least for now. I don't know what I am going to be writing about 10 or 20 years from now, but, God willing, I do intend to be writing, and I have learned to never say never when predicting the content or timing of future books. In any case, I can promise my readers that my first post-Cleveland volume will be a terrific murder story, and that it will contain many of the facets of my Cleveland tales: violence, sex, depraved evildoers, reversals of fortune, and a slam-bang surprise ending.

One of the greatest pleasures of writing is the opportunity to thank all those who have aided me in my literary ventures. As always, I owe incalculable debts to George Condon and Peter Jedick. I would never have dared to become a Cleveland storyteller without the challenging models of Condon's unsurpassed Cleveland volumes. And I would never have had the guts to try free-lance writing and slideshow presentation without the brave example of Peter's work. I also owe research debts to Faith Corrigan, Fred McGunagle, Doris O'Donnell, and Tom Barensfeld—tireless reporters all—who have aided me generously in my unholy pursuits. Not to mention the illustrious dead: stellar reporters like Howard Beaufait, Robert Larkin, and Bus Bergen, terrific storytellers all, whose columns still shock, entertain, and awe even these many decades afterwards.

More specific debts that are particular to the present book and its contents include: William Barrow and his terrific staff over at the Cleveland State University Library Special Collections (thank God Joseph Cole donated the *Cleveland Press* morgue to them); Dr. Judith Cetina and the staff at the Cuyahoga County Archives; David Holcombe and his staff at the Cleveland Police Historical Museum; the staff of the Cleveland Public Library Photograph Collection; and Dennis Dooley of *Northern Ohio Live*. I would also like to thank Sherrill Paul and her terrific drivers—especially Agnes—over at Lolly the Trolley. They have rendered my adventures as a murder 'n' disaster tour guide pleasant and easy without fail.

I should mention here the even more intangible but distinct obligations owed to my fellow staff members at the Cuyahoga County Public Library. Over many years, they have labored unsuccessfully to keep me humble, and their tragically futile quest should be recognized. They include: Holly Schaefer, Vicki Richards, Pamela DeFino, Avril McInally, David Soltesz, Mary Ann Shipman, Sara Lindberg, Christy Igo, Roberta Tyna, Laurie Evanko, Karen Rabatin, Dan Jezior, Clara Ballado, Christy Wiggins, Mary Ryan, Abbey O'Neill, Karen Kraus, Marty Essen, Rebecca Groves, Jennifer Gerrity, Judy Vanke, Dave McInally, Nancy Pazelt, Catherine Monnin, and Nick Cronin. And thanks, always, to Mary Erbs, uncrowned Empress of the Fairview Park Library's Children's Room. A special thank-you is also due to Joan Patrici ("Joanie the Cop"), best of sisters-in-law, to whom chapters 8, 17, and 22 are dedicated.

It only remains for me to thank my greatest sources of strength and inspiration. My mother, former Hearst reporter Jean Dessel Bellamy, did not live to see this book, but it and its companion volumes would never have happened without her unfailing love and support. And this book is dedicated to Laura: wife, lover, friend, companion, and loving critic.

DEATH RIDE AT EUCLID BEACH

Chapter 1

"HE'S GOT A GUN!"

The Tina LaMont Story (1956)

Heroes just happen; they are not born or made. Prolonged study of Cleveland murders and disasters has convinced me of at least that: there is simply no knowing who will become a hero. A building catches on fire. One man, to the horror of his friends and even himself, stomps over his own grandmother in his panic to flee; another risks his own life to save others, almost as if he had been rehearsing for such an act all of his life. There's no predicting it: all you can be sure of is that heroes and heroines will arrive in the most improbable places, at the most unlikely times, and with the most unpredictable personalities. Consider, for example, the case of Tina LaMont.

We don't know much about Tina LaMont. Yes, she was a dancer, and she danced at the kind of establishment that "decent" middle-class folk of the 1950s didn't have much respect for. We know she was 32 years old, probably a little old for her line of work, and divorced. (That, too, meant something in the 1950s that it doesn't mean now.) We know that her real name was Mrs. Dorothy Kochs, she lived at 1644 Ansel Road—not exactly a fancy address, then or now—and that she had a little girl, Jody, three years old. We also know she did a very brave thing for which she paid a terrible price.

About Richard Peter Storino, the villain of this story, we know much more. Twenty-nine years old in 1956, he had a shabby resume befitting the nasty little punk he was. He was born in 1927 in Watertown, New York. He and his two sisters had lost their father when he was five and their mother when he was 11. Richard started filling police blotters and reform school registers when he was 10, mostly on charges of auto theft and larceny, and offenses linked to or aggravated by his precocious and prodigious drinking problem.

The Gay 90s nightclub, 1024 Walnut Ave., from
The Plain Dealer.

After stints in various reformatories and prisons, in 1951 he went
to Elyria, where a relative lived. He worked there for almost five
years as a machinist before coming to Cleveland on August 5,
1955. Living at the Hawley House Hotel at West 3rd and St. Clair
Avenue, he worked for several months as a night manager at the
Kamm's Corner Royal Castle Restaurant, quitting just before
Christmas. He then took a job at J. & J. Wholesale Jewelers in the
Scofield Building.

Ignorant of his past, the manager at the Hawley House thought
that the small-statured, quiet Richard was a desirable tenant. His
older sister Shirley, who tried to look out for him, hoped that
Richard might finally be reforming his wayward life. Indeed, in the
second week of January 1956, she said to him, "Aren't you glad that
you've straightened out?" "Yes," he replied, "but it cost me a lot to
change." Richard Storino had not straightened out, nor had he

changed. At about 8:30 on the evening of January 18, 1956, Richard walked into the Scott Drug Store at 2030 West 25th Street. Showing his .38-caliber gun to the cashier there, he departed with $26. A little over four hours later, at about 1 a.m., he entered the Tastyburger Shop at 1806 East 9th Street. Pulling out his revolver again, Richard demanded money from night manager Lester Babington and left with $30.

Some thugs would have quit right there. It was a chilly January night, and Richard had reason to believe that the cops might be looking for whoever had pulled two heists that night. But he only had $56 to show for two armed robberies, so it must have seemed perfectly logical that he pull one more job before calling it a night.

Richard sidled into the Gay 90s bar at 1:45 a.m., just before

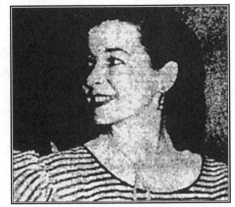

An unexpected heroine.
Cleveland Press, January 19, 1956.

closing time. Sitting quietly on a barstool, he nursed his Scotch and soda as he waited for most of the customers and staff to leave. Gradually they trickled out, and by 2:30 a.m. Richard was satisfied with the crowd. The only ones left besides him were co-owners Aaron "Goldie" Goldstein and Hy Wolfson, porter Benjamin Jones, and dancer Tina LaMont. Goldstein was sitting at the bar, while Wolfson counted up the day's receipts. Tina was downstairs changing out of her work clothes, and Jones was standing near the door.

Goldstein hardly noticed as Storino slipped off his barstool and walked beside him. He didn't even hear Storino the first time he said, "Look at this." But he did hear him when he said, "You'd better look at this," and he definitely saw the .38-caliber revolver that Storino suddenly pulled out of a waist holster. Sitting down beside Goldstein, Storino said, "Don't make a move, this is loaded. If you move I'll blow your brains out. I want you to stay here until the other man leaves, and then you get me all the money."

By this time, Wolfson was aware that something was going on.

He saw Goldstein stiffen and then he saw the gun. Walking slowly by porter Jones, he whispered, "Get the police. That guy's got a gun on Goldie." Jones noiselessly slipped out the front door, just about the time Tina LaMont reappeared in the bar and sat down on a stool. Goldstein called to her to go home, but Storino said, "Never mind that. Tell her to come over here." She walked around the bar and sat beside him.

Owe Our Lives to Entertainer, Say Police Who Shot Robber

Cleveland News, January 19, 1956.

Meanwhile, Jones had run down to East 9th Street and Walnut Avenue, where he flagged down a police car with Lieutenant Norman Bayless, 43, and Sergeant Melvin Stahley, 47, sitting in it. Bayless was no stranger to such situations. The previous May he had killed a robber attempting to hold up the Mechalovitz Co., a tobacco wholesaling firm at 640 Broadway. He had just recovered from wounds suffered in that shootout, and both he and Stahley knew what to expect as they entered the Gay Nineties front door with their guns drawn.

It happened so fast. Storino, Goldstein, and Tina were right in front of the police officers, sitting sideways at the bar as they came in. As the officers approached the group, 12 feet away, Goldstein shouted, "He's got a gun!" Spinning sideways, Storino fired at the officers. That is, he tried to fire—because Tina LaMont grabbed at his hand and gun as he brought them up. The gun fired—but the bullet was deflected into the ceiling 10 feet above. And Storino didn't get another chance. Before he could get control of his gun, Stahley fired three times and Bayless twice. Four of the slugs hit Storino in his neck, chest, abdomen, and right thigh, killing him almost instantly. The fifth drilled Tina LaMont, burrowing into her back and lodging next to her spine. In the struggle to prevent Storino from shooting, she had been pulled right into the line of fire.

Even as Storino crumpled to the floor, Stahley grabbed the fallen dancer, saying, "Are you hurt?"

"No, I don't think so," Tina said. "But my legs, I can't move my legs!" Stahley called an ambulance and did his best to comfort her until it arrived. In critical condition, Tina was rushed to St. Vincent Charity Hospital, where doctors labored feverishly through that night to save her life. Thanks to their skill and multiple blood transfusions they were able to so. But her condition was still so precarious that they could not operate to remove the police bullet next to her spine.

In the meantime, Clevelanders awoke on January 19 to find that they had a new and unexpected heroine in their midst. Clevelanders have never responded as warmly to a noble soul as they did to Tina LaMont. How was it, they asked themselves, that this humble little lady (really a stripper, for God's sake!) had possessed the courage to risk her life for two policemen that she didn't even know?

The lives she saved.
Cleveland Press, January 19, 1956.

Bayless and Stahley initiated the paeans, telling reporters over and over how they owed their lives to Tina LaMont. Stahley rhapsodized:

> I'm satisfied that girl saved our lives. We're both very thankful to her. Storino's mind was ready [to shoot] and his reflexes were ready. He probably would have fired all five shots before we were ready if it hadn't been for that girl.

Bayless added, "The girl was quite courageous. I think she deserves all the credit in the world. How many other people would do something like that?"

The outpouring of public admiration was intensified by Tina's modest and unpretentious explanation of her heroism. When asked what she had been thinking when she saw the policemen come through the door, she simply said:

Dancer Faces Up To Cripple's Life

Cleveland News, February 4, 1956.

> I saw they were dead pigeons. They were just drawing their guns, and Storino wheeled and aimed his gun and I threw myself at him to save the police. . . . I guess I knew instinctively that whoever came in that door would be shot.

The showering accolades were nice, but Tina LaMont soon learned the real price she had paid for her instant of sublime courage. The day after she was shot, she told reporters from her hospital bed that her doctors said she wouldn't be able to dance for a year. It was clear then that her legs were at least temporarily paralyzed, but an operation on February 2 disclosed the harsh truth everyone had tried to avoid facing: Tina LaMont would probably never walk or dance again. She took her fate with characteristic aplomb:

> I've got plenty of spirit. People have been and are being wonderful to me. Things will work out all right, even though it will take time. . . . I've never done much but dance, but I hope I can buy a rooming house to support myself and my little girl.

Tina was right about people being wonderful. Her plight brought out the best in thousands of Clevelanders, beginning with the ranks of the Cleveland police force. In what was accurately described by the *Cleveland Press* as a "history-making act," Cleveland police chief Frank Story proposed on the day after her shooting that a fund for Tina be raised by policemen and the general public. The response was immediate and generous. Thousands of dollars for Tina were raised over the next few weeks, and thousands more by other public and private groups.

HEROINE IN GUN FIGHT in a downtown night club, Mrs. Dorothy Kochs lies in a hospital bed with a bullet in her back.

VICTIM'S CHILD: Jody Kochs, 3, plays with her toys and wonders why her mother doesn't come home.

Police Chief Proposes Fund for Heroic Wounded Dancer

Cleveland Press, January 19, 1956.

Downtown restaurant proprietor Charles Rohr and Theatrical Grill owner "Mushy" Wexler solicited contributions from the owners of downtown restaurants, including the Tavern Chop House, Hickory Grill, Kornman's Restaurant, and Joyce's Cafe. The Grotto Circus gave a benefit performance for Tina on February 23, the opening parade of which was led by her three-year-old daughter, Jody. Such fundraising efforts for Tina climaxed on April 5 with the presentation of the "Tina LaMont Benefit Show" at Public Hall. Hosted by popular disk jockeys Bill Gordon, Bill Randle, Bob Forster, Wes Hopkins, Hal Morgan, and Norman Wayne, the show featured Morey Amsterdam, Joe E. Lewis, Harry Belafonte, comedians Smith and Dale, tap dancer Tito Cavalero, and many other singers, dancers, comedians, and performers. The benefit show raised $20,000 for Tina, an amount supplemented by a three-year grant of $50 a week from the American Guild of Variety Artists. Six months later, Tina received national recognition of her heroism when she won a Carnegie Hero Award. Presented to her on October 27, 1956, the medal came with a $50-a-month stipend paid through 1965.

The rest of the Tina LaMont story followed the tone set from the outset by this plucky woman. She finally got out of Charity Hospital on March 10, after almost two months there, and tried to resume her interrupted life. Defying medical expectations, she soon learned to walk without braces, eventually graduating to the use of canes and walkers. Carefully managing the money raised for her, she bought that rooming house she wanted, a house for students in University Circle, and eventually purchased a home for herself and Jody on Carlyon Road in East Cleveland. There, she was able to do her own cooking and most of her housekeeping. In 1968, she moved to Conneaut, eventually living in a trailer next door to her daughter Jody's family, which included two grandchildren. Tina died in 1981 at Richmond Heights hospital, while undergoing surgery for intestinal problems.

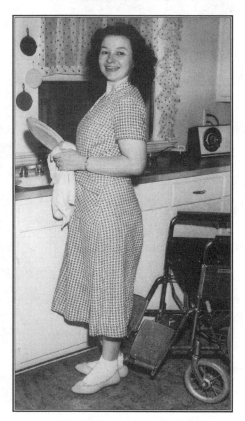

Three years later: Tina LaMont at her home, July 1959.

When last heard from publicly in 1966, she was still the same plucky Tina who had put her life on the line for two strangers without hesitating for a moment:

> And even now—even with what the incident has done to my life—I would do the same thing again. I have no regrets, no bitterness. I feel a great peace. For me, every day is Christmas.

It was still the same credo of optimism that she had expressed seven years earlier:

> You know, I'm beginning to think I was lucky. I could have stepped off the curb and got hit by a car, you know, and none of these nice things ever would have happened.

As for Richard Storino, well, he left behind two quite suitable epitaphs. One came from his sister Shirley, whose reaction to his death was a heartfelt "He's caused my sister and I nothing but trouble." The other was pronounced by assistant Cleveland police prosecutor Richard Matia, who ruled Richard's killing "justifiable homicide" practically before they took his cold, dead corpse out of the Gay Nineties.

Chapter 2

THE LION SLEEPS (FOREVER) TONIGHT

Death at Public Hall (1934)

Cleveland's Public Hall has witnessed its share of Cleveland woe. The first recorded human fatality there occurred when Horace Neighbors fell to his death down an elevator shaft on February 23, 1934. Thirty-nine persons were injured when a railing gave way on July 15, 1935. A balustrade collapse 11 years later hurt another four persons attending a dance there. More recently, and spectacularly, Metropolitan Opera veteran Betty Stone snagged her costume in a backstage elevator on May 1, 1977 and was fatally injured.

Cleveland's circuses have likewise had their quotient of calamity. Most notoriously, a flash fire of unknown origin killed scores of animals on August 4, 1942. Some of the badly burned animals were taken to the basement of Public Hall for medical treatment. Some of them didn't make it, including two elephants who had to be machine-gunned by Cleveland police officers.

Probably the most brutal event ever recorded in Public Hall occurred there in January 1934. The Grotto Circus was in town, and renowned animal trainer Clyde Beatty was entertaining two rapt audiences a day with his menagerie of 40 lions and tigers. All went well until the morning of January 29, when a routine rehearsal of Beatty's big cats turned deadly. Things began normally as Beatty led five lions and four tigers into the big cage and whipped them to their pedestals. He then drove six of the younger lions into the cage. The first two entered without incident, and then another two, a lion and lioness, followed them in. That was Death's cue, for as Bessie, the two-year-old female, trotted in, one of the older lions decided he'd had enough. His name was Sammie, he weighed twice as much as Bessie, and he hurled all of his enormous bulk at her throat as she came into the cage.

The next 20 minutes provided a spectacle of pandemonium beyond the experience of even the most hardened circus folk. As lions and tigers around him roared and snarled, the frantic Beatty vainly tried to separate the two beasts locked in mortal struggle. When his whip, blank pistol, and chair proved ineffectual, he ordered his assistants to turn powerful fire hoses on the two animals. When that, too, proved futile, Beatty began beating Sammie with an iron bar to make him disengage from his killing embrace. Sammie was finally beaten unconscious about 20 minutes after his initial attack, and the two lions were at last separated. It was too late: Sammie had gotten his mouth around Bessie's neck and had shaken and strangled her to death.

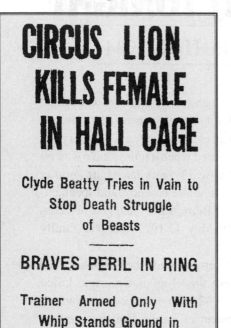

CIRCUS LION KILLS FEMALE IN HALL CAGE

Clyde Beatty Tries in Vain to Stop Death Struggle of Beasts

BRAVES PERIL IN RING

Trainer Armed Only With Whip Stands Ground in Jungle Fight

Cleveland Press, January 29, 1934.

The experienced Beatty knew what to do next. He'd had his fill of animal troubles before, although he described Bessie's killing as the most dangerous fight of his career as an animal trainer. After Sammie regained consciousness, Beatty brought him right back into the cage for the rest of his interrupted rehearsal. The point, as Beatty put it, was to "show him who's boss." Beatty then brought in two sibling lions, Leo and King, who as Beatty anticipated and wished, gave Sammie a mauling he wouldn't soon forget.

Beatty may have been overly optimistic about Sammie's reform. It is recorded that the unrepentant Sammie knocked a chair out of

Sammy, Lion-Killer, Cowed and Tamed by Snarling Companions

Murderer of Young Female Takes Fancy Beating and Quits Cold in Steel Cage; Battle Royal Prompted by Trainer Beatty

Cleveland Press, January 30, 1934.

Beatty's hands at that evening's public show. In any case, Beatty thought the fault for the fatal incident lay less with Sammie than with the proportion of younger lions in his entourage and ongoing tensions between the male and female cats. The most interesting comment on the episode came from Beatty's new wife, an animal trainer named Harriet. When informed of that morning's lethal combat, she said, "I wish I'd seen the fight."

There will always be dangers whenever wild beasts are mixed with humans or each other. On February 14, 1948, one of Beatty's assistants was badly clawed by a big cat in another Public Hall Grotto show. And on May 5, 2003, Rosey, an 18-year-old lioness, was found murdered in her lair at the Cleveland Metroparks Zoo. No witnesses came forward to describe her killing, but suspicion swirled nastily around Moufasa and Chloe, two five-year-old sibling lions.

Chapter 3

BLIND MURDER

The Killing of Thomas Martin (1907)

You don't have to be a policeman or saloon keeper to know that many killings happen around bars. Alcoholic refreshment is notorious for loosening inhibitions, and it seems especially potent and effective at disarming scruples about the Sixth Commandment. As with most saloon killings, the murder of Thomas Martin involved excessive alcohol, an unsavory cast of characters, and a fatal outcome. It was different enough, however, to warrant inclusion in the calendar of unsolved Cleveland murder mysteries.

There were only two other persons in his West 58th Street saloon as Thomas John Martin prepared to close it during the last minutes of January 2, 1907. One was Henry Engel, a stationary engineer, who lay stationary, indeed, in an alcoholic stupor on a tavern table. The other person was John Anderson, a blind man and, if not blind-drunk, certainly no stranger to strong drink. What happened in the last seconds of January 2 was something the two men could never agree upon. Engel's story was that a stranger came into the bar and ordered a drink. Downing it quickly, he ordered another, but Martin said, "No, your tab is big enough already." The stranger retorted, "Take that!" pulled out a gun, and started shooting. Martin, again according to Engel, pulled out his own revolver and returned fire. Seconds later, Martin's wife rushed into the room, drawn by the sound of gunfire. "Where's John?" she asked Engel. "Don't know," muttered the stupefied sot. Mrs. Martin then stepped forward and saw her husband lying on the floor, bleeding heavily. He died minutes later on his way to the hospital.

Cleveland police chief Fred Kohler's men were baffled from the start. True, Martin was a rough customer with plenty of old personal enemies and a talent for readily acquiring new ones. He was

The victim and scene of the crime.
Cleveland Press, January 3, 1907.

also a crack shot with a revolver. Martin's idea of fun was to sit on a bluff overlooking the Old Riverbed and shoot the lunchpails out of the hands of weary laborers as they trudged home from a hard day's labor on Whiskey Island. He had recently sold another saloon on nearby Cass Avenue and then dropped by later to pepper the place with buckshot. Martin was a hard drinker, a bully with a hair-trigger temper, and it is likely that someone would have killed him sooner or later.

ASSASSIN ESCAPES

Mysterious Murderer of West-Side Man Commits Crime in Presence of Blind Man and Another.

Cleveland Press, January 3, 1907.

But how had it been done? Martin took a bullet in his forehead and one in his abdomen. A third slug hit the bar, and there were two more bullet holes in the opposite wall. But the bullet holes in the wall didn't look fresh, and neither of the .38-caliber bullets in Martin nor the one in the bar matched those in Martin's own revolver, a .32-caliber weapon found in a drawer in back of the bar. The police speculated, but could not prove, that the bullets in the wall had probably been fired sometime before, perhaps as part of Martin's celebration of New Year's Eve.

The situation was further muddied by the sightless John Anderson, who denied there had been an exchange of gunfire or that he had heard a stranger come into the bar. Both Engel and Anderson were held for vigorous interrogation by the police, as was Charles Shay, an inebriated railroad switchman found wandering on the West Side the following morning. Neither Engel nor Anderson identified Shay as Martin's killer, and all three men were eventually released by Kohler's men.

The police duly surmised that the apparently drunk Martin never had a chance to get to his own gun and that all three bullets had been fired by his killer. The most likely scenario was that, after he was refused a second drink, the stranger had pretended to leave. Concealed behind a screen at the front door, he waited until Martin came to lock the door and then shot him. On January 7, after repeated announcements that the crime was almost solved, Chief Fred Kohler told reporters that he had given up hope of solving the crime. Martin's murder remains a mystery to this day.

Chapter 4

SEDUCED AND ABANDONED

Jennie, a Girl of the Cleveland Streets (1871)

It is commonplace that we know little about the sexuality of our ancestors. There will never be a history, for example, of the sex lives of late-19th-century Clevelanders. If hardly ascetic, 19th-century Victorians—English or American—were reticent about their sexual behavior and habits and unlikely to chronicle them in print. Because most 1870s Clevelanders were representative Victorians, much of what little we know about Forest City sexual proclivities of that decade comes from the criminal record. And most of that documentation comes from the era's celebrated murder trials, for it was usually only the egregious rupture of civic norms implicit in homicidal acts that exposed ugly, or at least indelicate, sexual realties to public view.

The Galentine-Jones murder case of 1870 was one such revealing episode. Superficially, of course, it was the edifying tale of a wronged man enforcing the "unwritten law," for such was the claim made by dentist Jay Galentine after he shot down Dr. William Jones for the crime of "raping" Jay's wife, Mary. The trial, to the pious titillation of Clevelanders, exposed the indelicate truth that Mary had whiled away her husband's prolonged absences by allowing Dr. Jones access to her person as many as five times a day. (For more details of this entertaining scandal see "Cold Lead For Breakfast" in the author's *They Died Crawling and Other Tales of Cleveland Woe*, 1995.)

It's a safe bet that no one living now, even you, gentle reader, has heard of the Jennie Droz affair. That's a shame, because it is at least as illustrative of the gamy sexual realities of the era as the Galentine-Jones burlesque. True, it lacks that aspect of comic absurdity that informed the latter scandal from beginning to end. But its sordid details bring to light matters never discussed in more "proper" histories of Cleveland: prostitution, venereal disease, the sexual victimization of female servants, and the plight of the "fallen

A woman scorned: Jennie Droz, 19. *Cleveland Leader*, February 21, 1871.

woman." Not to mention the fact that it offers an entertaining tale with a satisfying and surprising ending.

We could begin the Jennie Droz story in a number of places. One would be 1850, when Jennie Droz was born in Mecklenburg, Germany. The daughter of Ferdinand Droz, a jeweler and sometime foreign passenger agent, she came with her family to Cleveland in 1851, one of the many German immigrants who flooded into the city after the failed 1848 Revolution. Another place would be Jennie's childhood home at Pearl and Detroit Streets on Cleveland's West Side, where she grew up during the 1850s. (The West Side is also where Drs. Galentine and Jones resided at the time of their unfortunate 1870 interchange.) There the Droz family flourished: Ferdinand, his wife, his sons Louis and Philip, and his daughters Jennie and Lucy. As testimony of their status as new Americans, Philip and Louis were employed by the Cleveland Fire Department in 1869.

That year is probably the best place to pick up the Jennie Droz tale, for here commenced her undoing. Like many teenagers before and since, Jennie chafed at the rules and discipline of her respectable bourgeois West Side home. Her discontent flared up in the summer of 1869, when at the age of 18 she came under the sympathetic influence of a Mrs. Rachel Duffy, the wife of a bartender at Blanchard's saloon on Detroit Street. Ferdinand Droz would later publicly blame Mrs. Duffy for luring his daughter into secular temptations, but Jennie herself denied at her trial that she needed assistance in being led astray. Whatever their relationship, it is a fact that Jennie stole away from her parents' home one summer night in 1869, possibly with the material assistance of Mrs. Duffy. Several weeks later, in August, Jennie's outraged parents discovered she was working as a maid at the Cliff House, a splendid luxury hotel on the eastern banks of the Rocky River. Because she was 18, there was nothing her anguished parents could do but worry that young Jennie might succumb to worldly and impure snares in such a place.

Worldly and impure snares were not long in presenting themselves. Capitalist Daniel P. Rhodes and other Cleveland investors had opened the Rocky River Railroad "dummy line" two years earlier, in 1867, and they opened the Cliff House in January 1869 to provide a diverting destination for moneyed Clevelanders weary of city scenes. The Cliff House was initially managed by Lucien Phillips, but before the end of its first year its affairs were turned over to brothers Edward and Julius Fisk. By January of 1870, Julius was fully in charge of its operations. Thus and so smoothly was the scene set for Jennie's ruination.

As is so oft the case, more is known about the killer of Major Julius Fisk than about the victim himself. He must have been, as his contemporaries would have said, a "man of parts." Born in 1828, he enlisted in Company S of the 2nd Kansas Cavalry Regiment in 1862 and was wounded at Cane Hill, Arkansas, on November 28, 1862. Mustered out of the same regiment with the rank of major on April 18, 1865, he turned up five years later in partnership with his brother at the Cliff House. Described by his friends as affable, courteous, extraordinarily generous, and possessing an iron constitution, the Major seems to have been a moderately handsome man, albeit a bit on the fleshy side. He was above medium height and sported dark Burnside whiskers. It's probably fair to say, too, that the 42-year-old Julius was something of a ladies' man, judging from his behavior toward Jennie Droz.

Jennie's downfall proceeded apace from the moment Julius arrived at the Cliff House. Julius quickly took note of the comely dining room girl, and a week later he invited Jennie to his room. He behaved himself properly on that occasion, but his demeanor soon changed. Some days later he began to woo her in earnest, telling her she was too good to be working as a hotel maid, that she deserved fine clothes, that she ought to be his mistress. He also took to lurking in corridors and staircases, touching and grabbing the girl as she toiled through her menial chores. Jennie refused his initial proposition, and then, after telling her he would go to Kansas and then send for her, he tried to be intimate with her. She angrily repulsed him but quickly found Julius Fisk was a hard man to circumvent. Luring her again into his Cliff House quarters on some pretext one night, he offered her a glass of wine. Either it was drugged or Jennie had no tolerance for alcohol, for she passed out and Fisk thereupon "accomplished his purpose." Jennie predictably wept when she recovered her senses, but the affable Julius assured her all would be well.

Contrary to Julius's bland assurances, Jennie's life quickly deteriorated. Edward Fisk's wife Adeline had noticed the growing intimacy between her brother-in-law and the dining room girl—and she didn't like it. The Cliff House was already developing a reputation as a dissolute and lewd hotel, and Adeline decided to arrest its moral decline. On March 2, she summarily fired Jennie Droz. Very shortly afterwards, Jennie discovered that she was pregnant and that she was showing unmistakable symptoms of "a loathsome disease."

Indeed, Jennie had contracted a virulent case of syphilis from the hearty major. There weren't very effective treatments for the disease in 1870, and Fisk didn't try very hard to help her. Jennie apparently first consulted a physician herself (who of all people turned out to be Dr. William Jones, soon to be shot down by Dr. Galentine). His treatment failing, she begged Fisk to help her in her diseased, pregnant, and penniless state. She probably threatened him with exposure, too, doubtless the wrong tack to take with the steely Civil War veteran. Upon hearing her threats, Fisk coldly warned her that if she uttered a word against him, he would denounce her as a "woman of the town," and she would be put in jail. He also procured some mail-order patent remedies for her worsening infection, none of which helped alleviate her symptoms or mental distress.

Late in August or early September of 1870, an unwelcome Jennie showed up at the Cliff House again. Her mother had died earlier in the year, her death hastened by sorrow over Jennie's disgrace, and Jennie was too ashamed to return to her father's home. Living with various relatives or in cheap hotels and boarding houses, she tried to make a living by sewing and, eventually, as a prostitute on the streets of Cleveland. But by late August both her pregnancy and her disease had taken their toll, and she now threw herself on the tender mercies of her seducer.

What happened after that is murky. Major Fisk, still wishing to conceal his relations with her, put Jennie up in a nearby barn for eight or nine days. There she gave birth to a baby, but whether it was stillborn or strangled by Major Fisk she never knew. What she did know was that Major Fisk soon ejected her from Cliff House with warnings not to return.

Jennie resumed her life as a prostitute on the Cleveland streets. Often too sick to work at anything else, she took in sewing when she felt well enough and wrote several heartbreaking letters of appeal to Major Fisk. He apparently remained deaf to her appeals. And so it continued for several months more, as Jennie got sicker, more indigent, and desperate.

The bottom fell out on Thursday, February 16, 1871. Jennie was down to her last two dollars, and her landlord had attached her trunk in lieu of back rent. Multiple appeals to the major had proved fruitless, but Jennie decided she would give him one more chance. Walking from her current quarters at the Cleveland Hotel at Ontario and Prospect, Jennie went to Michael and Thomas Powers's gun store on Superior Hill (now the site of the Western Reserve Building). She entered the store about 11:30 a.m. and said she wanted a gun, and Thomas showed her a $7.50 revolver. She couldn't afford that, so he brought out a $2.50 pistol. Even that was beyond her slender means, but after consulting with Michael, Thomas allowed her to depart with the pistol after she gave him $2 and a ring as security on the 50 cents owed. (Gunsmith Thomas Powers became the father of two Catholic priests, one of them the legendary John Mary Powers, the charismatic pastor of St. Ann Church in Cleveland Heights. For more details on the remarkable Powers family see the author's *Angels on the Heights: A History of St. Ann's Parish, 1915–1990,* 1990.)

That evening Jennie walked over to Erastus Briggs's livery stable on Detroit Street. She said she wanted to rent a horse and buggy for several hours and that she would pay Briggs the hire on her return. She then drove the horse and buggy out the Detroit Street toll road, telling tollgate keeper Edmond Ruhill that she would pay him on her return trip.

Jennie arrived at the Cliff House about 8:30 p.m. Fisk soon became aware of her presence, and they chatted amiably in front of several witnesses, including maid Margaret Twohig and hostler William Albon. Their conversation continued in a desultory fashion until sometime after 9 p.m., when Jennie mentioned there were two lively girls over at William Patchen's hotel, across the Rocky River. She asked Julius if he would send William Albon to bring them over to the Cliff House.

Jennie's pretext worked like a charm on the susceptible Fisk, always agreeable to the company of attractive young women. Albon left the hotel about 9:30 p.m., and Jennie immediately began her real business, which was to beg Fisk one last time for emotional and financial support. Their interview took place in the hotel's reception room, a comfortable 10-by-12-foot area, and lasted almost an hour. Again and again, Jennie reiterated her desperate poverty and the ravages of venereal disease, all too visible on her face. But Major Fisk remained a cad to the end. It was not in his nature to help the woman he wronged, and he summarized his feelings even as he and Jennie heard the sounds of Albon's buggy returning, shouting, "I'll be damned if I help you at all."

That was all Jennie Droz needed to hear. All of the miseries of the past 13 months were now heartlessly punctuated with the finality of Fisk's callous retort. As Jennie later put it, "If he had said one kind word, I could not have shot him." That not being the case, she removed the single-shot revolver from her purse and fired once.

They were both standing as the gun went off. The bullet hit Julius just about an inch or so above the right ear. The lead ball penetrated three or four inches, inflicting mortal damage and flattening itself before coming to rest at the base of the brain. Without further ado, Jennie replaced her pistol in her purse and calmly walked out to the piazza. William Albon was there, having just returned from his futile errand at the Rocky River Hotel. "William," she said, "I have shot him. Will you drive me to town and give me up to the police?" "Shot who?" he replied. Jennie merely repeated, "I shot him" several times and then jumped in her buggy and drove off.

Major Fisk was still alive at about 10:40 p.m. when William Albon found him in the reception room. He was sitting in a chair, with a dog on his knee and blood coming out of his mouth. He was breathing hard and unable to speak. Dr. William Carter was sent for, but it was too late by the time he arrived about 45 minutes later. After he certified that Julius Fisk was dead, Albon was sent into the city to notify the police and Cuyahoga County coroner J. C. Schenck.

Meanwhile, Jennie calmly drove back the way she had come. Passing through the tollgate, she told keeper Ruhill that she was unable to pay him and continued on her way. Arriving at Briggs's stable at 11:40 p.m., she simply sat in the buggy until the stable clerk came out to see what was the matter. She was apparently in a state of shock, simply muttering over and over, "I wonder if the major is dead. I wonder if the major is dead."

Assisted out of the buggy by the puzzled clerk, she sat down in the waiting room, saying, "I feel so queer." She repeatedly asked the clerk to check and see if there was still a bullet in her pistol. There was not, and when she explained that she only had a penny left, the clerk took the gun as security for the buggy hire.

Jennie walked back to her room at the Cleveland Hotel. About an hour later, when Cleveland police sergeant E. B. Gaffet and patrolmen H. A. Cordes and Thomas Thompson tracked her down there, Jennie was lying fully dressed on her bed, with the door unlocked and a lamp burning. Rising as the officers came into the room, she immediately agreed to go with them to the Central Police Station; she told them that her pistol was at Briggs's livery. She refused to answer most of their direct questions but volunteered some information, which Cordes later recalled at her trial:

> She said she went out there to see if Fisk would not do something for her and give her some money. He would not, and she shot him in the head. She said Fisk had seduced her and given her a loathsome disease. Said she should not be glad to have him die, that she loved him. Said she had received letters from Fisk saying that if she did not shut up he would put her in the workhouse.

Astonishing everyone by her calm demeanor, Jennie Droz was taken off and locked up in a jail at the Central Police Station. When she was arrested she had but one cent and two receipted doctor bills in her purse.

Criminal justice procedures in 1870 were not quite what they are now. Almost as soon as Jennie was ensconced in her cell, a *Cleveland Leader* reporter was allowed to interview her for that day's edition. Repeating what she had told her arresting officers, she added more details about her seduction and shabby treatment. She was more reticent at the murder inquest the next morning. Convened in the very murder room itself by Coroner Schenck at 10 a.m., the proceedings included appearances by Margaret Twohig and William Albon, Dr. Carter, and Herman Patchen. The only interesting item to emerge from their testimony was Patchen's disclosure that he had found a seven-shot, loaded pistol in the pants Fisk was wearing when he was killed. Then Jennie took the stand, accompanied by her defense attorneys, Samuel E. Adams and Robert Davison. Still calm and collected, she gave her testimony in a quiet voice, wiping away a furtive tear several times. Forthcoming on her tenure at the Cliff House, she refused to answer a number of questions about the actual shooting. When the testimony concluded, Coroner Schenck quickly ruled that Fisk had died from a pistol ball at the hands of Jennie Droz.

Taken back to her cell, Jennie more freely unbosomed herself to another *Cleveland Leader* reporter. Enlarging on her wrongs, she denied that she had led an immoral life before she met Fisk. Though she admitted she had been a prostitute for the past four or five months, she pleaded penury as her excuse, claiming she didn't know there was a retreat for "fallen women" in Cleveland: "I know nothing but my sin and I had no way to live but to make it deeper." She admitted shooting Fisk but allowed that it was "awful," as she had loved Mr. Fisk. She said she had hoped she had only wounded him and that "he would live to be a better man."

CITY NEWS.

A SEDUCER SHOT.

A Young Girl Does the Deed.

Her Account of the Tragedy.

SEDUCTION AND DESERTION.

The Fatal Shot,

SHE IS ARRESTED.

Cleveland Leader, February 17, 1871.

The *Leader* correspondent amply repaid Jennie for her interview, writing that although there were two sides to the story:

> Everything connected with the fearful tragedy gives an appearance of candor to the prisoner's statement. It hardly seems possible, if she were ruined, that she would have singled out for her vengeance any one except the person who had wrought her disgrace.

The day after the inquest, Jennie was arraigned in the Cleveland police court. Her attorneys waiving an examination, she was incarcerated in the Cuyahoga County Jail, then located on Frankfort and Seneca Streets (West 3rd Street). The following day, at 3 p.m., funeral rites for Major Fisk were held at the Cliff House. The services were conducted by the Rev. James Erwin of the Franklin Street Methodist Church, who told the grieving mourners that Fisk's unexpected end demonstrated the shortness of life and the need to be prepared for death at any time. It was noted that Dr. Carter had done a splendid job in repairing the violence to Fisk's person. As an admiring reporter wrote,

Aside from the slightly livid appearance of the skin, and large purple spots about the shoulders where blood seemed to have settled, one might have believed that Major Fisk was but sleeping.

The wheels of justice commenced their regular, if not always predictable, grind. On Friday, May 12, 1871, Jennie was indicted by a Cuyahoga County common pleas court on a charge of manslaughter. The newspapers reported that she "manifested much joy" at news of this, as well she might. Considering the methodical way she had gone about acquiring a weapon, arranging transportation, and contriving to be alone with Fisk, it seems the all-male jury had likely stretched the bounds of chivalry to accommodate Jennie Droz.

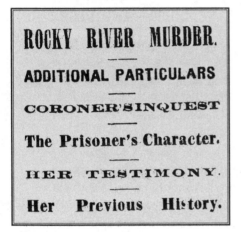

ROCKY RIVER MURDER.

———

ADDITIONAL PARTICULARS

———

CORONER'S INQUEST

———

The Prisoner's Character.

———

HER TESTIMONY.

———

Her Previous History.

Cleveland Leader, February 18, 1871.

When she came before Judge Foote to hear the indictment, she appeared much as she had at the time of Fisk's slaying: a small woman with large black eyes, short black hair, and even features, although the effects of syphilis had taken their toll on her once fine complexion. She was dressed entirely in black, complete with a black-beribboned black hat and a black cross at her throat. Her face was covered with a black veil. When asked how she pled, she whispered, "Not guilty," and her trial was scheduled for June 5. A bail bond of $3,000 was immediately arranged and accepted, and Jennie returned to her father's home to await justice.

One hopes that her sojourn there was more pleasant than her stint in county jail. There, she claimed, she was chronically subject to dreams in which Major Fisk would appear before her or she would waken on her cell bed with pistol shots ringing in her ears. However nightmarish her nights, however, her days were enlivened by frequent visits from her friends and the sympathetic society of fellow prisoner Kate Tracy, confined there on a grand larceny conviction.

It was rumored at the time of Jennie's indictment that the manslaughter count had been chosen over more grave charges in hopes Jennie would plead guilty to this lesser charge. If so, her prosecutors were disappointed, because she stuck to her stance of innocence even as the date for her trial was continually postponed for one reason or another. By the time she actually went on trial, in late May of 1872, the charge had been readjusted to murder in the second degree. When her case was called on May 29, she was ready to be prosecuted in Judge Paine's court by H. B. DeWolf and Samuel Eddy. Jennie, still dressed in her all-black outfit, was represented by Samuel E. Adams and M. S. Castle.

DeWolf's opening statement made it clear he would simply let the facts speak for themselves. He detailed Jennie's careful arrangements for the murder, methodically citing the many circumstances of motive, means, and opportunity. Samuel Adams, on the other hand, made it clear he would rely on the jury's emotional sympathies. Deftly, he painted the portrait of a trusting, then ruined, virgin, who had so foolishly "reposed confidence in his honor and promises of marriage." Then followed the catalog of her woes: her dismissal, her pregnancy, her "loathsome disease," and her desperate poverty. Skillfully, Adams reiterated Fisk's refusals to aid the wretched Jennie and led the jurors up to the winter of 1870–71 and the climactic day of February 16, when, he intimated, Jennie decided to kill *herself,* not Fisk:

> She was then in a boarding house without a dollar, her trunk had been seized by the landlord, and at that time her disease had assumed a most aggravating character. It was almost a moment of life or death to her. At that eventual moment she applied to Fisk and asked him to make some provision for her. He promised to do so but did not, and her last hope was dissipated. If she bought the pistol it will be proved that she bought it for purposes of self-destruction. She had become wearied of life. We expect to show that this girl, if she shot that man, did not buy that pistol for that purpose, and she shot him at a moment when her reason was overthrown.

Given the emotional appeal of Adams's presentation and the sordid character of the murder victim, it is likely that the trial might as well have ended there. But it continued, as witness after witness recounted the shocking details of Jennie's relations with Fisk and the events of February 16. Coroner Schenck, Erastus Briggs, Thomas Powers, Edmond Ruhill, William Albon, Margaret Twohig, and several newspaper reporters took the stand before Dr. N. M. Jones testified late that afternoon. A physician and brother of the murdered Dr. William Jones, he had also treated Jennie for the secondary stages of syphilis. His testimony was particularly crucial, as there had been persistent rumors that physicians had concluded Jennie suffered from no venereal disease at all.

Shortly afterwards, the state rested, only to make way for defense witnesses Drs. W. J. Scott, H. F. Biggar, E. Sterling, N. Schneider, and P. Thayer. Their subject was the secondary stages of syphilis, in particular its psychological effects. They were united in proclaiming that the disease in that stage often produced "not only depression of spirits but often affects the brain and prompts to suicide or impulsive acts belonging to the emotional insanity class."

The stage was now set for the star witness, and Jennie did not disappoint her enthralled audience. (Readers of the *Cleveland Herald* may have been disappointed: it refused to print the more earthy details of Jennie's testimony, piously noting that the "disgusting details of her testimony were eagerly listened to by the prurient crowd of spectators.") Testifying for two days, she detailed the lurid circumstances of Fisk's seduction, his subsequent spurning, the onset of her disease, and the gothic scenes in the Cliff House barn.

During cross-examination Prosecutor DeWolf attempted several times to suggest she had been less than a pure maiden when she met Fisk, but she disarmed his imputations with firm but demure denials. DeWolf also successfully attempted to introduce her letters to Fisk into the trial record, but the letters only supported the defense portrait of the accused as an innocent, trusting, if feckless ingenue. Full of girlish endearments ("Mr. Fisk, don't be mad at me will you, for I will do most anything for you," "I send you a hundred kisses and my love," "I hope that you didn't sleep with no girl yet") and pathetic pleas for money, they simply reinforced Jennie's image as Fisk's artless victim. More seriously, during rebuttal, DeWolf put Rocky River Railroad superintendent George G. Mulhern and Cliff House bartender on the stand in an attempt to besmirch Jennie's character. Mulhern related a conversation in which Jennie boasted of sleeping with a young man named Charlie Knapp, and Dolan testified that she had expressed a sexual preference for one of his fellow employees. Judge Paine promptly struck Mulhern's testimony from the record, and the opposing attorneys made their final arguments.

We have no copy of the closing arguments. That's a pity, because Adams, Eddy, DeWolf, and Castle were among the finest attorneys of the day, all of them celebrated for their rhetorical powers. But we do have Judge Paine's charge to the jury. In it he properly stressed the meaning of "malice" pertinent to the second-degree murder charge and the importance of judging Jennie's intention when she went to Cliff House with a loaded pistol. Although Paine did not tip his hand, he was careful to caution, in light of the defense's medical evidence, that the jury not be fooled into permitting a "license of crime" by accepting a "counterfeit insanity." The case went to the jury late in the afternoon on June 4, 1871.

Twenty-five hours later, the jurors reported to Judge Paine that they were hopelessly deadlocked. Despite many ballots, they had never come close, and Judge Paine immediately discharged them. It was said that the final ballot stood ten to two for acquittal; another report stated the voting at nine to three. The courtroom emptied, and Jennie Droz returned to her father's home to await another murder trial.

It never came. Jennie Droz was never reindicted for the murder of Julius Fisk and never stood trial again. One surmises that Prosecutor DeWolf and his cohorts saw the writing on the wall and decided to let the matter rest. And that writing was the "unwritten law"—for women. Although not articulated as often and publicly as the one for men (i.e., it's okay to shoot your wife's lover if you catch him in the act), a perusal of 19th-century murder trials suggests that a corollary rule operated for women. And the rule was that if a virtuous woman was treated badly enough—and certainly seduced, abandoned, *and* poxed Jennie qualified—then it was understandable, albeit regrettable, if the woman took her fatal revenge.

The rule worked for Jennie Droz in 1872, and it worked again for Mrs. Anna George in 1899, when the latter was accused of murdering President McKinley's brother-in-law George Saxton in Canton. Say what you will about the sexism implicit in all-male juries, you have to admit that justice was surely done in the case of poor Jennie Droz.

Chapter 5

DEATH ON THE HOOF

The Cleveland Stockyards Fire (1944)

Disasters, like murders, often reveal the priorities and social maladies of the societies in which they occur. The Cleveland Union Stockyards fire of 1944 was just such a tragedy. The investigation into the fire, which killed two firemen and injured three others and two civilians, highlighted both the treatment of mentally ill persons and the neglect of the city's infrastructure.

Long gone now, the Cleveland Union Stockyards were once the seventh-largest livestock center in the United States. Sometimes called the "Hotel de la Hoof" and constructed in 1881 on Scranton Road in the Flats, the stockyards moved to Gordon Avenue (later 3200 West 65th Street) in 1892 after a landslide destroyed the facilities. During their peak years in the Roaring Twenties, the stockyards embraced more than 60 acres of buildings, pens, troughs, and walkways, and a hotel to accommodate visitors involved in the livestock trade. In 1923, according to the *Encyclopedia of Cleveland History*, the stockyards handled 125,000 cattle, 145,000 calves, and 308,000 sheep and lambs. As a recurrent reminder of their prodigious size and social impact, there were frequent complaints about the mephitic stench pervading the neighborhoods surrounding the bustling stockyards, especially in the years from the 1890s through the 1920s.

As with all other Cleveland institutions, the Cleveland stockyards had their share of mishap and misfortune. A fire of unknown origin broke out in a hay barn on the afternoon of July 18, 1892, and destroyed virtually the entire facilities, including 200 to 300 tons of hay, several Big Four Railroad freight cars containing feed corn, and 200 head of cattle. Great numbers of Clevelanders came

A Judas goat leads lambs to slaughter: Cleveland Union
Stockyards.

out to watch the fire, which rapidly destroyed 10 acres of buildings
and livestock. Following the fire, the stockyards were completely
reconstructed.

Disaster struck again in the early morning of December 26,
1903. A fire originating in an overheated flue rapidly burned its
way through the two-story Cleveland Stock Yards Hotel at the corner of Gordon and Clark Avenues. Fortunately, the fire was discovered by Mrs. Frank Hearn, the leather-lunged wife of the hotel
proprietor, and she quickly roused the 25 sleeping guests to their
peril. Although the hotel soon burned to the ground in the near-zero
temperatures, the only serious casualty was aged invalid O. C.
Bradley. Several men risked their lives to rescue him from the
flames, but he was quite seriously burned by the time he was
brought out of the building. The hotel was rebuilt, and stockyard
operations resumed their wonted tenor.

Like the East Ohio Gas Company disaster that same year, the
March 11, 1944, Cleveland stockyards fire came in the middle of a
pleasant afternoon. Originating in a pile of hay at the Earl C. Gibbs
Co. packing concern, the fire rapidly swept through buildings,

The neighborhood smelled it: Cleveland Union Stockyards livestock pens.

pens, provender, and hundreds of cattle, hogs, and sheep. The first alarm was turned in at 4:03 p.m., the second at 4:12. The third came in at 4:16, and a "triple-five" alarm came at 4:26 p.m. Virtually all available equipment from the West Side and the downtown area—15 engine companies, two pumpers, a high-pressure truck, and five hook and ladder companies—were rushed to the fire scene. A crowd of perhaps 25,000 spectators soon formed to watch the battle with the flames.

All fires are dangerous, confusing, and scary. Those aspects of the Cleveland stockyards fire were intensified by a number of factors. The first was a steady, 20 m.p.h. wind, which drove the flames rapidly through the acres of buildings and livestock. The second was poor water pressure in the hydrants near the southwestern sector of the stockyards where the fire started. The third was the presence of hundreds of frightened animals, some of them large and most of them maddened by panic.

Early attempts by stockyard employees to escape the flames, like firefighters' efforts to battle them, were hampered by stampeding beasts in the stockyards proper and the surrounding West Side streets. The hogs were particularly difficult to steer toward safety, often having to be paddled forward, dragged by the ears, or even carried bodily out of harm's way. Eventually, two lines of neighborhood volunteers managed to form a human corridor, through which the animals were hustled to safety. Others were captured by men who ran foot races with the animals to bring them back in line.

Police Probes Open in Fire At Stockyards

Cleveland Press, March 13, 1944.

These animal rescuers were joined in their efforts by United States Coast Guard personnel from their nearby West 65th Street office, U. S. Army soldiers, and units of the Navy Shore Patrol. Some of the animals were so burned or stunned that they were unable to walk. One cow gave birth to a calf during the initial phase of the fire; both animals were burned to death minutes later. In all, 50 cattle and 25 hogs died in the conflagration, and more than one spectator was heard to bemoan the waste of meat ration points. Several observers, too, remarked on the irony of heroic attempts to rescue animals who were inevitably fated to end up as bacon, steaks, mutton, and veal in due time.

The hungry flames quickly consumed some of the stockyard buildings, sheds, and open pens. Then they advanced toward the covered pens and the livestock exchange, sending sparks toward other dwellings in the West 65th/Clark Avenue neighborhood. Cleveland firemen fought a desperate and ultimately successful battle to save the livestock exchange building and the covered pens. Sparks drifted over a house at 2251 West 65th Street, setting its asphalt shingle roof on fire. But firemen managed to put the fire out before it did much damage.

The Cleveland stockyards blaze was remarkable for the unusually good behavior of the large crowd of spectators it attracted. As readers of these chronicles know, Cleveland disasters have frequently drawn mobs of misbehaving civilians, whose antics have often compromised the work of Cleveland's safety forces. (For a prime example see the author's account of the 1953 West 117th

Cattle stampede from the flames. March 11, 1944.

Street explosion in "Smithereen Street," *The Killer in the Attic*, 2002.) Cleveland fire chief James E. Granger paid a rare compliment to the stockyards fire spectators when he commented, "These people did us a wonderful service. We are badly undermanned and appreciated the help we got. In fact, it was the finest assistance we have got since I've been in the service." That was really saying something, as Granger had been with the department since the early 1890s.

The central tragedy of the day came toward the end, as it often does in firefighting dramas. A group of firemen were standing next to the 14-foot-high wall of one of the meat processing buildings. As they did so, a fireman directed a stream of water against the same brick-tile, hollow-fill wall. The superheated wall immediately exploded, burying the men next to it in bricks and debris. Five firemen went down with the wall—and only three of them came out alive. When they finally put the fire out, about 6 p.m., firemen dragged out the bodies of Patrick Mangan and Norman Kitzerow. Injured firefighters James P. Ginley, James J. Leahy, and Raymond Horan were rushed to area hospitals.

Patrick Mangan, 52, lived at 1909 Walton Avenue. He was a 30-

year veteran of Engine Company No. 20. Mangan was survived by his wife of 25 years, Lillian, and three sisters. Kitzerow, also of Engine Company No. 20, left his wife Margaret and sons Jimmy, two, and Norman, Jr., six. James Ginley, a member of Hook and Ladder Company No. 9, was taken to St. John's Hospital, where he was treated for injuries incurred by falling bricks. James J. Leahy of the rescue squad, Engine House No. 33, was treated at City Hospital for burns. Raymond Horan, a member of the same rescue squad, was treated at St. John's Hospital and released. Meanwhile, a second fire, caused by "spontaneous combustion," broke out in the fire ruins at 12:38 a.m. and brought weary Cleveland fire units back to extinguish it.

The shock of the fire deaths and injuries soon engendered a sordid civic squabble. Chief Granger set it off the next day by charging that his firemen had been badly hampered by low water pressure in the stockyards area. Granger speculated that the water mains were too small and in bad condition. His comments set off an acrid exchange among city officials, especially after his complaints were echoed by Safety Director Anthony Celebrezze in his call for an investigation of Granger's charges. An angry Acting City Water Commissioner G. W. Hamlin retorted that he had not been "informed of any water pressure condition at the fire," and that, furthermore, it was the job of fire underwriters—not his department—to ascertain whether area water pressures were adequate to firefighting needs. The following day, March 13, Emil J. Crown, Cleveland Public Utilities director, weighed in, rejecting Granger's accusations wholesale. Noting that the 30-inch water main serving the stockyards area was as large as any in the city, Crown asserted that "there is not one iota of truth in the statement that there was insufficient water pressure available at the fire." He also claimed that some of the hydrants in the stockyards area were unusable simply because they were engulfed in flames at the time of the fire. At this point, Chief Granger climbed down, pledging to make his own private investigation. That was the last heard of the matter in public and no one ever took responsibility for the water pressure situation.

Meanwhile, the stockyards were already reviving. Almost as

soon as the flames were extinguished, 75 carpenters were at work constructing new livestock pens and temporary offices, and Cleveland Union Stockyards president A. Z. Baker vowed that his institution would be open for "business as usual" on Monday. He estimated the fire loss at $100,000, much lessened by the fact that the fire occurred on a Saturday afternoon, the lowest point in the production cycle of the stockyards. Had the fire occurred on a weekday, it is likely that both the human and animal tolls would have been higher.

Stockyard carpenters weren't the only ones working feverishly in the fire's aftermath. Cleveland arson investigators began combing through the ruins as soon as the embers cooled, searching for a clue to the unexplained inferno. They soon zeroed in on the southwest corner of the pens as the likely point of origin, and their suspicions focused on a group of neighborhood boys known for trespassing repeatedly in the area. But their investigation plodded along uneventfully for almost a year before they found a real clue, which came while they were investigating another fire. Someone had set the old Clark Elementary School at 5412 Clark Avenue on fire on January 12, 1944, two months before the stockyards fire. Arson probers had been working on the Clark School case for over a year when in February 1945, a neighbor remembered seeing an adolescent boy watching the Clark School fire, standing a bit apart from the other spectators. The neighbor had particularly noted the boy's tasseled stocking cap, and Cleveland Police detectives John Ungyary and George Connors soon identified the suspect. He was a 15-year-old retarded pyromaniac and a familiar figure to those who fought or chased West Side fires. Though he stoutly denied torching the Clark School, he readily confessed to Ungyary and Connors that he had set the stockyards fire.

The fact that the boy had been available to set the fire spoke volumes about the treatment of mentally challenged persons in the Cleveland of the 1940s. This youthful arsonist was the son of an epileptic mother who had already had two children taken away from her by authorities because she couldn't take proper care of them. Indeed, on January 6, 1944, the Cuyahoga County Probate Court had ordered the 15-year-old committed to a state institution

Rebuild Stock Pens, Fire Quiz Under Way

New pens and sheds, as nearly fireproof as it is possible to build, are planned for the fire-destroyed 15 acres at the Cleveland Union Stockyards, A. Z. Baker, company president, said today.

Cleveland Press, March 13, 1944.

for the feeble-minded. The boy's father had promised court officials to take him there, but somehow the committal had never taken place. Which is why the boy was sitting on a fence by the Earl C. Gibbs livestock pens on the afternoon of March 11, 1944, idly flicking matches at a pile of hay. His mother told the detectives that she thought he was telling the truth, and he was forthwith committed to a proper institution.

The Cleveland Union Stockyards quickly resumed normal operations after the fire. But the glory days of Cleveland as a meatpacking center were clearly on the wane, and livestock processing gradually shifted to other regions and cities. By 1968, when they closed down for good, the Cleveland Union Stockyards had shrunk from the 60 acres of its, er, salad days down to 35 acres. Seven years later, the structures on the stockyards site were razed, and a new shopping center rose where once cattle had brayed, sheep had bleated, and brave men had faced flames and died.

Chapter 6

DEATH ON DERBYSHIRE

The Newcomb Murder-Suicide (1934)

Where did things go wrong for Robert Newcomb? For most of his life he seems to have been Fortune's darling. After earning both medical and law degrees just before the turn of the 19th century, he soon rose to affluence and prominence in Cleveland's legal and social worlds. A partner in an illustrious and successful law firm, he was happily married and the father of two grown sons. He had a new home on a substantial street in Cleveland Heights and a wide circle of admiring friends. And yet it all came undone in a few minutes of violence one morning in 1934.

As was her habit, Maria Johnson arrived promptly for work that Monday morning, March 19, 1934. A domestic who lived at 2200 East 97th Street, Maria was always careful to catch a streetcar that would drop her off at 6 a.m. on Cedar Road, just a block away from the Newcomb residence at 2746 Derbyshire Road in Cleveland Heights. Following her settled routine, Maria let herself in the Newcomb house and went to the kitchen, where she put a kettle of water on the stove. It seemed a bit chilly that crisp March morning, so Maria's next task was to turn on the furnace in the basement.

Maria noticed two things when she got there. One was that there was a light on in the furnace room. The other was a red stain on the floor, running from the furnace toward a drain. Thinking it was rusty water, Maria walked around the furnace . . . to find her employer Robert Newcomb lying stark-staring-dead against the cellar wall. The red stain was not rusty water—it was blood coming from Robert's throat, which had been cut from ear to ear.

Perhaps not surprisingly, Maria momentarily yielded to hyster-

Lawyer Wields Ax On Sleeping Mate

Slashes His Own Throat With Razor; Leaves 4 Notes; Deed Attributed to Nervous Breakdown

Cleveland News, March 19, 1934.

ics. Screaming loudly, she ran up the cellar stairs to tell Faith New-comb, Robert's wife, what she had seen in the basement. Before she got to Faith's second-floor bedroom, however, she encountered Milliard R. Newcomb, 26, the younger of the Newcomb sons, who was living at the house. "Don't tell Mother," cautioned Milliard, and he went to the basement with Maria, where he found what she had seen. He then decided to awaken Mabel Warner, 72, Faith's mother, who was also staying at the house. He and Mabel then entered Faith's bedroom to give her the bad news.

Even the horrific scene in the basement could not have prepared Milliard and Mabel for what they found there. Faith was lying dead on her bed, her head smashed by two heavy blows. Beside her bed, on the floor, lay the instrument of her death—an ax, with its price tag of $1.35 still attached. On a nearby chair were her garments, and on another chair were Robert's trousers, his gold watch on top of them. His coat and vest were hanging from one of the bedposts.

The Cleveland Heights police and Cuyahoga County coroner Arthur J. Pearse soon arrived and rapidly came to some conclusions about what had occurred. Robert Newcomb had apparently awakened about 5:30 that morning. He then went to the basement and got an ax, which he had recently purchased. He climbed the stairs to Faith's bedroom, where he hit his sleeping wife twice with terrific force, using the blunt edge of the ax. (Mabel Warner had heard her daughter cry out once in the early morning, but she did not investigate.) Then Robert carefully placed the ax on the floor, returned to the basement, and there, by the furnace, methodically slashed his throat with a razor, employing all the skill that only a trained physician could bring to the task.

Why had this terrible thing happened? Nobody knew then—and nobody knows now. Apparently, behind his facade of personal, professional, and social success, something terrible was going on in the mind of Robert Newcomb. He had suffered a nervous breakdown in 1919 but had subsequently made an apparently complete recovery. Then, in early 1934, he began to experience the troubling symptoms of a reoccurrence. Robert began to hear voices again, and it wasn't long before he was eschewing his legal practice for almost daily "treatments" at the Cleveland Clinic. What exact malady he suffered is unknown, but some hints can be gleaned from the guarded comments of his brother Adrian, who described his final illness:

> He had been suffering from delusions at various times in recent weeks but never was there any indication of violence. And the encouraging thing about the delusions was his ability to laugh at them later.

What Robert's Cleveland Clinic "treatments" were is unknown. Whatever they were, Robert seemed to be recovering as mid-March of 1934 rolled around. He had resumed some of his office work, and his friends—the few who were aware of his psychological disturbance—seemed to think he was recovering his old upbeat and sociable self again. Although a lingering fear of crowds made him beg off an invitation to the Nisi Prius banquet at the Hollenden Hotel on March 17, he spent the following afternoon playing a strenuous round of golf-archery with Dr. Harry B. Kurtz, a medical school chum, at the Mayfield Country Club. Kurtz thought Robert was normal, and that evening, Sunday, March 18, Robert read quietly while his family and some guests played bridge at the house. He and Faith retired without incident at 11 p.m.

News of the Newcomb murder-suicide sent shock waves through the ranks of Cleveland's Social Register. Born in 1872 to a respectable New York City clan, Robert Burton Newcomb, whose family had come to Ohio when he was three, had grown up in Berea. Abiding his parents' wishes, he had attended Western Reserve University Medical School and graduated a physician several years later. But Robert Newcomb didn't want to practice medicine—and he never did—although the nickname "Doc" stayed with him until his death. Obtaining an undergraduate degree at

The first victim: Faith Newcomb.

Baldwin University, Robert entered Western Reserve University Law School and passed the bar in 1899, a year after he married Faith Warner. In 1900 he became a partner in the firm of Hopkins, Bole, Cobb & Newcomb, and five years later he joined with his brother Adrian and H. J. Nord to form a new law firm, Newcomb, Newcomb & Nord.

Over the next quarter-century Robert's law firm achieved eminent success. Prominent in the field of personal injury suits, the company prospered further from its role as legal counsel for the Brotherhood of Railroad Engineers. As tokens of their legal status, brother Adrian was honored with a brief appointment as a Cuyahoga County common pleas judge in 1923, and Robert earned professional and public kudos from his work to help reform the Cuyahoga County jury system and procedures.

It wasn't all roses and unstinting acclaim, however. Newcomb, Newcomb & Nord hit a rough patch in the early 1930s. Closely associated with the dealings of the Standard Trust Bank (of which Adrian was a director), the law firm was tarnished by accusations of making false entries after the Standard failed in 1931. Simultaneously, the firm came under fire from the Cleveland Bar Association, which charged its attorneys with violating rules designed to curb personal injury "ambulance chasing." But after two years of legal struggles over these matters, neither of the Newcomb brothers had been put in jail, and there was every reason to believe that the firm would weather its vicissitudes, as it eventually did.

Robert Newcomb also had much more to live for than just his struggling law firm. He had been married to Faith for 35 apparently happy years. He was on good terms with his sons Milliard and Robert, Jr. He had a wide circle of friends, socially cemented to him by memberships in the Mayfield, Hermit, and Athletic Clubs, the Cleveland Bar Association, and the Cleveland Chamber of Commerce. In addition, he nursed a passion for which he was well known: the Canadian wilderness. In the early years of the century Robert had discovered the wilds of northern Ontario, near Lake Tegami. He had soon become so besotted with the region that he purchased eight islands in the area and built eight fishing camps on them. He knew every inch of forest and water in the region, and his particular and persistent pleasure was to entertain his friends in the beauty of the frozen forests. He loved his frequent sojourns there with Faith every winter, and their home was filled with pictures from their many happy vacations. It was said in Ontario that he was worshipped as a near-god by the Ojibway Indians he encountered and employed at his Canadian camps. Moreover, Robert Newcomb had labored for years to foster better relations between Canada and the United States, leading goodwill delegations there and entertaining Canadian dignitaries in the United States.

A man on the brink: Robert Newcomb.

Coroner Pearse tersely disposed of the bloody doings on Derbyshire. Pronouncing Robert Newcomb mentally deranged through no fault of his own, Pearse conjectured that the lawyer had simply snapped without warning. Indeed, Pearse opined to reporters, the doings at 2746 could have been far more unfortunate:

> Without doubt, Mr. Newcomb was out of his head as a result of a nervous breakdown. It is fortunate that Mrs. Warner and Milliard did not get up at the time. If they had, he surely would have attacked them. Considering the mania that assailed him, it is surprising that Mr. Newcomb did not go through the house with the ax.

In making that judgment, Pearse may have had the benefit of information that he chose not to share with the public. It was reported in the newspapers that Robert left four penciled notes in the pocket of his coat found on Faith's bedpost. They were said to be unintelligible but containing "vague" references to his childhood.

Services were conducted at the Highland Park Cemetery chapel by a family friend, the Reverend Dilworth Lupton, on March 21. The bodies of Robert and Faith Newcomb were then cremated and their ashes buried in the cemetery. Twenty Canadian officials attended the last rites, and on August 5, 1934, a tablet honoring Robert's Canadian activities was dedicated in the Temagi Forest Reserve on Bear Island in Canada. The Derbyshire house was soon sold, and little remained of the Newcomb presence in Cleveland except for Adrian Newcomb's subsequent career. He survived his legal troubles to become a Cuyahoga County common pleas judge again in 1941, serving in that role until his death of a heart attack in 1953. At that time he was living in the former John Hartness Brown house at 2368 Overlook Road, a dwelling touched by tragedy in a previous era. (For details, see "Horror on the Heights" in the author's *They Died Crawling*, 1995.) Newcomb's Derbyshire Road death house eventually became the childhood home of the Reverend Nelson Callahan, the third pastor of St. Raphael Roman Catholic Church in Bay Village.

The reasons for Robert Newcomb's terrible acts remain unknown.

Chapter 7

THE VANISHING COED

The Disappearance of Ruth Baumgardner (1937)

Whatever happened to Ruth Baumgardner? Although her 1937 disappearance is not as famous an Ohio vanishing act as those of Melvin Horst or Beverly Potts, it remains a shocking and poignant mystery. It may have been a kidnapping perpetrated by a pervert, a phenomenon rare in Ruth's era but only too well known in the 21st century. It may have been a case of amnesia, a psychological explanation given more credulity back in the Great Depression years than now. Or it may have been a desperate attempt to begin a new life, free and far from the constraints and propriety of her middle-class existence. The only thing we know for sure is that we don't know any more of Ruth Baumgardner's fate than folks did in 1937.

We do know some details of her last day at Ohio Wesleyan University in Delaware, Ohio. Just a few weeks away from graduation, Ruth, a 22-year-old art major from Lakewood, was last seen by her fellow Delta Delta Delta ("Tri-Delt") sorority sisters in her dormitory, Austin Hall, shortly after 11 p.m. on May 4. Ruth had her hair in curlers and pins, and she exhibited no particular symptoms of distress or strain. Sometime before midnight, she said goodnight to her friends—and was never seen again by anyone who knew her.

Ohio Wesleyan University was a very small, tightly knit campus. When Ruth failed to attend any of her classes the following day, her Tri-Delt sisters alerted campus authorities at 10:30 that very evening. Organizing themselves into a virtual detective squad, the

Tri-Delts began checking with Delaware taxi drivers, railroad station and bus station personnel, and at all the campus hangouts. By the next day, May 6, everyone in Ohio and neighboring states was on the lookout for Ruth Baumgardner: 5 feet, 5 inches tall, 110 pounds, blue-gray eyes, and blonde hair with an irregular light streak on the left side.

The vanishing coed:
Ruth Baumgardner.

The mystery of Ruth's disappearance only deepened as authorities probed deeper into the case. Someone, presumably Ruth herself, had carefully left her dormitory room key on the back corner of an Austin Hall staircase, between the second and third floors. Her flame-red new Dodge automobile, an early graduation present, was found in its regular garage, with the key in the ignition. Ruth's room, rather uncharacteristically, was left in "apple-pie order," and her alarm clock, set for 6 a.m., had apparently run down that morning, suggesting that Ruth had arisen at 6 and left the dormitory without anyone seeing her. It seemed likely, from an inventory made of her clothes, that she had been wearing a brown suit, a sport hat, and brown "gillie" shoes and was carrying an old handbag when she left.

The initial theory of her disappearance, strongly embraced by her frantic parents, was that Ruth had suffered an attack of amnesia and was likely wandering God-knows-where amid Ohio's rural roads. Much stress was laid on her recent comment to a college chum that she was worried about earning all of her needed credit hours. This echoed a line she had written in her last letter to her father Carl in Lakewood, saying that "she had so many things to do she did not know how she was going to do them, and that she was extremely tired."

Disappearance of Coed Still Is Mystery After Three Years

Mystery surrounding the disappearance of attractive Ruth Baumgardner from the campus of Ohio Wesleyan University in Delaware remains as shrouded today as it did on May 4, 1937, the last day the art student, then 22, was seen alive by her sorority sisters.

On the third anniversary of her disappearance, her family, associates and the Burns Detective Agency, which investigated tips and rumors for more than a year, know no more than they did at the start of the nation-wide hunt.

Mrs. Richard Hardwick of 15802 Fernway avenue, a sister of the missing girl, said her parents have no idea whether their daughter is dead or alive.

"Time has somewhat soothed their grief," she said.

Mrs. Hardwick denied the most recent rumor heard here that Ruth had since returned home and that she is now in a sanitarium.

Many theories were expressed after the girl vanished from Austin Hall, girls' dormitory at the campus. Mrs. Baumgardner feared the disappearance was due to a nervous collapse, probably amnesia. The girl's mother stated that in the last few letters received at their home at 2093 Arthur avenue, Lakewood, Ruth wrote of being "very, very tired."

The only tangible clew in the case was supplied by two Zanesville women who reported to authorities

Ruth Baumgardner . . . still missing

ter. The trail could never be picked

Cleveland Press, May 3, 1940.

The amnesia explanation didn't fit well with the clues about Ruth that soon began accumulating from the multistate search for her. Mrs. Wilmer Smith, a resident living by the Oletangy River near the Ohio Wesleyan campus, reported hearing three eerie wails between 2 and 3 a.m. on the morning of May 5. Smith said they sounded like the cries of an hysterical person.

A barber in Worthington, Ohio, reported seeing a woman there matching Ruth's description about noon the same day. He said she was pacing back and forth on Grandview Road and wearing a brown suit.

Two women reported seeing Ruth in Zanesville the same day, shortly before noon. Mrs. Edward Hiehle and Mrs. R. A. Earick said she was hitchhiking, apparently with a young man whom they described as "collegiate."

H. B. Matthews, employed at the Baltimore & Ohio Railroad signal tower in Grafton, Ohio, reported seeing a girl matching

Grieving parents: Carl and Emma Baumgardner, 1937.

Ruth's description hitchhiking alone near his tower late in the day on Thursday, May 6.

Several days later, traveling salesman Joe W. Smith notified authorities he had given a lift in his automobile to a young man and a girl resembling Ruth Baumgardner in Nashville on May 7. Smith reported he had taken the pair to Memphis and that the young man had called his companion "Ruth."

Other sightings of Ruth were reported from West Springfield, Pennsylvania; Buffalo, New York; Henning, Tennessee; Pomona, California; and La Mesa, New Mexico. The most bizarre Ruth sighting came in New York City, where an unstable young woman passed herself off as the missing Ohio coed until being unmasked as a poseur from Fulton Street.

Inevitably, as one dead-end clue after another was probed and discarded, suspicions began to grow that Ruth had arranged her own disappearance. The alleged sightings of Ruth with a young male companion did much to foster such conclusions. But why would Ruth have done such a thing and in such a manner? As far as anyone knew, Ruth was happily engaged to her steady boyfriend back in Lakewood, and none of her friends was aware that Ruth had nourished any alternative passion. Moreover, it seemed likely that Ruth could not have had more than $5 on her person when she vanished, hardly the hefty bankroll needed to subsidize a new life and identity.

The alternative theories, that Ruth had been the victim of a kidnapper or a mishap, had no evidence for or against them. An exhaustive search, especially of the nearby quarries popular with Ohio Wesleyan students, failed to turn up any trace of Ruth. There seemed nothing in her personal or campus life to suggest that Ruth had run afoul of anyone on campus. Authorities were unable to discover which young man had made repeated—and unsuccessful— attempts to contact Ruth by telephone the evening before she disappeared.

And so the search ground on, day after day, and as May stretched into June, and then into July, the hopes of her heartbroken parents began to fade. A search for Ruth by operatives of the Burns detective agency was likewise unsuccessful, and all active attempts to find her eventually ground to a baffled halt.

To this day, no one knows what happened to Ruth Baumgardner, and her fate remains one of the saddest of Ohio's unsolved mysteries.

Chapter 8

THE BLACK SILK HANDKERCHIEF

The Murder of John Shipp (1900)

Cleveland has had its share of racially charged cop killings. Most recent was the murder of Patrolman Hilary Cudnik in December 1996. Both the ensuing trial and its startling denouement (killer Leonard Hughes's life was spared by the stubborn will of a lone juror) aggravated the racial tensions and animosities that ever percolate throughout Cleveland's civic life. Older readers will recall the incomparable horror of the 1968 Glenville Shootout, when African-American militants killed three Cleveland policemen and wounded 14 others. Truly antique readers may even recall John Leonard Whitfield's 1923 slaying of Patrolman Dennis Griffin and the thrilling, multistate manhunt that enthralled Roaring Twenties Clevelanders. (For more details of the Whitfield sensation see the author's "God, the Devil, Man or Beast," in *They Died Crawling,* 1995.) There have been other police murders with racial overtones, the level of civic tensions usually corresponding roughly to the overall state of race relations in the Forest City. But for sheer violence coupled with unique touches of the bizarre, it would be hard to exceed the first of the breed: the slaying of Cleveland Police patrolman John Shipp by Ed Rutheven in 1900.

This tale, like so many others, begins with the acute intuition of a woman. Rose Nienhuser of 26 Charles Street (now East 26th Street) must have been restive that warm spring evening of May 6, 1900. Instead of focusing on her own domicile on the east side of the street, she was keeping a careful eye on the house next door. The two-story frame dwelling just south of hers was the residence of the Henry W. Lueking family. Rose knew that Henry had taken his family to visit a relative in the country (which is what citified Clevelanders called Newburgh Township in that bygone era). So Rose was somewhat surprised when she heard a window raised in the Lueking house shortly after 8 p.m. She was even more intrigued when she saw someone light a match near one of the windows. Seconds later, the match flickered out. Then, at frequent

John Shipp, the victim.

intervals, the dim figure inside the Lueking house lit more matches, as it moved from room to room. After watching for several minutes, Rose Nienhuser had seen enough. Turning to her husband, she said, "George, I think there's a burglar in the Lueking house!"

George Nienhuser didn't hesitate a moment. Going to his front porch, he called across the street to George Fluck, who was enjoying the pleasant Sunday evening on his porch at 25 Charles. Fluck departed immediately in search of a policeman. Walking a block south to Woodland Avenue, he turned left and soon found Patrolmen John Shipp and Charles Dangler at the corner of Woodland and Sterling Avenue (East 30th Street). Informing them that there was a burglar in the Lueking house, Fluck accompanied the officers back to Charles Street.

It is likely that few present-day lawmen would endorse the tactics used by Shipp and Dangler that fatal evening. Arriving at the Lueking residence, they decided that Shipp should stay put at the front, northwest corner of the house, while Dangler went around the south side to the rear. But as soon as Dangler departed, Shipp apparently began walking toward the rear of the house on the north side. A few seconds later, Dangler heard him mutter, "He's inside, Charley; I can hear him." (That was Dangler's story; Rose Nien-

THE CENTRAL-AV SHOOTING.
The smaller picture shows the house at Central and Greenwood from which the suspect escaped.

The Central Avenue shootout. *Cleveland Press*, May 7, 1900.

huser would later testify that she heard Shipp imprudently call to the burglar inside, "Now I've got you. Come out of there or we'll blow your head off!") Meanwhile, Dangler stepped up onto a side porch and tried to open a door and adjacent window, but they were locked.

Shipp's death came without warning. Just as Dangler left the porch to go around the back, he heard three shots ring out. The shots were apparently coming from a pantry window on the north side near the back, and Dangler was close enough to see the flame from a revolver. Pulling out his own revolver, he shouted, "Don't shoot, Shipp, the bullets will hit me!" Then he saw Shipp, tottering slowly around the corner toward him. Shipp stumbled a few feet, mumbled, "Charley, I'm shot," and sat down heavily on the ground. He was bleeding profusely from wounds in his neck, chest, and leg and was dead within two minutes.

A moment later, the stunned Dangler saw a head masked with a black silk handkerchief lean out the pantry window. Dangler fired twice and missed, as did the gunman inside. Retreating for cover to an outhouse in the rear, Dangler waited for the gunman to make the next move. It came a minute later when the gunman smashed the glass out of a kitchen window in the southeast corner of the house. Dangler got ready to shoot him as he came out.

The broken window was just a clever ruse. While Dangler patiently waited, the gunman stealthily moved to the front of the house. Opening a front window, he scanned the street. He spied George Fluck and neighbors Frederick H. Meyer and Mrs. Charles Koester on the street, so he fired a warning shot, which struck Mrs. Koester in the foot and knocked her down. As the other neighbors fled for cover, the gunman leaped out the front window and began running north. As he passed Mrs. Nienhuser on her porch next door, he menaced her with his revolver and she fled indoors. He then turned to run east down the side of her yard, tripped over a low wire fence, and went sprawling. As he hit the ground, a revolver, a box of cartridges, and the black silk handkerchief all went flying from his grasp. Before he could retrieve them, however, he spied the tardy Dangler, who had been alerted to his escape by the shot fired at Mrs. Koester. The gunman picked himself up and fled to the back of the Nienhuser lot, leapt over a fence, and ran north on Jackson Court (East 27th Street) toward Scovill Avenue. Seconds later, Patrolman Dangler tripped over the same low wire fence, tore his uniform, sprained his arm, and dropped his gun. By the time he got up, there was no trace of the gunman or any clue as to where he had gone.

It didn't take the Cleveland police very long to focus on a suspect. Although the descriptions of the burglar/gunman tendered by witnesses were vague, the police already had an excellent candidate in mind. For some weeks, Police Chief George Corner's men had been aware that Ed Rutheven (alias Harry Flick), an African-American career criminal specializing in house burglary, had returned to Cleveland and was practicing his nocturnal craft on Cleveland's East End. Recently arrested and incarcerated for shooting at policemen in Galion, Ohio, Rutheven had escaped from

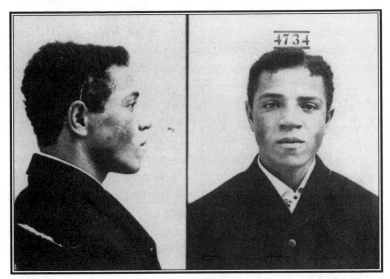

Not at his best: Cleveland Police Department mug shots of Ed Rutheven.

the Crawford County jail in Bucyrus on April 16, thanks to a steel saw smuggled into his cell by his girlfriend, Lizzie Fisher (alias Lizzie Chilia). Given Rutheven's lengthy record of burglary and shooting at policemen, Police Chief Corner and Sergeant of Detectives James Doran were quickly persuaded that he was the probable killer of John Shipp.

Indeed, Chief Corner had assigned his stenographer, African-American patrolman Charles Smith, to the task of finding Rutheven several weeks earlier. By early May, Smith had located him in a house at the southeast corner of Central Avenue and Greenwood Street (East 28th Street), where he was living with Lizzie Chilia and another couple, James (Ed Rutheven's brother-in-law) and Ida Belle Fearon. Ironically, it was that very same evening of May 6, at 7 p.m.—barely 90 minutes before Shipp was shot—that surveillance of Rutheven's residence had begun.

It was never explained how Ed Rutheven evaded the notice of the policemen who watched his house that night. Neither of the officers assigned to the 7 p.m. to 1 a.m. shift saw him return to his house after the Charles Street shootout, nor did Detective Albert Walker and Patrolmen Charles Smith and Harry Wilmore, who took over the stakeout at 1 a.m. Shortly after 10 the following morning, Detective James Doran and Patrolman Arthur Lacey arrived on the scene. Conferring hastily with the officers already there, Doran made the decision to move in. They posted Lacey to guard the rear of the house and entered the building with guns drawn. Wilmore remained on the landing while Doran, Smith, and Walker climbed to the second floor and opened the door.

A worthy mate: Lizzie Chilia, November, 1900. *Cleveland Leader*, November 19, 1901

Ed Rutheven wasn't there, but Lizzie Chilia greeted them sullenly as they filed into the room. Also present were James and Ida Belle Fearon and the landlady, an ancient African-American female named Emma "Aunty" Davis. It's not likely any of them were ready to cooperate with the police—but then it's only fair to say they never got much of a chance. Doran had just begun his interrogation when the first shot resounded outside.

Somehow, Ed Rutheven had seen the police coming. Apparently escaping through an unguarded window on the first floor, he silently slipped to the ground. While running through several back-yards he encountered an African-American woman, Jennie Hilton, at the door of her residence. He put a revolver to her head, thus persuading her to be quiet while he ran through her flat and out a door onto Central Avenue. As he emerged into the morning sun, he spotted Patrolman Lacey, still standing sentinel at the rear of Rutheven's house. Squatting in the middle of Central Avenue, Ed Rutheven took careful aim with his revolver and fired two quick rounds at Patrolman Lacey.

Amazingly, Rutheven missed, even at such point-blank range. After two bullets whizzed through his hat, the surprised Lacey began returning fire, a fusillade in which he was soon joined by Smith, Wilmore, and Walker as they stormed out of the Rutheven house in support. Not that they helped the situation much: the running gun battle that now developed only further compromised the rapidly fraying reputation of the Cleveland Police Department. As many as 50 shots were exchanged as the shootout raged up Central Avenue, down Greenwood Street, up Pine Avenue, and then north on Sterling Avenue. It was a miracle no one was killed, for the evidence of the indiscriminate gunfire could later be charted in the bullet-marked storefronts, lead-riddled utility poles, and shattered plate-glass windows in the affected streets. Not to mention the trauma suffered by dozens of terrified civilians who found themselves trapped for some endless minutes in the Wild West–like melee played out in the Central Avenue neighborhood. Astonishingly, the only casualty of this ballistic free-for-all was John H. Rimes of 581 Central Avenue, whose leg was grazed by a bullet as he ran for cover.

The Central Avenue shootout came close to causing another tragedy when Charles Smith stumbled while trading shots with Rutheven on Greenwood Street. Leaping toward the prostrate policeman Rutheven chortled, "Now I've got you," and raised his revolver to shoot. But the wily Smith was too quick: twisting away from Rutheven's shot, he fired a slug into his shoulder. Rutheven vaulted a fence, clutching his arm in pain, and ran up Pine Street to Sterling Avenue, where he kept on going. He was last seen running toward Prospect Street by a frustrated Patrolman Wilmore, who had to abandon pursuit when he fell and his antiquated service revolver disintegrated on the pavement.

Meanwhile, back at Rutheven's flat, Sergeant Doran was conducting his unfriendly interview with Lizzie Chilia. Although she proved uncommunicative, Doran eventually became curious about the sunbonnet she nervously clutched in her hand. Suddenly snatching at it, he uncovered a loaded .44-caliber revolver clutched in her hand. He took it from her and remarked, "I may have more use for this than you would." He then arrested everyone on the

A caustic view of police marksmenship.
Cleveland Press, May 7, 1900.

premises as "suspicious persons" and had them carted off to cells at the Central Police Station on Champlain Street. Doran now turned the apartment upside down, and his searches were not in vain: stolen goods from at least two dozen East End burglaries were stashed in the flat and the outhouse to the rear, including items of jewelry and a perfume bottle taken from the Lueking house the night before.

Public reaction to the Central Avenue shootout was uncharitable to Cleveland's Finest. Journalists at the *Cleveland Press* were particularly withering, running a brutally sarcastic cartoon that mocked their failure to capture Rutheven and reportage that excoriated the marksmanship of the police:

> . . . [the] most bungling piece of work ever done by the Cleveland police. One lone man was trapped by six able-bodied

police. The lone gunman escaped and managed to shoot holes through the clothing of policemen, while the police could only hit telephone poles, windows, and almost kill innocent civilians.

Doran and his squad were ultimately excused when the public learned that his officers had been carrying obsolete revolvers and that virtually no Cleveland policeman was afforded regular target practice. On May 8 a patrolman demonstrated to a sympathetic *Cleveland Leader* reporter that it took fully two minutes to reload his antique Merwin & Hubbard revolver, whereas the average Cleveland criminal sported modern guns that could be reloaded in just 15 seconds. An alarmed Mayor John Farley immediately ordered regular target practice for the police and promised them new revolvers.

Attention now turned to Patrolman Shipp and the hunt for his killer. Shipp, an Englishman by birth, had joined the Cleveland police force on December 2, 1892. A brave and conscientious officer, he was well liked by his peers and esteemed by the 3rd Precinct residents he had served for almost eight years. Police Lieutenant John Schriber recalled the time that Shipp attempted to arrest a belligerent rowdy in a Woodland Avenue dive. As soon as Shipp collared him, the rowdy's confederates attacked Shipp and tried to wrest his prisoner away. Although outnumbered five to one, Shipp managed to bring his man in, and the next day he returned to the saloon and arrested one of his assailants. During another such altercation in front of a saloon, Shipp was beaten so badly that he became blinded by his own blood. Despite his distress, however, he retained enough presence of mind to remember there was a barrel within arm's reach. Picking it up, he slammed it down over his foe and kept him trapped until help arrived.

The 45-year-old Shipp left a wife and four children to grieve for him at their home at 190 Seelye Avenue (East 53rd Street). He had two boys by his first marriage, Arthur, 20, and Frank, 18. Some 18 months before his death the widowed Shipp had married Florence Covill, herself a widow with two children of her own, Clyde, 26, and Bessie, 17. And, as sympathetic newspaper coverage soon made clear, Shipp's murder left his family in dire financial straits. There were no pensions for the families of murdered Cleveland policemen in 1900, and Shipp had not been eligible for membership in the officers' voluntary insurance pool. Arthur Shipp was a cripple with little earning capacity, and the family had no capital assets, not even a claim on their rented home. When it was learned that Florence Shipp lacked even the money to pay for her husband's interment, Cleveland's newspapers sprang into action. Within three days of the murder the *Cleveland Leader, Cleveland Plain Dealer,* and *Cleveland Press* had set up special funds for the relief of the Shipp family. The list of subscribers to these funds, published repeatedly in the newspapers, included such elite citizens as Samuel Mather, Jeptha Wade, and chewing gum magnate Dr. Edward Beeman. More significantly, the *Cleveland Press* organized a benefit concert, which took place at the Cleveland Chamber of Commerce on the evening of Friday, May 18. It featured the acclaimed "Meistersingers" and a galaxy of local musical talent, concert tickets went for $1 apiece, and the final proceeds amounted to $1,147. Together with the newspaper funds, it was enough money to save Florence Shipp from penury and to buy her a home of her own.

John Shipp's funeral took place at his Seelye Avenue home on Wednesday, May 9. The services, conducted by the Reverend C. Frederick Brookins of St. Mary's Episcopal Church, attracted a throng of over 1,000 persons. Shipp's casket was flanked by impressive floral displays, including one contributed by his undertaker, J. & W. Koebler: a floral re-creation of his badge number, "178." Following the rites, a solemn procession of policemen and members of the Knights of Malta and the Sons of St. George accompanied the coffin to the receiving vault at Woodland Cemetery.

The official investigation of Shipp's murder did not much accelerate the hunt for his killer, but it did collect a useful catalog of the largely circumstantial evidence in the case. Shipp's autopsy, conducted by Dr. Guy H. Horwell on May 7, found three .38-caliber slugs in Shipp's corpse. The first bullet had hit his neck and severed the jugular vein; the second had drilled through his right lung and hit the spinal column; the third had hit him just above the right knee, shattering his femur. The .38-caliber slugs caused some initial confusion, as the weapon dropped by Shipp's killer when he stumbled at the low wire fence was a .32-caliber revolver. The confusion was soon cleared up by Henry Lueking, who reported that the burglar had stolen *his* .38-caliber revolver and a box of compatible cartridges.

The loot from Henry Lueking's home that was found at Rutheven's flat tied Rutheven to Shipp's murder. In addition, $7,000 worth of loot found there—the swag from several dozen other burglaries—was eventually identified by the East Side victims of Rutheven's prodigious larceny. Among them were items stolen from the Lueking home, including three pairs of cufflinks, a gold watch chain, two shirt studs, a garnet brooch, and the box of .38-caliber cartridges. By May 9 the Cleveland police had enough information to send out a circular to every police station in the Midwest. It identified Shipp's killer as one Ed Rutheven (alias Flick), and described him as a Negro, about 5 feet, 5 inches, 150 pounds, with black eyes, dark, curly hair, and a freckled face. He was said to wear a dark, double-breasted sack coat and a soft black hat. He was also reported to be a morphine addict.

Like the frantic 1887 manhunt for cop-killer "Blinky" Morgan (see the author's account of the Morgan affair, "Bring Out Your Man!" in *The Maniac in the Bushes and More Tales of Cleveland Woe,* 1997) and the inept 1923 dragnet for John Leonard Whitfield, the search for Ed Rutheven was replete with silliness, hysteria, and folly. Stimulated perhaps by the $1,000 reward offered by the City of Cleveland and Cuyahoga County for Rutheven's capture, citizens from all over the United States were soon reporting his sighting or capture. One man had seen him hopping a freight out of Linndale; another espied him imbibing in a Broadway Avenue saloon; another found him sleeping in a Cedar Avenue barn; while still other perspicacious souls saw him in Elyria, Hudson, and Columbus. Even the police were not free from such mass hallucinations: on May 10 the Cleveland Police Department received a telegram from the Buffalo, New York, police announcing that Rutheven had been apprehended as he attempted to enter Canada at Niagara Falls.

None of these reports had any substance to them, and the lack of progress in the Rutheven manhunt soon produced predictable recriminations. On the day of Shipp's funeral, Mayor John ("Honest John") Farley bitterly denounced the judges of the Cleveland police court. Claiming that they were partially responsible for Shipp's murder, Farley charged that Detective James Doran had arrested Rutheven in May of 1899 on a concealed weapons charge. Subsequently, Police Court judge William F. Fieldler had fined Rutheven $10 and sent him to the Workhouse until it was paid. Only three days later, however, Judge Fieldler had succumbed to the tearful pleas of Lizzie Chilia. Claiming to be Rutheven's lawful wife, the persuasive Lizzie bleated that Ed was the sole support of her and their two young children—a farrago of lies, to say the least—and Judge Fieldler reduced the fine to $5, which a grateful Lizzie paid. Thus it was, Farley thundered, that a bleeding-heart, wrist-slapping judge had freed a brazen killer to go out and murder Cleveland policemen.

Judge Fieldler responded to Farley in kindred dudgeon. Expressing extreme doubt that he had ever even sentenced Rutheven, Fieldler stoutly defended his alleged judicial conduct:

> [Rutheven] had no criminal record at the time that the police were aware of. Anyway, how could I anticipate even if he were the man that he would kill the policeman a year later? I have never knowingly allowed a bad man his freedom, as the mayor has. Soon after he took office, the mayor pardoned Shurleff and Wilson, who had tapped the wires of the Western Union Telegraph Co. Instead of aiding the courts, the mayor clogs them and he is clogging the wheels of justice now.

Thankfully, such unseemly civic bickering came to a halt precisely at 2:30 p.m. on Saturday, June 2, when word came from Indianapolis of Rutheven's capture. The police there were well acquainted with Rutheven and had suffered some unpleasant dealings with him in recent years. They also knew that he sometimes consorted there with a woman named Fanny Demares, Lizzie Chilia's sister-in-law, in a house at 1134 Lafayette Street. After receiving the circular on Rutheven sent out by the Cleveland police, they staked out Fanny Demares's house. By June 2, they were satisfied that Rutheven was there, and they decided to bring him in.

The Indianapolis police were probably aware of the May 7 Central Avenue fiasco. In any case, they didn't take chances when they came to arrest Rutheven. Wielding shotguns and revolvers, Detectives Thomas Dugan and Samuel Gerber and two patrolman barged in the back door at 1134 Lafayette, while Captain of Detectives Jerry Kinney and a Detective Splan came in the front door. Rutheven saw Kinney as he came through the door and ran the other way, only to find Dugan and Gerber coming at him. Kinney's squad had been warned to "take no chances" with Rutheven, so when Gerber saw him raising a revolver toward Kinney, he shot him in the back. Even as he fell to the floor under a pile of policemen, however, Rutheven continued to fight like a wild animal until a blow from Splan's pistol knocked him out. Taken to a heavily guarded hospital room, Rutheven was identified two days later by Patrolman Charles Smith, who reported that Rutheven cried when he saw him, perhaps recalling the bullet that Smith had fired into his shoulder on Greenwood Street.

Ten days later, a rapidly recovering Rutheven was brought back to Cleveland and placed in a special hospital cell at the Cuyahoga County Jail. Lizzie Chilia, who was also a guest there on a charge of receiving stolen property, somehow learned of his arrival and hollered, "Hello, Ed!" as he was hustled past her cell window. Although she otherwise refused to talk about her "husband" or his doings, Ed Rutheven gave expansive interviews to several Cleveland reporters during his first days back in Cleveland. Apparently convinced that he had a permanent license to shoot at policemen, he insisted that it was only bad luck and the poor sportsmanship of the Indianapolis Police that had brought him low on Lafayette Street:

> If I had only seen those Indianapolis police coming, there would
> have been a cleaning up in the police department had they
> attempted to prevent my departure. The trouble was that a
> policeman in citizen's clothes got into the house and into the
> room where I was sitting before I saw him. Rushing to the back

door I came face to face with another. He shoved a gun in my face. I reached for mine. It was old-fashioned [Henry Lueking's .38-caliber revolver] and the hammer clung to my pocket. Then he shot me. When I got my gun out I would have laid him low but the bullet, which had entered near my spinal column, paralyzed my shooting finger and I could not pull the trigger. Then they knocked me down with a club. . . . They couldn't have caught me in ten years if I had seen them coming. There were plenty of fences and posts for me to dodge behind and I could have kept them pretty busy with my gun while I got away. . . . I would have shot my way out as easily as I did in Cleveland. When the Cleveland officers came for me in Greenwood Street I saw them and I knew I'd get away. I didn't want to shoot any of them and didn't use my gun until Policeman Smith sent several bullets at me. One of them struck a coin in my pants pocket and came near landing me. Then it was time to shoot my way out, which I did. Smith and another officer dropped to the ground for protection when I began banging.

Rutheven also admitted to reporters that he had escaped from Cleveland only seconds after the Central Avenue shootout by boarding an interurban streetcar bound for Painesville. But he refused to discuss either the Lueking burglary or Shipp's murder, and he expressed a breezy fatalism as to what would have happened if Gerber's bullet had hit his spine: "Oh, that wouldn't matter much! I've got to die sometime . . . it doesn't make any difference to me. They can do what they please with me, send me to the electric chair or let me go."

The record of Ed Rutheven's stay at the Cuyahoga County Jail affords a glimpse of the relative casualness of local penology at the turn of the last century. Like Lizzie Chilia, Rutheven was a morphine addict and, like her, was allowed to purchase and consume needed quantities of the drug during his tenure in the county jail. Indeed it was reported in the August 10, 1900, edition of the *Cleveland Press* that Rutheven was clamoring for the county to pick up the tab for his drug habit.

Another episode during his incarceration speaks volumes about the casual ubiquity of firearms in turn-of-the-century Cleveland. On the morning of July 4, Rutheven was drawn to his cell window by the sound of gunfire. Peering through the bars, he saw a young boy firing a revolver into the air. Rutheven called out, "Say, why don't you give me that pistol?" The boy looked at Rutheven and said, "What do you want it for?" Rutheven replied, "Well, I would make things a little warm around here for the police." The boy declined to give Rutheven his gun, retorting, "No, you already know how to use it too well."

Rutheven's trial on four counts of first-degree murder finally got under way on October 29, 1900. A marathon of almost four weeks, it was a dramatic and acrimonious affair from start to finish. Held in Judge William B. Neff's common pleas courtroom in the county courthouse just north of Public Square, the trial took place behind a hastily constructed barrier, which included a six-foot-high iron railing topped with a heavy metal curtain. Designed to keep curiosity-seekers from too closely pressing upon the business of the court, the barrier was immediately denounced by Rutheven's counsel. Insisting that it was a "cage," they charged that it was designed to prejudice Rutheven's jurors into believing that he was some sort of wild beast in need of unprecedented restraints. If there were any wild beasts present in the courtroom, however, they were more likely Rutheven's energetic attorneys, Harrison J. Ewing and Robert S. Avery. Fighting for Rutheven's life without quarter or civility, they objected to almost every word uttered by prosecutors Harvey Keeler and Thomas J. Ross during the lengthy trial. And although they failed to save their client's life or even to have most of their hundreds of objections sustained by a supremely patient Judge Neff, they did succeed in persuading some elements of Cleveland's African-American community that Rutheven's trial was a racist farce. Even before jury selection ended, a protest was framed by local black leaders and sent to Judge Neff:

> Whereas the crime charged against [Rutheven] is no more foul and inhuman than in the cases of Smith, Arden, "Blinky" Morgan and others know as notorious criminals, they were not confined in a cage like some wild animal or ferocious beast. And in

view of these facts we feel it has, and will continue to intimidate
and influence the jurors to prejudice against the prisoner.

While the lawyers wrangled over jury selection—with Ewing
insisting that each successive venire was illegally drawn—
Rutheven entertained the standing-room-only crowd with a demonstration of his theatrical prowess. Early on the afternoon of the first
day's session, he suddenly paled, pitched backwards over his chair
onto the floor, and began vomiting, foaming at the mouth, and
writhing in spastic convulsions. Then he fainted dead away and
could not be roused even when a bucket of water was thrown into
his face. Taken apparently unconscious back to his cell, he continued his convulsions for several more hours. Although Judge Neff
was impressed enough to recess the court until the following day,
remarking that it was excessively hot, a more cynical James Doran
opined that Rutheven had deliberately made himself sick by eating
a bar of soap. When he returned to court the next morning,
Rutheven vigorously disputed Doran's charge, blandly insisting,
"Why, I swallowed a cud of tobacco and then took a drink of water.
I like good eating too much to eat soap."

Thanks to Ewing and Avery's incessant objections, it took a full
week to impanel Rutheven's 12 male jurors. But the inevitable
tedium of the process was enlivened by a few moments of
unscripted humor. When prospective juror William Smith, a white
ex-policeman, was asked by Ewing if he were related to Rutheven,
he angrily snapped, "Do I look like it?" And when Bartholomew
Lucy, a retired Irish factory worker, was asked by Ewing if there
were not "some race prejudice between Irish and colored people,"
Lucy tartly riposted:

> Ask me something personal to myself, sir, and I'll answer. I am
> an Irishman, but I don't feel called upon to answer questions
> relating to my entire people.

More sensibly, the defense lawyers asked each prospective juror
if he had race prejudice, whether he belonged to any secret society,
and whether he would believe a colored witness as readily as a
white one.

From beginning to end, the Rutheven trial revolved almost entirely around circumstantial evidence. Try as they might—and they strove heroically—Ewing and Avery were unable to diminish the impact of that evidence as it was paraded before the jury over the following two weeks. All the goods stolen from the Lueking home that turned up 13 hours later in Rutheven's apartment were identified by the Luekings. A most damning item of physical evidence was the revolver taken from Rutheven when he was captured in Indianapolis. The .38 Smith & Wesson had originally belonged to Henry Lueking, and he readily identified it in court. Even more damning for Rutheven was the black silk handkerchief, seen by numerous witnesses masking the face of the Charles Street burglar and later retrieved by Frederick Meyer where the fleeing killer had dropped it by the low wire fence. Not only had Rutheven stolen that handkerchief from the home of Carrie Scheible at 156 Commonwealth Avenue on April 25, he had actually admitted to Scheible's husband, during one of his voluble jailhouse interviews, that he had taken it. Worse yet, the talkative Rutheven had told James Doran, again during one of his loquacious jailhouse interviews, that "he trusted no one" and that "if anything was in [his apartment] he took it there himself." So, despite the lack of an eyewitness who could identify Rutheven as Shipp's killer, Keeler and Ross were able to link him firmly and fatally with the stolen goods, the murder weapon, and the burglar/killer's black silk handkerchief.

Just to make sure, Keeler pulled a surprise witness out of his hat at the end of the state's presentation. Placing C. M. Vorce, a prominent "microscopist," on the stand, Keeler led Vorce through a painstaking ballistics tutorial for the benefit of the jury. Based on his comparison of exploded revolver shells left by Shipp's killer on the floor of the Lueking pantry with some shells fired from the revolver taken from Rutheven in Indianapolis, Vorce used enlarged illustrations (magnified 67 times) of the shells to support his conclusion that all of the bullets had been fired from the same revolver. His impressive, meticulous performance left Ewing sputtering with objections and put Rutheven ever closer to the hot seat. As if that weren't enough, Vorce also persuaded the jury that the marks of forced entry found on the windows of the Lueking house perfectly matched the business end of a burglar's "jimmy" found at

Rutheven's flat. After winning a two-day recess from Judge Neff, Ewing returned to the fray with his own "expert witness," R. W. Whitney, who attempted to dispute and disparage Vorce's illustrations and qualifications. But Whitney proved an ineffective witness, especially after he was forced to admit that he had little experience with microscopes or magnification.

The relentless and cumulative impact of the circumstantial evidence eventually forced Ewing and Avery to take the supreme risk of putting both Ed Rutheven and Lizzie Chilia on the witness stand. This gambit was particularly perilous, as the two had not been permitted to converse privately during their months of incarceration and could not have concocted a mutual alibi. Lizzie went first, on the afternoon of November 19, 1900, and her appearance did not disappoint the standing-room-only crowd of spectators, as the next morning's *Cleveland Leader* reported:

> She appeared, not as if she had stepped from her cell in the jail where she had been confined for almost five months, but from a hansom cab at the door of the Court House. Her feet were encased in patent leather shoes, the soles of which had only been soiled by the walk from the women's department of the County Jail to the witness stand. Her black silk dress was of an elaborate pattern and expensive material, and she wore an elegant sealskin jacket. Her hat was a large one and completely covered with ostrich feathers. She affected a most solemn mien.

As she passed by Rutheven on the way to the witness stand, Lizzie bent over, took both of his hands in hers, and kissed him long and tenderly.

Lizzie's testimony on the stand may have lacked for plausibility, but it did not fail on the score of invention. She claimed that on the evening of May 6, between 9 and 10, she had encountered a man known to her only as "Jacobs" at her front door. She knew him as a vague acquaintance of Ed Rutheven's, and when Jacobs asked to see him, she told Ed that he was there. Then, as she discreetly watched, she saw Jacobs hand Rutheven a bundle covered with a white cloth. She heard Jacobs say, "Get what you can out of this," and then saw him hand Ed a burglar's "jimmy." Although Lizzie claimed she didn't know Jacobs's full name or where he lived, Keeler could not shake her basic story. But he took quick revenge. Without warning, he suddenly demanded that Lizzie admit that she was not, in fact, Rutheven's legal wife, as she claimed to be. When she blandly admitted the fact, Keeler dramatically asked the bailiff to call William Fisher to the stand. Sure enough, out trotted Lizzie's real husband, who identified himself to the jury and calmly told the tale of how Lizzie had deserted him for Rutheven. His appearance was, as Ewing angrily charged, a "grandstand play," moreover one of negligible tactical value. But it may have served its purpose of further unnerving Ed Rutheven, for his own testimony that afternoon, following Lizzie's, was a disaster.

After telling the jury he was born in Memphis in 1871, Rutheven told them of coming north in the 1880s, working as a circus roustabout, and the circumstances of his two-year term in an Indiana prison on a burglary rap. When queried aggressively by Keeler as to what he had been doing after his escape from the Bucyrus jail on April 16, Rutheven merrily replied, "Hidin' from the police." After admitting that he had been living with Lizzie at the Greenwood Street house in May, he simply repeated her crude fictions about a man named Jacobs. Asked if he could describe Jacobs, the rattled Rutheven got into a screaming match with Keeler, shouting, "Yes, but I won't, I won't tell you and you will never learn from me. It's none of your business, anyway." After some prodding by Judge Neff, Rutheven availed himself of his constitutional right to remain silent on all matters except his insistence that he knew nothing about the Lueking burglary or the murder of John Shipp. When he finished testifying, Prosecutor Keeler mocked his refusal to reveal anything about Jacobs, sarcastically reading out the names of every "Jacobs" listed in the Cleveland City Directory and subpoenaing one of them at random.

For all of Ewing's rhetorical concern about race prejudice against his client, there was little overt evidence of it at the trial. True, Prosecutor Keeler got so carried away at one point as to say that Rutheven had no more rights than a "dog," but as Judge Neff noted, such oratorical excesses were normal in capital cases, regardless of the defendant's race. Indeed, the most explicitly racist exchange of the trial was initiated by defense lawyer Ewing, during his cross-examination of African-American patrolman Charles Smith about the May 7 Central Avenue shootout:

> Ewing: Were you not riveted to the spot and didn't every kink in your hair stand up straight when you saw Rutheven running towards you?
> Keeler: I object to the witness being insulted.
> Ewing: What clap-trap.

Ewing's talent for abuse blossomed further as the parade of state witnesses and physical exhibits put Rutheven ever closer to the electric chair. During his sarcastic interrogation of Indianapolis detective Jerry Kinney, Ewing clashed with both Keeler and Assistant Prosecutor Thomas Ross:

> Ewing [to Kinney]: Did you get any of that blood money [the reward for Rutheven's capture]?
> Keeler: I object.
> Neff: I'll sustain the objection.
> Ewing: Did you get any of the scalp money?
> Ross: I object. [To Ewing]: You couldn't be decent if you tried.
> Ewing: I appeal to the court for protection from Mr. Ross's caustic remarks.

Relations between opposing counsel deteriorated further as the trial moved toward its end. On Monday, November 19, fraying tempers provoked the following dialogue during C. M. Vorce's testimony about the bullets fired from Henry Lueking's revolver:

> Keeler: You may state, Mr. Vorce, whether or not the three shots found in Lueking's house were fired from the revolver taken from Rutheven at Indianapolis and which you examined.
> Avery: Oh, shut up!

Ross's turn came next, when he wearied of Ewing's innumerable objections to Vorce's complex testimony, objections that came, as the *Cleveland Press* reported, "at every period and at almost every comma":

> Ewing: I object.
> Ross: Don't act like a chump!
> Ewing: I object to being called a chump!
> Ross: You take up enough time with your trivial objections to try three lawsuits!

Perhaps the most juvenile and comical of such rude exchanges took place during Detective Dugan's testimony about Rutheven's capture in Indianapolis. When Ewing asked him what kind of gun he was carrying at the time, Dugan whipped out a large revolver and flourished it. A nervous Judge Neff asked, "Is it loaded?" Dugan replied, "Sure, .38s." "Well, for heaven's sake, point it some other way," scolded Neff. The incident prompted more nasty dialogue between Ewing and Ross:

> Ewing [to Judge Neff]: I demand that the witness be taken from the room and relieved of his weapons.
> Ross: Not getting scared, are you Ewing?
> Ewing: If this man is going to be allowed to carry a revolver, I insist that we be furnished with them, too.
> Ross: What do you want a Gatling gun for? Are you getting scared?

The fireworks between the lawyers, however diverting, probably had nothing to do with the trial result. Rutheven's pathetically thin alibi spoke volumes to his 12 jurors, as did the almost too voluminous circumstantial evidence. The most fatal witness against Rutheven was probably Carrie Scheible. She identified the black silk handkerchief dropped by Shipp's killer as one of her husband's and offered the infallible and irrefutable detail of a conscientious housewife: she said she knew the handkerchief by the particular manner in which it was folded and the types of creases she had made while ironing it.

Ewing's summation for the defense was, predictably, an emotional appeal that rigorously skirted the mountain of damning circumstantial evidence against Ed Rutheven. Audibly sobbing, Ewing dwelt on the graphic horrors of Rutheven's possible execution.

He pictured the prisoner being led from the courtroom to the county jail and from there to the penitentiary in Columbus and finally to the electric chair. He pictured him as he would appear ready for the electric chair, and even during the scene when the fatal current was turned on.

Attempting to discount the impact of Vorce's ballistic illustrations, Ewing disparaged his sketches of the murder bullets, demanding, "Would you swear a boy's [Rutheven was 29 years old] life away on the mark of a brush?" Less sensibly, Ewing virtually blamed Shipp's death on the victim himself, insisting that his tactics in confronting the Charles Street burglar had led to his unfortunate death and were, moreover, of a piece with the indiscriminate use of force demonstrated in the Central Avenue shootout.

The more confident Harvey Keeler largely eschewed emotion and devoted his final argument to a methodical catalog of the circumstantial evidence linking Rutheven to John Shipp's murder. Reply to Ewing's sly insinuation that Detectives Walker and Doran had solicited false testimony from some of the state's witnesses, Keeler shouted dramatically, "So help me God, I'll resign this office and go to shoveling dirt in the streets before I'll ever ask a jury to try a case on fixed testimony." Noting Ewing's criticism of the forceful methods employed by Cleveland policemen against burglars, Keeler revealed that Ewing himself had discovered a burglar in his home some years before—and shot him dead on the spot without warning.

After rather perfunctory instructions by Judge Neff, Rutheven's jury retired to deliberate at 12:55 p.m. on Saturday, November 24, 1900. They returned at 10 that evening with a verdict of murder in the first degree. Interestingly, Rutheven was only convicted on one of the four capital counts, which was killing Shipp by shooting him in the neck while committing a burglary. A complication developed, however, when the jurors were polled and juror Joseph Bell blurted out his wish that mercy be shown to Rutheven. This automatically nullified the verdict, and Ewing and Avery took advantage of Keeler's momentary absence to try and pressure Thomas Ross into accepting a life term for Rutheven instead of the death penalty. When Keeler returned and discovered the maneuver, he angrily accused Ewing and Avery of jury tampering and threatened to "send someone to the penitentiary" if the death verdict were nullified. The upshot was that the jury again retired—and returned 30 minutes later with an unequivocal death verdict. Rutheven showed no emotion when it was read, nor did he show much feeling when Judge Neff pronounced his sentence of death on December 20. Lizzie Chilia did not take the news as well, pitching a violent and prolonged fit of hysterics when the news filtered back to her jail cell.

Perhaps owing to his race, there was little organized effort to save Ed Rutheven's life. There were few mass petitions to the governor of Ohio to exercise clemency, so oft a feature of 19th-century capital cases. The Reverend Edward D. Dandridge of Shiloh Baptist Church, an African-American congregation, did, however, issue a public plea to spare Rutheven's life. Asserting that he was still not convinced by the evidence, Dandridge argued that Rutheven's life should be spared even if he *were* guilty of Shipp's murder:

> I also believe that mercy should have been shown Rutheven even though he were found guilty. We must remember that the colored people have all been slaves or children of slaves. They are friendless, and are crowded from one part of the country to another. It is no wonder that a few turned desperate criminals.

If there *was* a racist component in the reluctance of Ohio authorities to grant clemency to Ed Rutheven, those authorities were not terribly concerned about it. After turning down Rutheven's final appeal for commutation, Ohio Board of Pardons member S. J. Hatfield addressed the racism issue obliquely in his report to Ohio governor George K. Nash. Citing the claim by Rutheven's partisans that Rutheven was being electrocuted for being a Negro, while other recent, white murderers from Cleveland escaped the death penalty, Hatfield stated:

Over this the pardon board has no control. If there has been a miscarriage of justice in those cases, that is no reason why the pardoning power should lend itself to a miscarriage of justice in Rutheven's case.

"GUILTY," SAYS RUTHEVEN JURY

FIRST-DEGREE VERDICT RETURNED SATURDAY NIGHT AFTER A FEW HOURS' DELIBERATION.

Cleveland World, November 25, 1900.

Governor Nash, for his part, made it clear that he would not lift a finger to save Rutheven's life until he produced the elusive "Jacobs."

Thanks to three successive reprieves, Ed Rutheven did not keep his original date with death on April 12, 1901. On the night before his June 28 execution, he yielded at last to the noisy solicitations of two preachers and an attending choir of 14 women and "got religion" in his Ohio Penitentiary death-row cell. His last public statement, issued that afternoon, was a far cry from his erstwhile, insouciant bravado: "I'll try to keep a stiff upper lip, but no one who hasn't gone through this can even guess at the torture of it all. I'll try to die game."

Lizzie Chilia, confined in another wing of the Ohio Penitentiary, comported herself more melodramatically. After a final meeting with Rutheven on June 26, she returned to her cell and slashed her throat with a clasp knife. Her half-hearted suicide try was unsuccessful, as was her attempt to assume the burden of Rutheven's guilt. The night before his execution, she confided to a sympathetic clergyman, the Reverend W. M. Langford, that it was *she* who had committed Rutheven's many burglaries and murdered John Shipp. Lizzie's "confession" did not gain added plausibility from her insistence that she had performed all of these alleged deeds disguised as a man. Informed of her story, Ed Rutheven stoutly repudiated it, and then sat down hungrily to his last meal. It included fried chicken, ham and eggs, watermelon, strawberries, ice cream, huckleberry pie, and chicken soup.

As the *Cleveland Leader* dryly remarked, Ed Rutheven's electrocution was "from the scientific standpoint . . . a perfect success." Just after midnight on June 28, 1901, he entered the Columbus death chamber while a choir sang "Nearer, My God to Thee," and he was strapped into the electric chair. His demeanor was calm, and he used his last breath on earth to reiterate his innocence of Shipp's murder and to insist that Lizzie was not involved in his criminal activities. As the black cap was put over his head, he said, "I want to say this much more, Warden, about my wife. She is innocent. Goodbye, all." A few moments later a current of 1,750 volts was passed through his body for seven seconds, and then reduced to 250 volts for 113 seconds. Rutheven's body was not burned by the current, and it was immediately turned over to his friends for burial in Greenlawn Cemetery in Columbus.

Florence Shipp was not present at Rutheven's execution, but she anxiously watched the clock in her Cleveland home as the hour scheduled for his electrocution ticked away. Recalling her fear that he would cheat justice by way of pardon or suicide, she told a *Cleveland Press* reporter:

> I only wish the prison authorities had given me permission to have turned on the electrical current to kill Rutheven. It would have afforded me the greatest satisfaction, and I could have done it without the least regret.

Neither John Shipp's killer nor his widow had the final word in the Shipp tragedy. That was reserved for the formidable Lizzie Chilia, who had been sentenced in January 1901 to a five-year term in the Ohio Penitentiary. Early on the morning of November 19, 1901, she became the first woman ever to escape from the Ohio Penitentiary. Carefully planned, her flight was a daring and complicated plot, involving ladders, ropes, dizzying ascents, masculine disguise, and an outside confederate. The latter was George Bailey, a career criminal, who had become smitten with Lizzie while a guest in the male section of the penitentiary. Lizzie was last heard of in the fall of 1902, when she was rumored to be back in Cleveland and burglarizing homes on her own account. In any case, she was never apprehended by the law, nor did she ever make good on her erstwhile threats to seek bloody revenge against James Doran, Charles Smith, and Emma "Aunty" Davis.

The best epitaph for Ed Rutheven appeared in the *Plain Dealer*

WATCHED THE CLOCK AS RUTHVEN DIED.

THE WIDOW OF HIS VICTIM KEPT VIGIL AS THE MURDERER'S LIFE WAS PASSING.

Cleveland Press, June 28, 1901.

on the day before his execution. Acknowledging his almost supernatural nerve and stoic indifference to death, a reporter noted the petty and childish impulses that had put Rutheven in the electric chair, as evidenced by an inventory of the items he had stolen from the Lueking house:

> A mania of perfume bottles, an undue regard for baubles and trinkets, an insatiable desire for weapons led to the terrible end of Ed Rutheven. . . . As usual in such great crimes, the discovery of the perpetrator was due to accident . . . the retention in his possession of a few articles of almost insignificant value, but on those small shreds the state wove a skein of evidence which had its beginning in one small perfume bottle and its end in the electric chair. . . . In the year in which he infested Cleveland he took thousands of dollars worth of goods, the greater part of which he sold for trifling sums. When sentenced he was penniless.

Patrolman John Shipp's name can be found inscribed on the National Law Enforcement Officers Memorial Wall, Judiciary Square, Washington, D. C. (Panel 41, West Wall, line 16).

Chapter 9

THE MAN WHO LED TWO LIVES

The Lawrence Bader Story (1957)

Is there really such a thing as amnesia? Is it possible to lose all memory of one's unique identity and personality? To those with a penchant for hard-headed facts, it may seem a dubious concept, more likely to occur in B pictures of the 1940s than in real life. Yet even hardened amnesia skeptics might waver in their cynicism when confronted with the unhappy tale of Lawrence Bader. It not only seems to have been a genuine case of amnesia, it happened right here in Northeast Ohio.

Kitchen appliance salesman Lawrence ("Larry") Joseph Bader liked to go fishing. So no one, least of all his wife, Marylou, raised an eyebrow when the 30-year-old Akron father of three announced in May 1957 that he would try to get in a little perch fishing on an impending business trip to Cleveland. Nor did this seem odd to Lawrence E. Cotleur, from whom Larry Bader rented a 14-foot outboard boat at his Rocky River livery on the afternoon of May 15. True, Cotleur was a bit puzzled that Bader insisted on a boat with running lights, as Larry assured Cotleur he would return before dark. And Cotleur did mention Coast Guard warnings of a looming Lake Erie storm—but Bader assured him that he would not venture beyond the Rocky River. Everything seemed in order to Cotleur, and he watched without undue concern as Bader chugged away in his boat, furnished with fishing gear, two life jackets, and a small suitcase.

Cotleur may have been the last person to see Larry Bader before he vanished. The United States Coast Guard encountered a fisherman matching Bader's description at the mouth of the Rocky River about 9 p.m. They warned him to avoid the gathering Lake Erie storm, and he told them that he would stay on the river. It may or may not have been Bader but, in any case, Bader did not return his boat to Cotleur's livery that night. The now anxious Cotleur notified the Coast Guard at 7 the next morning, and several hours later Bader's boat was found beached at Perkins Beach on Cleveland's

Lawrence Bader, 1957.

West Side. It was undamaged, except for a missing stern light, and both life jackets were still in the boat. There was no sign of Larry Bader or his suitcase.

It seemed an obvious case of death by mishap, an unremarkable drowning rather than a staged disappearance. By all reports, Lawrence Bader was a happily married man who reveled in the joys of life with his wife and three children, with a fourth expected in September. True, he had some trouble brewing with the Internal Revenue Service (he hadn't filed a return since 1952 and faced a $3,500 lien), and his $10,000 annual income was further pressured by debts and a mortgage amounting to $20,000. But these were not unusual or remarkably severe financial straits for a middle-class businessman, nor was his $25,000 in life insurance a startling figure. Indeed, the day he disappeared the methodical Bader paid the $45.85 due on his premium.

The Coast Guard search for Larry's missing corpse was thorough but futile. They gave up looking in July of 1957, and the legal and financial consequences of his disappearance lingered until a Summit County probate judge declared Lawrence Bader legally dead in 1960. Soon after that, the New York Life Insurance Co. paid Marylou Bader $24,579 on her husband's death claim. Following a legal battle with the U. S. government, Mrs. Bader also began collecting $254 a month to help in raising her fatherless brood of four children.

Eight years went by. It was a one-in-a-million chance—but it did happen on February 2, 1965. While attending the National Sporting Goods Show at McCormick Center in Chicago, (a forever anonymous) man from Akron stopped by the Sanders Archery Co. exhibit. A middle-aged man wearing an eye patch was there, demonstrating archery equipment. Suddenly, the Akron man looked at him and realized: *That one-eyed man looks just like Larry Bader!* After a casual conversation with the archery demonstrator, the Akron man called Bader's family in Akron and told them what he had seen. Larry Bader's brother, John, then called a Chicago niece, Mrs. Suzanne Pekia, and asked her to check out the Larry lookalike at McCormick Center. Two days later, she strolled up to the Sanders booth, took a long look at the one-eyed man, and said to him, "Pardon me, but aren't you my uncle, Larry Bader?"

Hunt Missing Man in Lake

Cleveland News, May 17, 1957.

No, the one-eyed man replied blandly. Of course he wasn't Larry Bader, a man he'd never even heard of. He was John ("Fritz") Johnson, the sports director of KETV television in Omaha, Nebraska, and an archery enthusiast. But Suzanne Pekia persisted, and she eventually persuaded the apparently unruffled Johnson to telephone Lawrence Bader's brothers John and Richard in Akron. After their conversation, Johnson admitted being struck by how much his voice resembled one of the brothers'. But he still insisted he was John Johnson, and he claimed to have no knowledge of Lawrence Bader or any previous life. But he did agree to call Marylou Bader in Akron, who was immediately certain that his voice sounded like that of her vanished spouse.

Richard and John Bader flew to Chicago the next day and met with John Johnson. He remained adamant that he wasn't Larry Bader, but he admitted being struck by his strong physical resemblance to one of the brothers. But Richard and John were now certain that he was Larry, and they pressed Johnson until he suggested that he have his fingerprints checked against the dead man's to clear this silly confusion up once and for all. As he put it later, "Wouldn't I have to be out of my mind to agree to that if I knew I was Bader?" Whatever his mental condition, he and the Bader brothers went to a Chicago police station, where Johnson's finger-

Wife Sees Lawyer as 'Dead' Mate Turns Up as Omaha TV Announcer

Cleveland Press, February 8, 1965.

prints were taken by Lieutenant Emil Griese. Griese sent the fingerprints off to the FBI, where they were compared with prints taken from Larry Bader when he joined the United States Navy in 1944. On February 6, Griese got the fingerprints report back. He took one look at it and said, "It's one and the same man—or else it's something from beyond." Or as a stunned Larry Bader later recalled the scene:

> Up to that moment I had no doubt that I was not Larry Bader. But when I heard that, it was like a door had slammed and somebody had hit me in the face.

A plastic cast of Lawrence's teeth that exactly matched Johnson's dentures amplified the already inescapable conclusion: John Johnson *was* Lawrence Bader.

The outcome of Johnson/Bader's unmasking was messier than anyone could have predicted. John Johnson now related the story of his life—as he remembered it—to astonished reporters and lawmen. He said he had been born a foundling in 1929 and reared in a Boston, Massachusetts, orphanage, where he was given the name "John Johnson." Serving in the United States Navy for 14 years, Johnson claimed he had been badly wounded in both World War II and the Korean War. After being discharged from a veterans' hospital in 1954, he had bummed around before arriving in Omaha on

May 21, 1957—just six days after Larry Bader disappeared in his boat. Working first as a steakhouse bartender, the charming and sociable Johnson had soon secured work as a radio personality for Omaha station KBON. Cultivating an eccentric public image, the popular deejay was well known for his unusual automobile (a hearse with a built-in bar) and his penchant for publicity-driven stunts and behavior. During a marathon fundraiser for polio, Johnson sat atop a flagpole, drinking martinis. When seated at restaurants, he was wont to suavely ask waitresses to "bring me a couple of dollars' worth of food." He was also widely recognized as a tropical fish enthusiast and a skilled archer. Capping his successes, Johnson married Chicago divorcee Nancy Zimmer, an eye-popping photographer's model, in 1961. The family-loving John adopted her daughter, Krista, by a previous marriage, and their son John was born in 1963. Lyle Davis, who knew Johnson well in his Omaha years, spoke for many when he characterized Johnson as "a man who enjoyed a good time and a good laugh, but he was completely responsible at all times."

The unraveling of John Johnson's seemingly idyllic life had actually begun even before he was recognized at McCormick Center. In March 1964, he had been diagnosed with a malignant tumor behind his left eye. He lost the eye to surgery and took to wearing a romantic-looking black eye patch and a pencil-thin mustache. But the loss of an eye didn't dampen his love for archery, a pursuit that Lawrence Bader had also shared. Johnson continued to excel at the sport, and it was his status as the Nebraska state archery champion that led to his fateful appearance at the Sanders Archery Co. exhibit.

No one ever seems to have doubted John Johnson's repeated assertions that he could not remember his life as Larry Bader. Although liable for prosecution on grounds of criminal fraud (the insurance money), bigamy, and nonsupport, Johnson was never prosecuted on any of these charges. His first wife refused to file any charges against him, believing that he had not consciously abandoned her and their children. "I know I've been wronged," she told Akron police detectives, "but I don't want to do anything about it." She was more forthcoming in an *Akron Beacon-Journal* interview,

2 Funerals Set After Double Life

Cleveland Press, September 17, 1966.

summarizing her husband's odyssey this way: "I felt had there been a disappearance, rather than drowning, that it would have to have been something out of his control, definitely."

Events moved rapidly after the fingerprints clinched Johnson's identity as Bader. As Marylou Bader, a devout Roman Catholic, refused to give John Johnson a divorce, he soon left Nancy Zimmer, although he continued to share in the rearing of their two children after their marriage was annulled on June 2, 1965. Two months later, he had what he described to *Cleveland Press* reporters as a "wonderful" reunion with Marylou and the kids at a La Grange, Illinois, motel. But he never returned for good to his first family, for as he sadly reiterated, he had no memory of them at all.

Larry Bader's imperfectly recaptured life didn't last long. The cancer that had taken his left eye returned that same eventful year, and it killed him a year later on September 16, 1966. In keeping with his bizarre destiny, two funerals were held for the man who had led two lives. After services in Omaha, his remains were taken to Akron for another funeral and interment in a local cemetery. His death occurred only a year after Summit County probate judge Nathan Koplin declared Lawrence Bader officially undead, and while the Fidelity & Deposit Co. of Maryland was trying to recover its $24,579 insurance bond from Marylou Bader.

The bottom-line question in the Larry Bader story remains the same after 40 years. Was John Johnson's story really true, insofar as he knew and remembered it? Like Larry Bader, he claimed to have been in the U. S. Navy, although he must have been aware that there was no documentary proof of such service under the name of John Johnson. Likewise, he must have known there were no records of his "war injuries" or his alleged and prolonged sojourn at a veterans' hospital. It is a remarkable fact, however, that he managed to convince virtually everyone that he had not deliberately faked his own death. So either Larry Bader was the greatest actor in Northeast Ohio history—or the victim of a terrible and still inexplicable malady. Perhaps it was the sudden onset of an undiagnosed mental illness or the long-delayed consequence of a head injury that he had suffered while he was in the navy. Whatever the truth, the Larry Bader saga remains a puzzling enigma, like the tale of Martin Guerre, an unsolved and tantalizing riddle. Or as writer Jay Robert Nash termed it in his 1978 account of the Bader mystery, "a weird story forever unanswered."

Chapter 10

MANHATTAN BEACH MELEE

The Bostock Animal Riots (1902)

Maybe it happened, and maybe it didn't. It was reported to be Cleveland's worst animal attack ever. Other voices insisted it was a lurid fiction made up of whole cloth. The only certainty is that it set Cleveland newspaper readers on their ears for three days in 1902.

Few Clevelanders remember a place called Manhattan Beach. A century ago it occupied the shoreline area on Lake Shore Boulevard at East 140th Street, later the site of the White City Amusement Park and now the location of the Easterly Waste Water Treatment plant. Back at the turn of the last century, it was the place where Frank Bostock's internationally renowned Animal Show put on its annual display of wild jungle beasts for the entertainment of susceptible Clevelanders. So it was that the morning of June 7, 1902, found Bostock's crew unloading wild animals from flatcars provided by one of Cleveland's street railway companies. It was a routine task, transferring the beasts from their traveling cages to the ones used for public display, and the routine usually went without incident.

It didn't this time. The carnage commenced about 9 a.m. After trying unsuccessfully to lure a recalcitrant grizzly bear from its cage, tamer Herman Wedder decided to go in after it. A big mistake: as Wedder entered the cage, the bear lunged at him and pulled him into a deadly embrace. Ignoring the nail-studded rod with which Wedder frantically beat him, the grizzly sank his teeth into Wedder's right leg, exposing the bone and inundating the cage floor with the tamer's blood. Alerted by Wedder's screams, Bostock show workers beat off the bear with pitchforks and pulled the fainting Wedder from the bloody cage. It was soon reported that his savaged leg would have to be amputated.

A few minutes later, leopard tamer Madame Millie Morelli was assaulted by one of her beasts. Although already nursing a bad wound inflicted by the same animal a week before in Boston,

Wild animal impresario
Frank Bostock.
Cleveland Leader, June 2, 1900.

Morelli insisted on bringing the leopard its breakfast. As she did so, the leopard sprang at her and bit into her right arm. The beast then knocked her down and sank its teeth into her right side. Like Wedder, she was soon pulled from the cage and rushed to medical attention.

The worst episode occurred at 2 p.m. When one of the Nubian lions refused to leave his cage, tamer Joseph McPhee, 23, decided to go in after him. Equipped only with the small whip used in the public shows, McPhee was no match for the enraged animal. Knocking him flat as he entered the cage, the lion bit McPhee's arm severely.

Even as Bostock workers began to poke the beast with pitchforks, the lion took bite out of McPhee's right leg, badly tearing the muscles and tendons. More attempts to stop the lion's rampage failed, and he finished by biting into McPhee's abdomen, exposing his bowels and triggering a fountain of blood. That seemed to sate the lion, and the tamers were finally able to pull McPhee's mutilated body out of the cage.

What happened after that is a murkier story. Although the next day's initial newspaper accounts reported dire prognoses for McPhee and Wedder, they were reported alive and recovering three days later. Madame Morelli, moreover, recovered so rapidly from

INFURIATED WILD BEASTS ATTACK THEIR KEEPERS

Bloody Happenings While Bostock's Animal Show is Being Unloaded.

Cleveland Leader, June 8, 1902.

her allegedly serious wounds that she repaired not to a hospital but rather to the more pleasant accommodations of a suite at the Hollenden Hotel.

The *Cleveland Press* was having none of this sanguinary tale. Perhaps chagrined that it missed the sensational story, which broke late on a Saturday (the *Press* had no Sunday edition), it charged in its Monday edition of June 9 that the whole story was a complete hoax. Claiming to have elicited the real story from Frank Bostock himself, the *Press* account related that all three of the animal tamers had actually been mildly wounded in animal attacks *the week before in Boston,* rather than at Manhattan Beach. The whole bloodcurdling story, the *Press* concluded, was a grotesque fabrication invented by the "Cleveland yellow papers." Going further— perhaps well beyond the bounds of good taste—the *Press* also published a facetious burlesque of the alleged attacks, a version in which a helpless bear, leopard, and Nubian lion were assaulted and mauled by ferocious trainers "Alonzo Weddo, Mlle. Sopellii, and Senor Deonda."

So what really happened that June day at Manhattan Beach?

Chapter 11

DEATH RIDE AT EUCLID BEACH

The Sad Fate of Joseph Senk (1943)

Cleveland's amusement parks have furnished an ample portion of Cleveland woe. Their most persistent nemesis has been fire. Euclid Beach Park's movie theater burned down in 1908, and the nearby White City Amusement Park was razed by fire in 1906 before its final destruction during a violent storm two years later. Puritas Springs Park was visited by devastating fires in 1910 and 1946. And Luna Park was hit by serious blazes in 1908, 1927, 1929, and 1938. (The 1908 fire destroyed its popular "Human Dry Cleaner" ride, a revolving barrel that, like Euclid Beach's later "Flying Turns," caused its male and female occupants to become delightfully entangled.)

Such mishaps have not been entirely unexpected. It's no secret, of course, that much of the enduring appeal of amusement parks has always been the genuine but controlled terror generated by their "rides." And no ride in Cleveland history was more terrifying—and thus beloved—than the Euclid Beach Park "Thriller," the unchallenged king of area roller coasters for almost half a century. Designed by the Philadelphia Toboggan Company and erected during the winter of 1923–1924, the Thriller enraptured generations of Clevelanders with its breakneck speed and high (71 feet, 5 inches!) elevations. Built for $90,000, it paid for itself in one season and was undisputedly the most popular attraction at Euclid Beach until the park's 1969 demise. Boasting three trains in nonstop rotation during its salad days, a Thriller unit was composed of three cars with four seats each. Many an aging Clevelander can recall both

The summit of all Cleveland fears:
the "Thriller" in action.

the exhilaration of its ride and the chilling rumors that clung to its
creaky wooden structure. Truly, a Euclid Beach visit was not complete until the inevitable moment an impressionable youngster was
told to be careful because "a boy once stood up on the Thriller and
fell off and was killed." How terrifying to a child! How scary even
to a cautious adult! And . . . how deeply pleasurable!

The remarkable thing about such minatory folktales is that they
contained a kernel of truth. There *were* two serious accidents on the
Thriller, and one of them cost the life of an imprudent 16-year-old
boy. The first mishap occurred sometime in the 1920s, probably in
the coaster's early years before its second hill was severely reduced
in height. An unidentified boy stood up in a car as a train rounded
the final curve. Someone tickled him from behind, causing him to
catapult out of the train, bounce off the guardrail and three high
tension wires, and then to carom off several branches of an adja-

cent sycamore tree. He landed badly bruised and shaken, but alive.

The second, fatal, and well-documented episode happened shortly before midnight on July 3, 1943. East Technical High School student Joseph Senk, 16, began horsing around in the front seat of a Thriller lead car the moment it left the station and began climbing that first, rackety monster hill. Twice he stood up as the train was whipped above the tracks by its momentum, and twice his companion, William Troscht, 17, pulled him back down in his seat.

1 Killed, 8 Injured on Roller Coasters

Youth Dies in Plunge From Euclid Beach's "Thriller"

Troscht didn't get a third chance. As Senk stood up a third time on the Thriller's final turn, he was hurled from the car in an instant. A second later his

Cleveland Press, July 5, 1943.

head smashed into the guardrail posts at the side of the tracks, and he was probably lying dead there by the time his train pulled into its station. All of the passengers on the train except for Troscht quickly dispersed into the anonymous crowd, and Euclid Beach Park personnel and Cleveland safety officials were left with little testimony as to exactly how the tragedy had occurred. It's even probable that none of the other riders on the train, save Troscht, were aware of what had happened. It looked like a simple case of sheer youthful folly, and probers were soon more interested in what caused a crash that injured eight persons on the park's "Aero Dip" ride the next day.

Senk's funeral was held in St. Casimir Church on July 7, and he lies buried in Calvary Ceme-

Rules Youth's Coaster Death Was Accident

Cleveland Press, July 6, 1943.

tery. The day before his final rites, Cuyahoga County coroner Samuel Gerber ruled his death an accident, finding no fault with either the Thriller's mechanics or the Euclid Beach Park management.

Chapter 12

FRACTIOUS FRIDAY THE THIRTEENTH

The Communist Relief Riots (1934)

The story of Cleveland in the Great Depression will probably never be fully told. The history of everyday people rarely is, obsessed as we perennially are with the doings of politicians, generals, celebrities, and the wealthy. Not to mention our tendency toward historical amnesia about the unpleasant parts of history. As with a bad marriage or a lost war, the sufferings of everyday people are soon forgotten, even when on as colossal a scale as Cleveland's social woes in the 1930s.

That's too bad, because the real story of the Forest City in the 1930s—more than just those timeworn tales of the Torso Killer and the Great Lakes Exposition—is a narrative replete with drama, pathos, and, yes, even a quotient of nobility. True, it was a rotten time for many people, but most Clevelanders never surrendered their highest ideals or their best impulses. Even under the unprecedented stresses of that time of torment, Cleveland preserved its commitment to liberal political values and public civility. And there is no better index of that commitment than the story of the 1934 Communist relief riots.

The relationship of American Communists and Clevelanders was an unhappy one from the start. Although Charles E. Ruthenberg, the leader who molded several disparate groups of leftists into the American Communist Party, hailed from Cleveland, the party had a stormy reception there from the outset. Grotesquely underestimating the hostility of Cleveland authorities and citizens to his foreign ideology, Ruthenberg organized the 1919 May Day parade that culminated in a total disaster for Cleveland Commu-

Cleveland News, July 13, 1934.

nists and their fellow travelers. Quite a few of them had their heads broken during a police-led riot in downtown Cleveland, and many more were jailed, deported, or harassed for their ideas and rhetoric. (For more details of this disgraceful episode see the author's "Red Dawn in Cleveland," *They Died Crawling*, 1995). The bombing of Mayor Harry L. Davis's home on June 2, 1919, an act of apparent retaliation for the May Day excesses, further unendeared Clevelanders to the methods of Cleveland Reds. Not surprisingly, police surveillance and occasional harassment of local Communists continued afterwards throughout the 1920s.

Beginning in 1927, Cleveland Communists began evolving more provocative tactics. Organizing themselves into activist groups with names such as the "Communistic Council of the Unemployed," the "Small Home and Landowner Association," or the "International Labor Defense Group," they began confronting both Cleveland leaders and citizens in more public ways. Often directed by gifted Communist agitator Israel Amster and his dynamic wife Sadie Van Ween, local Communists began holding frequent demonstrations at Public Square and other civic places.

They also began showing up at Cleveland City Council and Cleveland Board of Education meetings. Their rhetoric in public was loud and provocative; their behavior before governmental bodies was disruptive and confrontational. Usually presenting what were obviously unreasonable or even fantastic demands, they would frequently orchestrate tensions to the point where they were either ejected by Cleveland safety forces or their targets withdrew from public view.

A preview of the 1934 riots came on February 11, 1930, just four months after the stock market crash. A mob of between 1,000 and 1,500 unemployed, whipped up by Communist orators at Public Square, marched on Cleveland City Hall, demanding admittance to a meeting between city council members and a delegation from the Communistic Council of the Unemployed. When police refused to admit more than 500 of the marchers, the remainder outside rioted, manhandling several Cleveland police officers and knocking Police Inspector George J. Matowitz down the city hall steps. Three policemen and two rioters were injured, and nine of the alleged riot ringleaders were arrested and prosecuted. To the chagrin of Matowitz and other police officers, however, municipal judge Martin L. Sweeney (later U.S. congressman Sweeney, and first-cousin of No. 1 Torso Killer suspect Dr. Francis Sweeney) dismissed the charges against five of the rioters on March 4. Excoriating the Cleveland police for not allowing all 1,500 Communist marchers into the city council chambers, Sweeney also chastised Matowitz for his courtroom behavior, telling him, "You're not conducting this lawsuit, Inspector."

The Cleveland police didn't bide their time long in seeking

> # CITY'S JOBLESS BATTLE POLICE, CLUBS SWING
>
> ---
>
> ## Inspector Matowitz and 20 Officers Are Attacked by Hundreds.
>
> ---
>
> ### FIGHTING IS HAND-TO-HAND

Cleveland News, February 11, 1930.

revenge. It came just two days later on March 6, 1930, at a downtown rally, one of many called by Communists in U.S. cities to protest unemployment. This time the march to city hall was peaceful, as was the subsequent rabble-rousing by Red orators at Public Square. But after several hours of disparaging rhetoric, Cleveland police brass lost their patience. With no defensible justification, Cleveland mounted police suddenly provoked screaming pandemonium by attempting to disperse 10,000 persons from Public Square with repeated charges by mounted police forces into the crowd. Remarkably, only two people were hurt in the melee, one a Communist sympathizer who was hit on the head by a milk bottle thrown from a Public Square building by an apparent Communist unsympathizer.

Cleveland Communist agitators kept up the pressure. On the evening of October 5, 1931, 600 Communists invaded a city council meeting. When they refused to stop disrupting the proceedings, they were forcibly evicted by Cleveland police. That rough encounter proved but a prelude to the tragedy that occurred the following night. Three Cleveland police officers were sent to keep order as a crowd of 300 Communists surged around the scene of a house eviction at 2693 East 47th Street, near Woodland Avenue. As the officers approached the angry crowd, one of the female agitators shouted, "All right, let's go!" and several dozen members of the mob assaulted the police trio. Fearing for their lives, they pulled out their service revolvers and started firing. When the smoke cleared, four Communists and two policemen lay on the ground. Two of the Communists, John Grayford and Edward Jackson, were fatally wounded, and Cleveland police lieutenant Owen McAdams had accidentally shot himself in the arm and leg. Three other Communists were also wounded by police fire, and Patrolman Walter Wingate was beaten with clubs by the mob. Three thousand Communist sympathizers turned out for the last rites of Grayford and Jackson on October 10 at Harvard Grove Cemetery, where the two men were buried in a single grave. Later that year, three of the rioters charged with the assault on the three police officers were acquitted by a jury.

A similar, albeit nonlethal, disruption occurred at an eviction at

Communist May Day parade, Public Square, 1930.

3433 East 139th Street on February 10, 1932, when 300 Communists battled six squads of police. This time, however, two Communists were convicted of resisting arrest at their subsequent trial on March 22, 1932. Two months later, yet another disruption of a city council meeting resulted in the bodily ejection of seven or eight Communists from city hall. The scene was repeated eight months later on November 21, when mounted policemen turned back 300 Communists at city hall. Such obnoxious obstructiveness continued sporadically until the Cleveland City Council was forced to perform evasive maneuvers, such as rushing through their sessions before the Communists showed up.

Compared to Communist riots and disorders in such cities as New York, Washington, Chicago, and Detroit, Cleveland's troubles with Reds had, thus far, been mild affairs. The relative tolerance of Cleveland authorities for Communist disruptiveness was highlighted by the different treatment meted out to them in Mayor Frank Cain's more genteel Cleveland Heights. When Communist demonstrators tried to stage a nonviolent demonstration against the Hungarian Olympic swimming team at Cumberland Pool, they were attacked by a squadron of club-wielding policemen, who crammed them into a truck and deported them back to Cleveland. But the Cleveland disturbances were a warning indicator of both the increasingly provocative nature of Communist tactics and the rising anger of the unemployed citizens they aroused and recruited.

As the Great Depression ratcheted up, so did Communist agitation in Cleveland. There were more and more public demonstrations and parades (one observer would count as many as 200 Communist demonstrations in Cleveland between 1927 and 1934) and more shouting disruptions of Cleveland City Council meetings. There were also such clever novelties as the tactic of having several dozen Communists invade a restaurant, order meals, and then blithely inform the irate waiters that they could "send the bill to the Communist Party."

But the most persistent focus of Communist pressure remained the 13 district offices of the Cuyahoga County Relief Administration (CCRA). Scattered throughout Cleveland, these overburdened agencies were staffed by badly paid and predominately female social workers, whose task was to deal with and distribute relief to the often desperate 40,000 families and 13,000 single men and women who thronged their offices daily.

It was a woeful job for the CCRA workers, and Cleveland Communists insured that it became increasingly unpleasant as the Depression wore on. Crowding the small relief offices in organized and disciplined groups, they became adept at intimidating and tormenting the relief workers with incessant visits and shouted demands. Sometimes they went further, slapping, pushing, and knocking down the social workers. It was an ugly, dangerous situation, and it was bound to get worse as the Depression deepened by the day and local Communists became emboldened by the tolerance of Cleveland officials for their unreasonable, bullying behavior.

A typical incident in their campaign of harassment occurred on September 8, 1932. After some hours spent yelling at employees at the relief office at East 125th and St. Clair Avenue, a mob of Communists decided to attack policemen at the scene. A flurry of fisticuffs, nightsticks, and tear gas drove the Reds away, but the incident was a harbinger of things to come. The scene was virtually

Cleveland police arrest a Communist demonstrator, early 1930s.

repeated on January 24, 1933, when a Communist mob 300 strong was turned away with tear gas from an Associated Charities office at 3812 Superior Avenue. Several more incidents of this type occurred in 1933 and 1934, the Communist confrontations with the relief workers waxing nastier and nastier.

The deteriorating situation finally exploded on Friday, July 13, 1934. Operating with obviously premeditated precision, three groups of Communist activists attacked four CCRA district offices simultaneously, shortly before noon. A group of five men and one woman from the Council of the Unemployed forced its way into the CCRA branch at Miles Avenue and East 95th Street. They knocked down guard John Stiles, barged into the office of Assistant Director Edward Newman, and began harassing him with shouted demands. As that continued, a Communist relief client being interviewed by relief worker Johanna Winfield stood up and slapped her in the face. Finally, Cleveland police patrolman George Jackson intervened, and the six Communists were arrested, taken to Central Police Station, and charged with disorderly conduct.

At about the same time, two Communist activists, Mary Todorovitz and Nellie Halbreda, walked into the CCRA office at East 45th Street and St. Clair Avenue. Approaching relief worker Emma Maurer, 23, they assaulted her, punching her repeatedly in the stomach. They, too, were soon arrested and hauled off to Central Police Station cells. Minutes later, a crowd of 300 persons, led by leaders of the International Labor Defense group (ILD), surged about the entrance of the CCRA office at 2843 Franklin Boulevard and demanded admission. Squads of police, who had been tipped off that they were coming, turned them back with a show of force.

The worst of it came at the Prospect office, located at 2100 East 40th Street. At the same time the other relief offices came under siege, several dozen Communists forced their way through a back door and crowded into the small waiting room. They began badgering the relief workers, and 3rd Precinct Cleveland police patrolman James Vesely, who was on duty there, quickly realized he needed reinforcements and called the precinct station.

Lieutenant Charles Kissling and Patrolman Thomas Gibbons soon arrived in the crowded, chaotic office. As if by prearrangement, the Communists split into three groups, each attacking one of the policemen. A cadre of six assaulted Gibbons, attempting to knock him down. Vesely tried to come to his aid, but as he did so, one man grabbed his throat and began choking him. An instant later another man, Samuel Arsenti, pulled Vesely's service revolver out of its holster. He raised it and began shooting.

The first bullet hit Patrolman Gibbons in the leg. Twice more the police revolver barked, and two more people fell to the floor with gunshot wounds. One of them was Andrew Masisik, 42, who took a bullet in the shoulder. The other was his wife Anna, 40, who suffered a minor flesh wound in the leg. By this time Vesely was desperately wrestling with Arsenti for the gun, and as he did so it went off again. This bullet hit Mrs. Vinnie Williams, 37, killing her almost instantly. Ironically, both the Masisiks and Williamses had come to the CCRA office as part of the Communist harassment group.

Arsenti didn't get another chance. Even as Vinnie Williams went down, Patrolman Gibbons finally managed to get his gun out its holster. As Arsenti tried to flee out the door, he stumbled, and as he

Arresting a communist rioter at Cleveland City Hall,
February 11, 1930.

went down Gibbons fired once, drilling him in the stomach and
spine. As he fell dying to the floor, Lieutenant Kissling grabbed the
gun from his hands.

This was the version of the dramatic events provided by the
police and subsequently given to the public via Cleveland's three
daily newspapers. It's probably close to the whole truth, although
it's possible that the Masisiks were hit by police bullets in the
chaotic crossfire in the cramped CCRA office. Cleveland's Communist leaders, of course, were having none of the official version.
I. O. Ford, the Communist candidate for Ohio governor, stated
later:

> The shooting was not accidental, but follows a definite policy of
> the CCRA administration and the city administration to terror-
> ize the members of the unemployed councils and to shoot them
> if necessary to get them out of the charity offices.

A statement issued the next day by International Labor Defense leaders A. B. Lewis and Clifford David more specifically accused "paid assassins of the [Cleveland Mayor Harry L.] Davis administration" of having wantonly opened fire on helpless, innocent, and indigent civilians. The ILD also presented a list of demands including that: 1) A. V. Cannon be removed as CCRA chief; 2) Patrolman 845 [Thomas Gibbons] be arrested for the "murders" of Arsenti and Williams; 3) Cleveland police chief George Matowitz be removed; 4) the families of the slain Arsenti and Williams be compensated by the city; and 5) police guards be removed from the relief offices.

Law director and acting mayor Ezra Z. Shapiro (Mayor Harry L. Davis was out of town) rejected the ILD charges and demands categorically when Communist leaders came calling at City Hall the day after the riots. Lauding Cleveland police for their restraint, Shapiro laid down the law in unmistakable terms:

> As for the shootings, from what we know now, it was one of your own who took a gun from a policeman and precipitated the trouble. That is intolerable and we will not stand for it. We will not tolerate violence. As long as we have this form of government we will do our best to see it function in an orderly way.

Ordering Chief Matowitz to post more police officers as guards at the CCRA relief offices, Shapiro publicly vowed that further violent demonstrations would be vigorously quelled.

Meanwhile, the aftershocks of the riots continued. There were disturbances during the afternoon and evening of July 13 at a grocery owned by Jacob Blumenson at 5901 Quincy Avenue. It was a grocery used by the CCRA for distribution of relief staples and, like the CCRA offices, had already seen its share of angry, disruptive relief clients. That afternoon, a female client became angry and accused Blumenson of shorting her a jar of mayonnaise in her relief package. When he offered her a free jar to defuse the situation, she knocked it to the floor and stormed out. Soon afterwards, a mob gathered and began throwing stones and bricks at the grocery. One of the stones hit Blumenson, and his wife Dora was hit in the head by a bottle. The police came, arrested a few rioters, and dispersed the rest. That evening, a mob again formed, and the police had to return to suppress more violence and make more arrests. Many of those arrested, unsurprisingly, were familiar faces from the ranks of Cleveland Communists.

As expected, Cleveland officials quickly exonerated all of the policemen involved in the riots from any blame. The relief workers from the besieged offices supported police versions of the events and told of the systematic and frightening harassment that had culminated in Friday's violence. There were no witnesses to the Prospect office shootings except the police and the Communists in the room. But an investigation by Cleveland police ballistics expert David Cowles concluded that Mrs. Williams had been slain by Patrolman Veseley's gun and that Arsenti's fatal bullet had come from Patrolman Gibbons's revolver. Cuyahoga County prosecutor Frank T. Cullitan summarized official conclusions less than 24 hours after the riots, stating:

> I am convinced that the gathering constituted a deliberate and organized attack on the welfare office. But I am not sure that the killing of [Vinnie Williams] was anything more than the act of one irresponsible and misguided person. . . . Stern measures must be employed in providing proper protection for the administration of relief agencies. . . . [The police] handled themselves with admirable restraint and cannot in any way be held responsible for the loss of life that resulted from this most unfortunate occurrence.

The aftermath of the relief riots followed the scripted martyrology typically offered by Communist party leaders on such occasions. The bodies of Arsenti and Williams were dramatically displayed for public view in two coffins on the second floor of party headquarters at 3631 Central Avenue. The caskets were draped in red-and-black bunting, and large placards proclaimed that the Cleveland police had murdered two "comrades." A party worker sat at the building exit, soliciting coins for the funeral expenses. On July 18, following predictable eulogies, the bodies were escorted

Tireless Communist attorney Yetta Land and N.B. Davis,
Communist candidate for Cuyahoga County prosecutor, 1934.

by parading Communists to their final resting place in Harvard
Grove Cemetery. Most of the funeral spectators, estimated at
6,000, were merely the idly curious, excepting the 150 watchful
Cleveland policemen in attendance.

Who were these two supposed martyrs to the cause of world revolution? Thirty-seven-year-old Vinnie Williams was a widow and
mother of three children. She had come from Atlanta, Georgia, in
1918 and lived since then in Cleveland. She had allegedly come to
the relief office that day to obtain a stove grate. Less was immediately known about Samuel Arsenti, other than the facts that he was
42, unmarried, and on relief. But more significant illumination of
his character came after a beer parlor proprietor named Dan Ricci
noted Arsenti's photograph on the front page of the *Plain Dealer*
on Saturday, July 14. Ricci had been shot in the groin by one of
three robbers who had barged into his parlor the previous November. He thought the picture in the *Plain Dealer* looked familiar and,
sure enough, a casket-side visit evoked a positive identification of
the late Samuel as the thug who had shot him. Ricci's identification
of Arsenti was seconded by Clarence Biesinger, who had also wit-

nessed the holdup. Cleveland Communist officials made no public comment on this tarnishing disclosure about their latest casualty in the war against capitalism.

Those arrested in Friday's disturbances were handled with brisk efficiency by Cleveland's judicial system. A total of 19 people— 15 men and 4 women—had been apprehended in the various disorders, and their cases were tried before Cleveland Police Court judges Jacob Stacel and David Moylan within 24 hours of their arrests. Typical were the cases of John Fears and Arthur Davis, accused of throwing bricks and stones at the Blumensons. They were quickly convicted, given 30 days in the workhouse, fined, and assessed court costs. Those of the accused rioters who were not immediately tried or who could not make bail were remanded back to jail for a month or two. Communist defense lawyer Yetta Land protested the high bail demanded of her Miles Avenue rioters, telling Judge Stacel, "You might as well pickle them," but he ignored her protest, declaring, "It was time to end such disorders."

That was pretty much the end of it, although both the Depression and the disruptive antics of Cleveland's Communists continued for some time. Several hundred Communists held yet another rally at City Hall on July 16 to protest the riot dead. Increased security at CCRA relief offices prevented further tragedies such as that of July 13, and Cleveland Communists toned down—but did not cease— their perennial tactics of confrontation and disruption. They may have taken to heart Mayor Davis's comment, uttered several months later, when an overwhelming show of police force overawed a Communist mob bent on storming City Hall. "On a previous occasion when I was mayor," Davis remarked on October 29, "we settled once and for all who is the boss of this town and we'll do it again tonight if necessary." Davis's unsubtle reference to the indiscriminate police violence of the 1919 May Day Riots was a telling reminder of his willingness to use force in preventing any repetition of previous disorders.

All in all, the City of Cleveland came out pretty well in the aftermath of the relief riots. There was no wholesale retribution akin to the "Red Scare" excesses of 1919, and the rights of free speech and free assembly—even when unpleasant and repugnant to most citi-

zens and officials—continued in force in the Forest City. Indeed, as
several commentators pointed out, Cleveland Communists had
become emboldened to commit their July 13 excesses by the very
tolerance hitherto extended to them by city authorities. As Plain
Dealer staff writer Charles Lawrence pointed out, "Many a Communist head which would have been cracked open in New York,
Chicago, or Detroit" had
remained intact as Cleveland
Communists continually
pushed the envelope of permitted behavior in the months
before July 1934. Moreover, as
astute Plain Dealer analyst
Ralph Kelly argued, the violence of the Communist relief
riots was implicit in the anti-
democratic nature of the party

CLEARS POLICE IN DEATH OF 2 IN RELIEF RIOT

Cleveland Press, July 14, 1934.

and its commitment to revolution at all costs. Noting that although
only the latest confrontations had resulted in bloodshed, he
warned:

> Nevertheless, all the "demonstrations" have carried violence and
> bloodshed in incipiency. They have assembled various groups of
> persons with burning resentments against various conditions—
> resentments which could be easily released by the workings of
> mob spirit. . . . What happened Friday was the logical result.
> Whenever excited individuals gather in a mass, led by someone
> who tells them in terms, convincing at least to them, that they
> have been unjustly treated, violence of some kind is certain to
> follow. That the violence of Friday took the shape of murder is
> merely a side issue. It could have happened anytime in the past
> and it can happen anytime in the future.

Chapter 13

"SHE MADE ME SORE..."

The Ida Deli Murder (1920)

Joseph Deli, as one imaginative reporter put it, "made love with a pistol." Maybe he did, maybe he didn't—but that's what his two murder juries believed, and the second one sent him to die in the electric chair. While one could insist that Deli's murder of his child-wife was not so terribly unusual a crime, it was surely such an archetype of conjugal slaughter as to warrant its inclusion in these melancholy annals.

Hungarian immigrant Joe Deli was 23 when he met Ida Juhasz, 15, at a family christening. Two years later, Joe, now a machinist, persuaded Ida, now 17 and a West High School student, to elope with him to Painesville and get married. Some say he forced Ida to do it at gunpoint, others insist it was the more usual story of two youngsters carried away by passion. Maybe Ida had second thoughts, or maybe, as Joe always insisted, it was really her parents' opposition to the youthful nuptials. It is undisputed, however, that the marriage so quickly frayed that Ida filed for divorce a mere 10 weeks after her elopement. This provoked Joe to threaten her, which provoked her father, realtor F. J. Juhasz, to have Joe arrested for carrying a concealed pistol. F. J. did not succeed in having Joe prosecuted. Worse yet, he was unsuccessful in persuading Cleveland lawmen to let him carry a pistol with which to protect his daughter from Joe's continued promises of armed aggression. The stage was set for tragedy.

After several weeks spent stalking Ida at her home at 4658 West 21st Street, Joe succeed in luring Ida to a meeting on Broadview Road on the afternoon of January 14, 1920. When Ida once again spurned his pleas for a reconciliation, Joe pulled out a pistol. The terrified Ida ran down Broadview Road to the steps of George J. Senger's home at 3211 Broadview and tried to get in, but it was already too late. Joe fired five shots at Ida, missing the first four times but sending the fifth bullet straight through her heart. Joe's shots attracted the attention of some neighbors, among them Lieutenant John J. Riley from the Cleveland Fire Department station across the street from the death scene. The doughty Riley quickly marshaled a posse of 15 men and, armed with shotguns, they set off in pursuit of Joe Deli. Joe fired the last round in his gun at his pursuers without effect and they cornered him a few minutes later in a cellar at 4251 West 24th Street. Although he had by now reloaded his gun, Joe surrendered peacefully to his captors.

Cleveland News, January 15, 1920.

Tried twice for murder, Joe never wavered from the story he had told from the moment he was arrested. When asked why he killed Ida, he said, "I loved her and she loved me and we couldn't live together." While not denying that he shot her, Deli insisted that he couldn't remember shooting the gun and simply explained, "I was so much in love I went crazy."

Joe's murder juries weren't buying his crazy-love excuse. Cleveland was in the midst of its all-time worst crime wave in 1920, and Cleveland's judges, prosecutors, and juries were in no mood to extenuate Joe's *crime passionel*. Although his first death verdict was thrown out on a technicality, his second jury efficiently con-

Deli, Condemned to Die

Cleveland Press, March 6, 1920.

victed him in January 1921, and Judge Maurice Bernon immediately sentenced him to death. It was the first death sentence (not counting Joe's prior conviction) voted by a Cuyahoga County jury since 1913. When asked by Judge Bernon whether he had anything to say, Joe replied, "I would like to go and see my wife's grave."

ORGY OF MURDER
DELI PLAN, CLAIM

Assert Wife-Slayer Schemed to Kill Fath-
er-in-Law, Family Friend and Self; Read
"Love History" to Jurors.

**LATE NEWS
BULLETINS**

Cleveland News, March 2, 1920.

Joe was allowed to make that visit to West Park Cemetery before he was taken to his Columbus death row. It is reported that as he stood by Ida's grave, he said, "I wish I was lying beside her there."

He got part of his wish soon enough. On January 6, 1922, Joe ate his last meal of browned chicken, mashed potatoes with gravy, rice, hot biscuit, apple pie, and coffee. It is said that he dined indifferently on his final repast, a departure from the proverbial "hearty meal" customary on such grim occasions. Strapped into the Ohio Penitentiary's electric chair at 12:05 the next morning, Joe died without a murmur as two powerful electric shocks passed through his body. His last letter was to his parents in Hungary, to whom he wrote, "I'm sorry I killed Ida. I didn't know I did it. I loved her and love made me crazy. I am going to her and am happy." To the death-row barber who shaved his head for the electrodes just minutes before his electrocution, Joe said, "I didn't really do it. Yes, I did, too, but I wasn't to blame. She made me sore, honest she did."

Chapter 14

THE BOY WITH HITLER'S FACE

The John May Warren Photo Hoax (1938)

It may seem a long way from the ghastly melodrama of the Third Reich to the balmy, suburban breezes of Lakewood, Ohio. But history has its sardonic way of playing such jokes, and one such bizarre connection made worldwide headlines back in 1938.

It all began mundanely enough in 1933, shortly after Adolf Hitler's Nazi regime came to power in Germany. Hitler was already in bad odor with the British when, by some unknown chance, the photograph of a baby fell into the hands of a London newspaper. Taken in Westport, Connecticut, sometime before, it was a snapshot of John May Warren, the infant son of a woman living there during the early 1930s. Shot looking into strong sunlight, the squinting John May didn't look very happy, although his frowning face fell well within the range of run-of-the-mill baby pictures. But that wasn't the case after a skilled photographic retoucher was done with the picture—and so it was that John May Warren's clock-stopping fright of a baby picture was now presented to the world as the scowling visage of the *infant Adolf Hitler!* Although the photograph was instantly denounced as a hoax by German consuls around the world, it was already too late. Widely reproduced in newspapers and magazines, the photograph was readily accepted by millions as Hitler's picture, as well as visually compelling evidence that the baleful child had been but too much father to the man.

The hoax began to fray as the 1930s wore on. John's mother eventually saw "Hitler's baby picture" and, realizing it was her

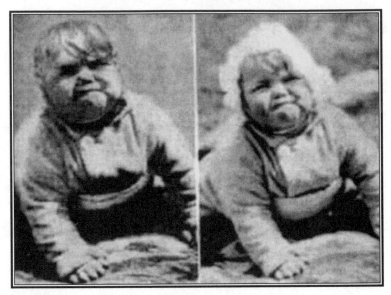

The "Hitler" baby picture. Photo on the right is original unretouched photo of John May Warren.

son's retouched photograph, tried to set the record straight. Finally, in April of 1938, *Life* magazine published the original photo and the retouched version side by side in a special issue devoted to the Third Reich. Other newspapers and magazines picked up the story, adding details about the fraud.

It soon made no difference to John May Warren. By now eight years old, he was living at 1225 Edward Avenue in Lakewood, and his concerns were doubtless far from the gathering storm of World War II. The late afternoon of June 27, 1938, found him riding his bicycle near his home and sucking on a candy sucker. He was carrying a glass milk bottle home in his left hand when he lost control of his bicycle. The glass bottle fell with him, and when he hit the ground a glass splinter stabbed into his chest and pierced his heart. Some neighbors rushed him to the hospital, but he was already dead when he got there.

No one has yet discovered how his baby picture became the infant image of the 20th century's greatest monster.

Chapter 15

BEHIND EVERY
SUCCESSFUL MAN

The Glengary
"Blue Book"
Killing (1930)

Murders in high society have always drawn a disproportionate share of public attention. It is perhaps unfair, certainly undemocratic, but eternally certain that the killing of a rich man has more entertainment appeal than the slaying of an obscure nonentity. There are hundreds of Cleveland homicides every year—but the ones we most remember are among the rich and celebrated: the Marilyn Sheppards, the William Potters, the William Lowe Rices, and the Marlene Steeles. And so it is with the most shocking killing to ever disturb the tranquillity of Cleveland's social register: the Glengary Road "Blue Book" killing of 1930.

The blood was blue, and the (illegal) liquor was flowing that night at a party at 2873 Glengary Road in Shaker Heights. Gracing an affair termed "brilliant" by Cleveland's society arbiters, the party guests were a living catalog of the pages of Cleveland's "Blue Book," that annual directory of the area's most socially prominent residents. The occasion was a prenuptial celebration for Andrew Jackson Duncan III and Miss Thalia Reese Fuller. The prospective groom was the son of William Duncan, a member of the Squire, Sanders and Dempsey law firm and chairman of the board of the Wheeling & Lake Erie Railroad, and he was a nephew of the late President William McKinley. The bride was the daughter of Ralph Lathrop Fuller, president of Ralph Fuller Associates. The host was Donald Dunham, son of the Glengary residence owner, realtor Raymond S. Dunham. Their 40 guests were of like social mega-

3 HELD IN MURDER AS ROBBERS ATTACK MANSION IN HEIGHTS

Student Is Slain as He Resists Gunmen in Raid on Guests at Pre-Nuptial Celebration

Cleveland Press, August 25, 1930.

tonnage. After the tragedy, all of them would recall having had such a good time before Death crashed the party.

It was after midnight on August 25, 1930. Most of those present thought it was a joke at first. Just as the party was beginning to break up, two men, dressed in suits and wearing handkerchiefs over their faces, barged through the back door of the house about 12:30 a.m. "Stick 'em up!" they shouted at the guests, shoving guns into the chest of host Donald Dunham and trying to steer him toward the front of the house. Even after they saw the guns, some of the guests remained skeptical, thinking this "robbery" scene was simply a joke—a joke in very bad taste—on the part of the host. One of the debutantes present even playfully attempted to pull the handkerchief off the face of one of the gunmen. When he cursed and waved the gun at her, she realized it wasn't a gag.

Herding Donald Dunham and several others into a corridor leading to the billiard room, the robbers locked them in and confronted the remaining guests, trying to move them toward the front of the house. It wasn't an easy task, and the appearance of a third gunman at the front door didn't accelerate the process. It was clear to at least some of the male guests, most of them Ivy League collegians, that the robbers were young, unconfident, and noticeably losing their initial bravado. At this point, perhaps five minutes into the robbery, the gunmen had failed to obtain any jewelry or cash, and the situation was deteriorating by the second. They began hearing taunts that the police had already been called and were on the way. So by the time the robbers and the robbed got to the front porch, their roles were reversed. Although the three robbers still had their guns, they were by now backing away from some of the more aggressive male party guests. Finally, one of the gunmen panicked. "C'mon, let's go!" he cried, and he and his two companions began a quick retreat, backing rapidly toward the street with their guns drawn.

It could have and should have ended right there. Nothing had been stolen, and no one had been hurt. Some of the guests, in fact, were not even aware that there was a robbery in progress. But the blood of some of the young collegians was up—there had been ample alcoholic refreshment at the party—and they thought they had taken enough guff from these three young punks. Four of the guests, Ransom Miller Wilkison, Frank Clark, Allan Thomas, and Cecil Webster, decided to confront the robbers. Advancing toward the nervous gunmen, they taunted them, sneering, "You guys are afraid to shoot. Why don't you start something?" A second later, Ransom Wilkison grappled with one of the gunmen, and the two went down, tussling on the lawn.

Wilkison had his hands on the throat of his gunman as Raymond Dunham came on the scene. One of the robbers was standing a few feet away with a rifle, screaming at Wilkison, "Let go of my brother or I'll plug you!" "You'd better let him go, Miller, or you'll get hurt," Ray Dunham cautioned the incensed Wilkison as he squeezed harder and harder. Dunham finally got through to him, and as the gunman staggered to his feet, Ransom shouted to the rifleman, "All right, here he is—come and get him!" A moment later, the first gun fired.

The next few seconds were a chaos of gunfire, as revolvers and a rifle roared in the hands of the robber trio. "Don't worry, they're blanks," someone shouted. They were not. As the party guests watched in horror, they saw two of the robbers fall to the ground. Then, Ransom Wilkison staggered and fell in the middle of the street. Shot in the head, he began to die in front of his friends. Everyone stood frozen for some seconds, until one of the gunmen ran toward a waiting automobile, and the two wounded robbers limped away from the scene.

The events at 2873 Glengary had not gone unnoticed by the neighbors. One of them was H. E. Gabriel, who lived across the street. Surmising there was some kind of fight, he called the police. Shaker Heights police officers Frank Maxom, Lawrence Horrigan, and Albert Schley arrived shortly after the shooting and set off in pursuit of the robbers. It was an easy task: the two wounded gunmen had limped away from the scene, closely pursued by an angry group of partygoers. When the police caught up with everyone, the two gunmen were trapped in a ditch by the Shaker Rapid Transit right-of-way on Shaker Boulevard, desperately ducking as their pursuers shied stones at them. They surrendered meekly and were hustled off for questioning at the Shaker Heights police station.

As murder investigations go, the "Blue Book" murder didn't take much unraveling. Enraged by the disappearance of their confederate, who had sped off in a car, the two wounded gunmen started singing to the police immediately. The older one, Angelo Bell, 20, was suffering from a leg broken above the knee, compounded by an adjacent bullet wound. The younger captive was his brother Mike, only 16, and in pain from a flesh wound in his shoulder. Within minutes of their capture they implicated the third man, Ross Valore, 19, and told police where to find him. He was arrested that morning at his parents' home at 2547 East 29th Street. That night, before Shaker Heights mayor William J. Van Aken, all three were charged with first-degree murder and bound over to the grand jury. Two days later, the funeral for Ransom Wilkison was held at his parents' home at 3075 Fairfax Road in Cleveland Heights.

The initial story told to police by the Bell brothers was not so much inaccurate as tantalizingly incomplete. The passage of time would uncover some of its more startling facets. But it was enough for Cuyahoga County lawmen to start planning efforts to send Ross Valore to the electric chair. A career criminal, Valore had most

Captor and captives: top: Shaker Heights chief of police Irvin; bottom left: Mike Bell; bottom middle: Angelo Bell; bottom right: Ross Valore.

recently been in trouble with the law the previous January, when he was arrested on a Lorain County robbery charge. Paroled soon after, he had returned to Cleveland and resumed his life of larceny. Then, on the afternoon of August 24, he had come to the Bell brothers with a proposition. He told them he'd read about a swanky Shaker Heights party in the newspapers. It gave him a bright idea: Why not leave the gas station jobs to chumps, he argued, and go where the *real* money was, at a rich people's party? Valore had known the Bell brothers since they were young children, and it wasn't hard to convince them. That evening, about 7:30, they all piled into Valore's automobile and drove away. A few minutes later they stole a Jordan automobile on Shaker Boulevard. Transferring to that, they motored to Valore's home at 10510 Way Avenue, where Valore picked up a .38-caliber revolver for Angelo and stuck a .25-caliber automatic pistol in his own pocket. They then departed for some several hours of aimless driving as they killed time.

It was about 12:30 a.m. when they pulled up to the well-lit Dunham residence. Their guns at the ready, Angelo and Ross went in the back way, leaving Mike to stand in the shrubbery near the front door, holding a .25-70 rifle that was almost as big as he was. Mike was still there a few minutes later, when his demoralized comrades came backing out of the house and across the Dunham lawn, pursued by belligerent collegians. It was Angelo who was tackled by Ransom Wilkison, and it was Mike Bell who threatened to shoot him. Seconds later, someone did start shooting. It was probably Ross Valore, by now frantic to escape his pursuers. But all three gunmen now fired their weapons. A bullet from Mike's rifle crashed into the home of L. S. Bing at 2920 Glengary, where it was found the next day. Two bullets from Ross Valore's .25-caliber gun found human targets, as both Mike and Angelo were wounded in the confusion by their own compatriot. It was the fourth bullet, fired from Angelo's .38, that smashed into Wilkison's skull, killing him almost instantly.

From the beginning, Cuyahoga County prosecutor Ray T. Miller was determined to send Ross Valore to the electric chair. Both of the Bell brothers were meekly cooperative, a stark contrast to Valore, who angrily insisted that he was completely innocent. It was initially believed, moreover, that Valore was the mastermind of the business, the smooth persuader who convinced the less clever brothers to help him. Refusing even to accept a court-appointed lawyer, Ross maintained his defiant, uncooperative stance right up to the opening of his trial. He didn't even change his tune when it was announced on October 13 that his wife Cecile, 24, had just been indicted on a charge of participating in some other robberies with him. Cecile was immediately incarcerated in the Cuyahoga County Jail in lieu of $25,000 bond.

Ray T. Miller was just biding his time. On October 27, Ross Valore's trial opened in common pleas judge Samuel H. Silbert's

The cast and set of the tragedy: top left; Thalia Fuller, the guest of honor; top right; Ransom Miller Wilkison, murder victim; middle right; Andrew Jackson Duncan III, fiance of Miss Fuller; bottom left; Mrs. Ralph Scott Mueller, party guest; bottom right; scene of the tragedy, 2873 Glengary Rd., Shaker Heights.

courtroom. He was defended by former common pleas judge Dan B. Cull and Ezra Shapiro, both of them appointed by the court. Miller took personal charge of the prosecution. The first week of the trial passed predictably. After a tour of the Glengary Road death scene, the jury of eight men and four women listened as a parade of guests at the fatal party recounted the details of that night. Much of their testimony was inconsequential: while most of them had eventually realized that there was a robbery in progress, none of them had seen Wilkison get shot and only one, Donald Dunham, could even identify Ross Valore as one of the robbers.

More important than the eyewitness testimony were two crucial legal struggles waged during the initial phases of the trial—and the defense lost both of them. The first was a fight over admitting the confession made by Mike Bell to Shaker Heights detective Daniel Candrow on the day after Wilkison's murder. Mike Bell's statement included damning detail about the planning of the robbery and passionately expressed the betrayal felt by Angelo and Mike when they realized Valore had left them in the lurch on Glengary Road. Candrow recalled in his own testimony that Angelo, confronted face to face with Valore, had called him a "dirty double-crosser," and told him: "If you had stuck with us, none of us would have been caught. I wouldn't squeal on you if you had taken care of my little brother."

The second, and equally critical, legal tussle came over the matter of Valore's prior robberies. Miller had considerable evidence ready to show that Ross had committed two previous armed holdups and that Cecile Valore had been involved in at least one of them. Defense attorney Cull fought desperately to prevent the state's witnesses to the robberies from testifying, arguing that Valore's previous misdeeds were irrelevant to the first-degree murder charge he was being tried on. On November 3, Cull lost the fight, Judge Silbert agreeing with Miller's contention that evidence about Valore's prior robberies was admissible as they were "like and similar offenses." Then, Judge Silbert permitted Harry C. Royal, a partner in the Cleveland office of Ernst & Ernst, to take the stand and describe how Valore and two other thugs had robbed him and several others in front of a house at 2630 Fairmount Boulevard on June 20, 1930. Royal could not identify Ross as the man who had relieved his party of their cash and jewelry, but Royal's chauffeur, Joe Simon, could and he very effectively fingered Ross. Several witnesses to another robbery on June 7, 1930, at the home of Mrs. William Evers, Jr., followed Royal on the stand. A man and woman had bluffed their way into her house at 1 p.m. and held her two servants and her young children at gunpoint until Mrs. Evers returned home. The two robbers had taken $2,000 in furs, cash, and jewelry, and two of Mrs. Evers's servants now identified Ross as the gunman and Cecile Valore as his armed companion. Maid Lola Lipscomb was a devastating witness against Cecile, recalling how she prodded the Evers children with her gun and snarled, "You shut up—if you let out one cry it'll be your last!"

It was clear to astute observers by the trial's second week that Prosecutor Miller was already looking beyond Ross Valore to his next judicial target: Cecile Valore. By now, Miller and other lawmen had come to believe that it was she, not Ross, who was the real mastermind behind the Glengary Road caper. Judge Silbert revealed publicly that she was a likely target just before the damning testimony of Lola Lipscomb implicated her in the Evers heist.

Taking the stand on November 5, Cecile proved to be a lousy witness both for her husband and herself. Stylishly arrayed in a black cloak trimmed with monkey fur, and described by reporters as "of the Amazonian type," Cecile almost shouted her denials that she or Ross were involved in either the Glengary Road tragedy or the two previous robberies. When queried as to how she knew Ross wasn't involved in the Royal robbery, she piously riposted, "Because he told me he wasn't, and I know he wouldn't lie to me." Quizzed as to what Ross did for a living, Cecile asserted that he worked, although she was unable to say for whom he worked or for how long. She also supported her husband's claim that he had spent the night of the Glengary robbery at his dying father's bedside on East 29th Street.

Ross Valore took the stand himself the next day. Well groomed, freshly shaved, dapperly dressed, and with well-pomaded hair (newspaper reporters described him as "sheikish-looking"), Ross blandly denied virtually everything that had been said about him by the state's 38 witnesses. He denied even owning a gun and reiterated his dubious claim that he had been at his dying father's side on the night in question. His tone of injured innocence became most emphatic as he swore that he had been severely mistreated during his interrogation by Prosecutor Miller and sundry other lawmen.

Ross was followed on the stand by Mrs. William Evers, who

pounded more nails in his legal coffin. She was allowed to testify that Cecile Valore had virtually confessed to robbing her on June 7. Her admission to Mrs. Evers came during a meeting at the Central Police Station, shortly after Cecile was arrested in October. During that same conversation, Cecile had promised to try and get some of Mrs. Evers's stolen furs back, whining that if she testified truthfully about the robberies some unnamed "Italians" would "bump her off." If Mrs. Evers was telling the truth, it must have been the most imprudent conversation of Cecile Valore's life, for Cecile capped her girlish confidences by blurting to Mrs. Evers that it was *she* who had driven Ross's gang to Glengary Road on August 25, and it was *she* who was waiting in the stolen Jordan as her frantic husband came running from the melee of gunfire at 2873 Glengary.

The final arguments for the prosecution and defense concentrated predominately on the emotional facets of the case. Ignoring the damning testimony of the Bell brothers and Mrs. Evers, Daniel Cull simply pleaded for his client's life, portraying Ross Valore as a poor boy who had never had a chance to go straight. Ezra Shapiro seconded his theme, warbling a starkly simple argument against the death penalty: "The state has no right to take this man's life— no man's life—that most precious possession which only God can give and only God can take away." Prosecutor Miller, too, eschewed the voluminous evidence, preferring instead to attack Ross Valore's moral character. Calling him a "yellow dog" and a "rat," Miller emphasized his betrayal of his confederates and demanded that he get "just the kind of mercy he meted out."

Maybe it was Miller's passionate denunciation. Maybe it was Valore's prior convictions. Maybe it was his wife's unconvincingly naive demeanor. Maybe it was the Bell brothers or Cecile's indiscreet confidences to Mrs. Evers. Maybe it was the unconvincing or just plain irrelevant testimony of the 15 witnesses called by the defense. Or maybe it was just Ross Valore's bad luck that the source of his only alibi—his father Joseph—had inconveniently died three days after Ross was arrested for the Glengary killing. (The death certificate said heart disease—his relatives said it was heartbreak.) Whatever it was, it only took his jury a little over five hours of deliberation and seven ballots to convict him of first-degree murder (with a recommendation of mercy) on November 7, 1930. Proving that he had learned nothing from his ordeal, Valore used his opportunity to speak before sentence was pronounced and whine, "I have only this to say. I think I didn't get a fair trial, because evidence of all the robbery victims was introduced in the case. I thought this was a murder trial, not a robbery trial." An incensed Judge Silbert retorted, "The trouble with you is that you are still defiant. You don't appreciate what has been done for you." He then sentenced Ross to life in the Ohio Penitentiary.

One month later, Cecile Valore was indicted for first-degree murder in the Glengary Road killing. Two weeks later Mike and Angelo Bell pleaded guilty in Judge Silbert's court to the same homicide. Angelo was represented in court by future U.S. congressman William E. Minshall, while Mike's counsel

MRS. VALORE SOBS AT TRIAL FOR MURDER

Bob-Haired Brunet Cringes-at Story of Killing of Student

Mrs. Cecile Valore, 26, bob-haired brunet, sobbed freely today when Coroner A. J. Pearse described the wounds that had caused the death of R. Miller Wilkison, whom she is accused of killing.

This was at her trial for first degree murder in the court of Criminal Court Judge Walter McMahon. Yesterday the trial began, and a jury was impaneled.

County Prosecutor Ray T. Miller is expected to ask that Mrs. Valore, alleged "brains" of a gang which murdered the young Princeton student in an attempted holdup Aug. 25, be given the electric chair as an accomplice.

A sob that was audible thru the

CRIES AT TRIAL

MRS. CECILE VALORE

Cleveland Press, February 10, 1931.

was redoubtable defense attorney Francis Poulson. Judge Silbert delayed pronouncing sentence on the two brothers, reasoning that their indefinite prospects might ensure their cooperation at Cecile's impending trial. In the meantime, while Cecile fretted and smoked cigarettes in the Cuyahoga County jail under an increased bond of $50,000, strenuous efforts were made to implicate her and her husband in the murder of Dr. Alfred P. Scully on March 3, 1930. (For details of the Scully murder, see "A Quiet, Middle-Aged Man," in *The Killer in the Attic and Still More Tales of Cleveland Woe*, 2002.) But the case fell apart when an eyewitness failed to identify Ross and Cecile as the couple he had seen near Scully's office just before the murder. It remained, however, an amazing coincidence that Scully's former secretary, Estelle Sogola, turned out to be Cecile Valore's sister.

QUIZ DETECTIVES AS WIFE NAMES VALORE SCULLY MURDERER

Cleveland Press, February 18, 1931.

Cecile's trial before common pleas judge Walter McMahon opened on February 8, 1931. Defended by J. Paul Lamb, Charles Krieg, and George M. Heil, Cecile was prosecuted by Ray T. Miller. Displaying a sunny optimism to reporters and spectators, she jauntily asserted at the trial's opening, "I'm not going out of here until I leave the front way." Wearing a dark-blue dress, flesh-colored stockings, and black pumps, the bob-haired Cecile deployed the full arsenal of her feminine wiles against Miller's devastating roster of witnesses. She sobbed audibly as Coroner A.J. Pearse described Ransom Wilkison's death wound. She indulged in paroxysms of weeping as Mike Bell told the jury how she had planned and managed the botched Glengary Road robbery. An indulgent Judge McMahon recessed the proceedings until she recovered her composure. When Angelo Bell, brought into court on a stretcher because of his unhealed wounds, testified on February 11, she interrupted him, screaming: "Angelo, Angelo, tell the truth—tell them everything. He's lying. He knows my life; he knows how [Ross has] helped you always; he's always been my friend."

Undeterred by her tears, Angelo amplified the prosecution's picture of her as the gang's chief and primary crime planner. It was Cecile, Angelo swore, who had told him the previous June that the "real money was in robbing houses." It was Cecile who cut out an item in a newspaper describing the upcoming Dunham party. It was

Cecile who had driven them to Glengary Road and told them what to do there. And it was Cecile who was waiting at the wheel of the Jordan at the end of the botched robbery, when Ross Valore jumped into the car and shouted, "Drive like hell."

Unlike her stubborn husband, Cecile Valore knew when to throw in the towel. By the time the Bell brothers finished testifying, it was clear to her and her trio of lawyers that the evidence that she had planned and participated in the fatal robbery was overwhelming. It was also obvious that she had no one to back up her ludicrous alibi that she had been scrubbing floors at her home the night of August 24. Dropping the tearful act, she watched with a calm smile on February 13 as her lawyers accepted a plea bargain to murder in the first degree. "It all seems like a bad dream," she sighed to Deputy Sheriff E. J. Dolan as he escorted her back to her County Jail cell.

It was initially hoped that the shock of her conviction might make Cecile willing to disclose underworld secrets, in hopes of mitigating her sentence. And at least at the start Cecile did not disappoint. On February 17, she told Cuyahoga County sheriff John M. Sulzmann that her husband Ross had not only killed Dr. Alfred Scully but also five other persons besides. Her revelations about the Scully slaying were especially dramatic: she said that Ross had told her about it the very night it happened. Early the next morning, about 4, there came an unexpected knock on their door at 10510 Way Avenue. Before Ross answered, he turned to Cecile and warned, "If that's the law, I'll kill you even if I burn." Cecile also accused Cleveland police detectives Charles Cavolo and George Zicarelli of lobbying Lorain County lawmen for the parole that freed Ross Valore in January 1930.

Cecile's bombshell revelations seemed almost too good to be true—and they were. A check of Ross's whereabouts during the chronology of his alleged murders cleared him immediately of most of them and rendered the remainder improbable. Detectives Cavolo and Zicarelli were exonerated of Cecile's charges after an official investigation. Even before Cecile was sentenced, most observers were beginning to agree with Ross Valore: "If she said it, she lied. They must have promised her something, or she wouldn't have made up a pack of lies like that. I'm not a killer. I don't go around killing people. Next she'll say I killed Abraham Lincoln."

On February 21, 1931, Judge McMahon sentenced Cecile to life imprisonment at the Marysville Reformatory. Immediately afterwards, Judge Silbert sentenced the Bell brothers. Although both were given life terms, Silbert convicted Angelo on a first-degree murder charge and Mike on a second-degree count. Judge Silbert explained the discrepancy on the grounds of Mike Bell's extreme youth and the fact that it was Angelo who had fired the fatal shot. Prosecutor Miller, for his part, lobbied for the lesser charge against Mike and promised that he would someday ask the Ohio governor to exercise clemency in his case.

The formidable Cecile made her last Cleveland appearance at a hearing to decide the custody of her daughter, Patsy, four. Cecile gasped, Cecile sobbed, and Cecile screamed anew in Judge Silbert's court as her mother, Marcella Barsky, fought it out with Kazmier Mazurek, Cecile's first husband, for possession of the child. Perhaps Cecile's theatrics were not in vain this time, for Judge Silbert turned Patsy over to Mrs. Barksy, as per Cecile's wishes. Four days later, weeping geysers, Cecile was taken away to the Marysville Reformatory.

Even in the 1930s and 1940s, "life in prison" was not life in prison. Almost 13 years after his conviction, Ross Valore was paroled from the Ohio Penitentiary on October 28, 1943. Although his initial behavior in prison was uncooperative, Ross apparently underwent a genuine character change there. He began to write to Judge Silbert and eventually cultivated the confidence of Ray T. Miller himself. He became a trusty, worked as a chauffeur for the Parole and Pardons Commission, and was described by Ohio Penitentiary officials as one of their best-behaved prisoners. It was reported at the time of Valore's parole that he was returning to Cleveland to take a job in his brother Sam's meat market. He died in Cleveland in 1967, 37 years after the victim of his Glengary Road crime.

Like Ray T. Miller and Dan Cull, Judge Silbert had argued for Ross's pardon on the grounds that his wife was the guiltiest party. As Silbert told a *Cleveland Press* reporter at the time of Ross's release, "I always was of the opinion that his wife, Cecile, who was

about five years older, really was the 'brains' behind him and that
she was the principal offender." Ironically, however, Cecile was
paroled from Marysville in 1941. Young Mike Bell had died in
prison only a year after his conviction, and triggerman Angelo
remained incarcerated at the time of Ross Valore's parole in 1943.

It is an interesting question as to whether Ross Valore, much less
his wife Cecile, could be convicted in today's more exacting legal
environment. Notwithstanding their probable guilt, there were
loose ends in the prosecution's case against them. Not a single witness presented at the trial could identify Ross as the gunman when
the actual shooting started. No ballistic evidence connected him
with the fatal shot. The state never did account for all the bullets
fired, or even the wounds Angelo and Mike Bell suffered—these
were just not considered important matters at the trials. In all probability, evidence of Ross's prior robberies would be suppressed in
today's judicial climate. And the prosecution's flexible emphasis
on just who was the mastermind behind the Glengary caper might
raise more than one contemporary juridical eyebrow. Ross Valore
was convicted largely because the state emphasized his dominant
role in the Glengary robbery. The state then turned around and
prosecuted Cecile Valore on exactly the same grounds. They were
certainly both morally guilty of Ransom Wilkison's murder and
may have deserved the actual sentences that they served. But the
justice meted out to them might seem sloppy by today's more strin-
gent, and often exasperating, judicial standards.

Chapter 16

ALCOHOL TO BURN

The Russo Wine Company Fire (1948)

It's just a parking lot today, but like almost every corner of Cleveland, the southwest corner of West 28th Street and Lorain Avenue has its tragic tale to tell. At this intersection two brave men died fighting the great Russo Wine Company fire of January 16, 1948.

On that date at about 4 p.m., Michael Russo and his brother Joseph had just handed out payroll checks to their 27 employees. They were then alone in the store with two salesmen when Michael smelled, and then saw, the smoke that was pouring out from a balcony area on the third floor. By the time the first of nine Cleveland Fire Department engine companies, four hook-and-ladder companies, and two hose companies arrived on the scene, the winery was a roaring inferno. Within minutes, 3,000 curious Clevelanders had turned out to watch as fireman fought the flames licking hungrily through paper cartons, wine labels, and 40,000 cases of wine.

Tragedy happened, as so often it does, when least expected. By 4:45 p.m. the fire was thought to be under control, and firefighters began to withdraw from the building's interior. Yet just as a group of five men emerged from a center door on the West 28th side, the building's brick wall collapsed on them, without even a warning creak. Three firemen managed to fight their way out of the debris, suffering severe lacerations and one broken leg. Left behind, however, were Paul I. Green, 57, of Hose Company No. 2 and Henry Spencer, 29, of Engine Company No. 6. Thanks to the persistence of the alcohol-fed flames, it wasn't until 7:20 p.m. that their com-

The smoldering ruins, January 1948.

rades were able to retrieve the bodies from the smoldering ruins. Green, a 33-year Fire Department veteran, left behind a wife, Hilda, and sons Donald and William. Spencer, who had transferred from the Cleveland Police Department to become a firefighter only seven months before, was survived by his wife, Grace, and daughter, Mary Lou. The two widows received $90 until their children turned 18 years of age.

The cause of the Russo Wine Company fire was never determined. The building loss was at least $200,000, plus the $300,000 cost of the wine stock destroyed. Older West Siders will tell you that the fire area stank for weeks afterwards with the smell of all that burnt wine.

Chapter 17

"A WRETCHED OUTCAST FROM SOCIETY"

The Murder of John Osborne (1853)

(This story is dedicated to Cleveland police officer Joan Patrici and the thousands of Cleveland policemen and policewomen, past and present, who have bravely, and often thanklessly, served, protected—and too often died for—the citizens of Cleveland.)

Cleveland in the 1850s was not for the weak or meek. Although its 1852 population of about 25,000 souls scarcely hinted at the sprawling metropolis to come, the nascent city was already experiencing the kind of social disorders we tend to associate with the more crowded maturity of our North Coast megalopolis. Drunkenness, street crime, prostitution, and murder were already present and beginning to claim the attention of both concerned citizens and enterprising journalists. By 1860, as the Civil War loomed, it would be evident from both the columns of Cleveland's several newspapers and the records of the criminal courts that the city had lost its innocence sometime during the preceding decade. And 1853, evidence would suggest, was the precise year in which that fall from grace occurred.

It wasn't just the increasing street crime that marked Cleveland's rancid civic maturation that year. True, it was bad and getting worse by the month. An egregiously cynical episode occurring in the late fall highlighted the increasing peril in Forest City streets. On the night of November 27, a man named Buck was found crawl-

Murderous Assault on a Watchman—Arrest
of the Offender.

Cleveland Leader, November 21, 1853.

ing painfully up the Water Street hill from the lakefront. Bleeding
from two severe cuts on his left ear and a fearful wound on his
cheek, he told a pitiful story of being assaulted, stabbed, and
robbed on the stairs by the Water Street docks. Thirty minutes later,
a report came in to the Cleveland police that yet another traveler
had been knocked down, stabbed, and robbed, on Euclid Avenue
near Sterling Avenue (East 30th Street). Alas, it was even worse
than appearances suggested. Investigation eventually revealed that
the perpetrator of the Euclid Avenue robbery was, in fact, Buck,
who had faked the story of his Water Street misfortune to deflect
the suspicions of Cleveland lawmen.

The year 1853 was likewise a vintage year for Cleveland murder. Particularly disturbing to Cleveland citizens (if diverting to
Cleveland newspaper readers) was the murder of Christiana Sigsby
in late April of that year. It was bad enough that Miss Sigsby was
found dead in her Muirson Street (East 12th Street) home, savagely
beaten and her throat cut ear to ear. But respectable Cleveland citizens were almost more upset by the disclosure that the young and
comely Christiana had been working, seemingly unhampered until
her last day, as a prostitute in a respectable Cleveland neighborhood. Nor were public anxieties soothed by the abject failure of the
authorities to solve her brutal murder. Clearly, Cleveland was no
longer a bucolic village, and its decay was further italicized at the
end of the year with an infallible index of moral and social deca-
dence: its first murder of a policeman.

Cleveland's police force at the time was a body barely worthy of
the name. Organized when the city was incorporated in 1836,
Cleveland's Finest were not so much a crime-fighting unit as a commercial security corps. Composed mainly of "Watchmen," the
force's chief duty was to watch for fires, especially in the commer-
cial-industrial area of the Flats and along the business area of Superior Street.

Little is known about John Osborne, the first Cleveland police-man to die in the line of duty. We know he was a relatively young man and that he had a wife, Isabella, children, and a father, Thomas. We know that he lived on Lake Street (now Lakeside Avenue) and that, like the other Cleveland watchmen, he was paid $300 a year. The only other fact we know about him is how he died.

It happened, as so many police murders do, in the dead of night. It was a Sunday evening, November 30, and it was raining steadily as Osborne and his partner, William Wilcox, walked their nightly round in the Flats. It was almost 11:30 p.m., but visibility was good, thanks to the new fangled gas lights that illuminated the area. Osborne and Wilcox had just come abreast of the New England House (one of Cleveland's premier hotels) on Merwin Street and were about to turn the corner and ascend Superior Hill (where the Western Reserve building today sits). Just before they turned, Osborne decided to seek a light for his cigar, and they walked toward the door of the New England House.

It happened in an instant. John Howley, a drunken sailor, had been watching the two officers from across the street. A habitual inebriate, Howley had arrived in Cleveland five or six days before and done little but drink since. That very evening he had imbibed in several River Street saloons before stumbling on a drunkard's dream. There, right on Merwin Street, were two kegs of whiskey just sitting in front of Crawford & Chamberlain's warehouse—*and the bungs of both of them were open!* The only moment Howley would later claim to recall was the instant he lay beneath one of the taps and turned it on . . .

Howley had probably been guzzling there for about two hours when he dimly espied Osborne and Wilcox walking through the rainy mist across Merwin Street. He lurched to his feet and began running toward the two watchmen. Wilcox was just eight steps behind Osborne as they turned toward the hotel door, and he didn't see Howley until the moment he passed him, running full-tilt. By that time it was already too late, and Osborne himself never saw him or the burly arm that suddenly reached around his neck.

It doesn't take long to slash a throat. It was an instant's labor, as Howley's sharp, four-inch case knife sliced through Osborne's neck scarf, cut through his rubber raincoat, and slashed into his jugular vein. Even as his blood began to arc in six-, then 10-foot jets onto Merwin Street, Osborne whirled and brought his heavy club down on Howley's skull. He was joined a second later by Wilcox, and they quickly beat Howley to the ground. Witnesses, including Thomas Patterson, ran up and took charge of the assailant, who was by now in no shape to escape, much less even to stand up.

Osborne was already in shock as Wilcox supported him with his arm and tried to maneuver him back to the New England House. Even as Wilcox hammered on the hotel door, the bleeding watchman muttered, "I guess I am killed." Wilcox's frantic pounding finally brought a boy to the door, but he was too frightened to unlock it, even after Wilcox screamed, "For God's sake, let us in, a watchman is stabbed and dying!" Two men now came up and helped drag Osborne up Superior Hill to Myron Cozzens's Franklin House saloon, where his bleeding was staunched with improvised bandages until Dr. Thomas G. Cleveland arrived and dressed his wound more professionally. Meanwhile, Wilcox had returned to the attack scene, where he found Howley still on the ground. He took him to the watch house on Water Street and turned him over to turnkey Joseph Taggert, who locked him in a cell. Before leaving, however, Wilcox asked Howley why he had stabbed Osborne. Howley replied that Osborne had once struck him and that he wanted to kill him for revenge. Howley repeated this assertion to Thomas Patterson, shortly before the bandaged Osborne arrived at the watch house. Despite his grievous wound, he, too, spent the night there and insisted on seeing Howley in his cell before being taken to his Lake Avenue home. The puzzled Osborne wanted to know why Howley had stabbed him, but he was certain after visiting Howley in his cell that he had never encountered him before.

The next morning Howley appeared before Thomas McKinstry in the Cleveland police court. Charged with assault with intent to kill, he was bound over to the February term of the common pleas court and returned to his cell in lieu of $2,000 bail. By now, the sobering Howley had modified his story, and he told McKinstry he had no idea why he had stabbed Osborne nor any memory of the event. He said he had come from Detroit the previous week and slept on the lakefront docks when he was drinking himself into insensibility.

It will never be known exactly what killed John Osborne. It probably wasn't the wound itself, although his family's successful opposition to an autopsy precluded a definite medical conclusion. Three inches deep into the neck, Howley's knife had slashed across the right side of Osborne's throat and severed about a third of the jugular vein. Dr. Cleveland later testified he thought it was a mortal wound from the moment he examined it but was encouraged when he was able to stop the bleeding. Several days later, however, bleeding resumed, and the worried Dr. Cleveland called in Dr. Horace Ackley, one of Cleveland's most respected physicians. The two doctors operated on Osborne on Saturday, November 26—but it was too late. Although Cleveland's testimony at Howley's trial was guarded on the subject of his patient's condition, it was clear that Osborne's neck wound was badly infected by the time the physicians reopened it. Osborne declined rapidly in the days that followed; he died at 3 p.m. on December 2. His funeral the following day was a solemn spectacle, attended by his fellow Hibernian Guards in full regalia, not to mention the sorrowing brothers of his Odd Fellows club chapter.

Almost three months later, on February 24, 1854, the trial of John Howley got under way in Cuyahoga County common pleas judge Samuel Starkweather's courtroom. Prosecuted by Samuel Williamson and Albert Gallatin Riddle (later a U.S. congressman and bosom friend of President James A. Garfield), Howley was defended by Robert F. Paine, Charles G. Finney, Jr., and N. W. Holt. As virtually none of the facts or eyewitness testimony was disputed by the defense, the burden of the trial focused on what weight Howley's jury should assign to his inebriated condition at the time of his murderous act. Striking a very modern note, almost all of the testimony and press coverage focused not on the murder victim but on the perpetrator of the crime.

Howley claimed he could not recall stabbing Osborne or even having any motive to do so. His lawyers quite shrewdly emphasized the facts of his shabby biography in an attempt to save his life. Born in Ireland in 1816, Howley had come to Toronto, Canada, with his parents at the age of 12. Living on an island in the St. Lawrence River, Howley had spent most of the next two decades as a fisherman or itinerant peddler. A confirmed sot by the age of 20, he had eventually worked as a sailor on the Great Lakes, a career frequently punctuated by prolonged alcoholic benders and stints in the Detroit poorhouse. He had arrived in Cleveland around November 13 and worked on the docks unloading cargo. Spending every cent he earned on alcoholic refreshment, he could recall nothing of the murder evening until he woke up in the Water Street watch house. A *Plain Dealer* reporter vividly captured the pathetic impression made by Howley on his courtroom audience:

> His appearance is that of a man who has been for long years on a prolonged debauch. He sits with his eyes on the floor and appears sullen and stupid. He never speaks except when questioned by his counsel, and the only explanation he gives of the murder is that he knew nothing about it—that he is totally unconscious of having committed the deed, and only came to his sense when he found himself in the Watch House. . . . Whiskey made him what he was before he committed the murder, and no one knows what influence it had on him when he did commit the deed.

After three days of testimony and argument, Judge Starkweather charged the jury on the morning of February 27. Noting Paine's emphasis on his client's alleged alcoholic insanity, Starkweather unequivocally insisted that "insanity produced by intoxicating liquors is regarded by the law as voluntary insanity, and is no excuse for crime." Howley's jury only took several hours to agree with Starkweather, returning a guilty verdict of first-degree murder against Howley that same afternoon. The jury was probably ultimately swayed by Starkweather's disclaimer on inebriation and the testimony of Wilcox and four other witnesses that they had seen no obvious signs of intoxication in Howley. Howley was only the second person convicted of first-degree murder in Cuyahoga County, the first being John Omic, the West Side Native American hung on

Public Square in 1812. (For details of that grimly farcical event, see George Condon, *Cleveland: The Best Kept Secret,* Doubleday, 1970, and the author's Internet-only publication, *By the Neck Until Dead: A History of Hangings in Cuyahoga County,* Cleveland Digital Library, 2000, http//:web.ulib.csuohio.edu/speccoll/bellamy).

Robert F. Paine's motion for a new trial was not heard until May 1854. Following Judge Starkweather's brusque rejection, 500 persons thronged his courtroom on June 6 to hear sentence passed on Howley. When asked whether he had anything to say, Howley muttered something inaudible, and then defense lawyer Finney was permitted to enlarge one more time on Howley's misspent life and diminished capacity. But Judge Starkweather, properly, had the last word. Addressing the prisoner, he pulled out all the rhetorical stops suitable to an audience familiar with the melodramatic moralism found in *Ten Nights in a Barroom* and similar tracts of contemporary temperance:

> The circumstances attending your commission of this crime, unexplained as they have been, by any evidence on your part, present it as one of an aggravated enormity. What your motive was in the commission of this awful deed, still remains concealed in mystery. John Osborne, the victim of your crime, was a peaceable and unoffending citizen of this city. . . . Your appearance in Court, as a wretched outcast from society, has plainly shown, that by habits of intoxication you have become reduced to the lowest degree of degradation, and have been brought at last, to end the wretchedness of a drunkard's life by an ignominious death. Be aroused now to a sense of your present awful condition, and with all diligence employ your remaining faculties, to meet your final Judge in peace.

Judge Starkweather then sentenced Howley to hang on September 8, 1854.

By the time Howley was sentenced, John Osborne was an all but forgotten man. The Cleveland City Council passed a unanimous motion on April 19, 1854, to pay his grieving widow Isabella $300 for her loss—but that was the last heard of the assassinated watchman, as public attention shifted to frantic efforts to save his killer's miserable life. A clemency petition requesting that Howley's sentence be commuted to life imprisonment was signed by hundreds of Clevelanders, and the city's newspapers unanimously emphasized Howley's pitiable state. As the *Plain Dealer* put it, "Appearances have indicated, since his arrest, that he is a man of inferior intellect, no education, and his senses have become thoroughly deadened by long years of beastly intemperance." The *Cleveland Leader*, no doubt expressing the temperance convictions of its crusading editor Edwin Cowles, waxed lyrical in its lament for the Merwin Street stabber, shifting guilt to the Cleveland's commercial purveyors of alcohol:

> At times [Howley] gives evidence of insanity, and again appears to realize his awful situation in all its terrors. . . . The prisoner is naturally of inferior mind, and that years of besotted drunkenness have left him in point of intellect very little above "the beasts that perish." What nature failed to do for him renders him an object of compassion; the deeper depth into which alcohol has plunged him, makes his poisoners as guilty as he.

Cooperating graciously with the crusade to save his life, Howley granted numerous jailhouse interviews. Sometimes calm, sometimes manifesting "evidence of insanity" to his interlocutors, he tirelessly reiterated his claims that he bore Osborne no malice and did not even remember stabbing him. During an interview in the last days of August, Howley allowed to a *Cleveland Leader* reporter that he would much "prefer" a commutation of his sentence to his looming Public Square execution.

Howley's partisans eventually had their way. On August 25, Ohio governor William Medill notified Cuyahoga County authorities and Howley's attorneys that he had commuted Howley's sentence to life imprisonment in the Ohio Penitentiary. Medill's decision elicited universal acclaim in Cleveland newspapers and doubtless gratified the many temperance enthusiasts who had fought for Howley's life. Would they have thought differently if they had known that Osbourne was to be but the first of more than

Howley's Sentence Commuted.

Cleveland Leader, **August 28, 1854.**

100 Northeast Ohio policemen to be callously murdered in the 15 decades to come?

Probably not. The shocks of Howley's assault and Osborne's death were soon effaced by another brutal murder in Cleveland's increasingly mean streets. Five days after Osborne died, a hunter named Richard West was stalking game in the woods near Dr. Seeley's Water Cure Asylum, just south of Kinsman and Case Avenue (East 40th Street). Tiring of his fruitless quest, he sighted a tame turkey on the asylum grounds, shot it, and then tried to conceal it for removal later. Several asylum employees had witnessed his illegal act, and one of them, Joseph Thompson, 22, confronted West and demanded that he pay for the dead turkey. West, a burly blacksmith, refused. When Thompson persisted, West shouted he would be damned if he didn't kill him, and promptly emptied his shotgun at Thompson at point-blank range. The heavy shot hit Thompson's leg, severing major arteries. He bled to death within an hour, and West subsequently served a term for second-degree murder, despite the protests of *his* tender-hearted partisans that his incarceration would seriously inconvenience his wife. The last heard of John Howley was in 1874, when it was reported that he was still serving time in the Ohio Penitentiary in Columbus.

Chapter 18

"A SWING FOR A SWING"

Slaughter on Cedar Avenue (1871)

Unlike the byzantine complications, elongated legal struggles, and ambiguous justice ensuing from many Cleveland murders, the 1871 J. H. Swing homicide offers a contrasting simplicity and blunt morality to its audiences, then and now. Consuming little more than one month from beginning to end, the case of the Swing killing featured a clear-cut villain, a sympathetic victim, and stellar police work by Cleveland's Finest. And if the legal defense given the accused was nothing to boast about?—well, John Cooper wasn't the kind of defendant likely to give the American Civil Liberties Union sleepless nights, even if had been around to render him aid.

The Swing affair began in the early afternoon of Tuesday, November 21, 1871, when rumors flew through downtown Cleveland that a terrible murder had been committed over on Cedar Avenue, just east of Perry Street (now East 22nd). It came to light about 1 p.m., when Jesse Palmer and John Yahraus ran into each other at the front door of tinsmith James H. Swing's shop at 32 Cedar Street. Palmer was there to make a purchase, and Yahraus had come to pay a visit to Swing, from whom he had learned his trade as a tinsmith. When repeated knocking failed to rouse Swing, the two men opened the unlocked door and entered Swing's workroom, which occupied the back part of the one-story house he owned on Cedar Street. They didn't find Swing there, nor was he in the backyard henery, where he kept his collection of prized domestic fowls. Walking past his bedroom window, they were unable to see inside, as the window was blocked by a large map of

Ohio someone had placed in front of it. Returning to the work-room, Yahraus and Palmer noticed pools of blood seeping from beneath the wooden partition that separated it from Swing's bed-room. Alarmed, they broke down the bedroom door and discovered what the next day's *Plain Dealer* justly termed a "sickening spec-tacle." Swing was lying more or less on his back, with his head leaning back. He was nearly naked, his clothes lay in mere shreds on his skin, and his arms and torso were covered with blood. His face was almost unrecognizable, his entire head merely a beaten pulp of blood, brains, and pieces of skull. There was blood on the walls and floor and thickly clotted on a heavy hammer that lay nearby. The room was a splintered wreckage of emptied drawers, ripped clothing, smashed dishes, and broken kitchen utensils. Most appallingly, a soldering iron was crammed into Swing's mouth and down into his throat, its four-inch copper handle sticking grotesquely out of his ruined mouth. The shaken Palmer and Yahraus immediately ran for the Cleveland police.

Superintendent Jacob Schmitt's men soon arrived, and they were as shocked as Palmer and Yahraus. It was obvious from the clotting of the blood that Swing had been dead for some hours and that his smashed body had lain undetected in his bedroom during that time. How could this have happened in the house of such a well-known man and on such a busy, well-traveled street?

James H. Swing was a substantial, reputedly wealthy, respected man, and this was likely no casual crime perpetrated on the spur of the moment. Two hours later, Coroner Schenck convened an inquest at Swing's house. After hearing testimony, he declared Swing had been murdered by an unknown hand. Several hours later, an aroused city council authorized a reward of $500 for the apprehension of Swing's killers, an amount quickly boosted to $750 by the Cuyahoga County commissioners.

Up until the moment he was found swallowing a soldering iron, James H. Swing had been one of the great success stories of Cleve-land's small but growing African-American community. Born in 1825, Swing had been the offspring of the unsanctified union between his slave mother and his father, allegedly a slave-holding aristocrat of the Lexington, Kentucky, area. Freed by his father as a youth and apprenticed to a tinner, Swing had mastered his craft and come to Cleveland to live and work in the early 1850s. Owning his own home, where he also conducted his business, Swing had become both a prosperous businessman and a figure of some political weight in the small circle of Cleveland's African-American Republican leaders. Known for his education and probity, Swing gave political speeches during local election campaigns (Cleveland African-Americans had gained the right to vote in 1870) and was also venerated for his abilities as a raconteur, often entertaining visitors to his shop with a genial flow of amusing anecdote. He was an amateur inventor, vintner, and expert checker player.

True, his life had not been without sorrow. Lately, he had been borrowing small sums of money and even coal from his neighbors, belying his reputed wealth. And his 1869 marriage to a German girl, Lizzie Lever, had ended disastrously in

HORRID MURDER !

A Colored Man Butchered on Cedar Street.

His Head Badly-Mangled with a Hammer.

A Soldering Iron Found Crammed Down the Throat of the Corpse.

The citizens of Cedar street were startled to-day by the announcement that a horrid murder had been perpetrated on that quiet little street.

Plain Dealer, November 21, 1871.

divorce after only three months when she deserted him to ply her vocation as a streetwalker. But Swing had hopes of a reconciliation, and it was said that he had recently offered Lizzie $1,000 to return to him. No one could verify that he had an enemy in the world, much less one who would have dispatched him in the orgy of violence that had occurred in the back bedroom at 32 Cedar Street. Not that Cleveland's 1871 newspapers were about to lavish unstinting praise on even a "good Negro," as Swing's obituary in the *Cleveland Herald* demonstrated:

> In personal appearance the deceased was rather repulsive than
> otherwise. He was tall and gaunt, and extremely awkward in his

motions. His face was pecked and pitted, and his coarse curly hair and whiskers presented an ungainly appearance. He had a low, receding forehead and as far as intellect was concerned he certainly appeared very inferior.

The solution of the Swing murder was a classic of solid, dogged, and unromantic police procedure. The first clue came from a little African-American boy, who told detectives that he had seen a mulatto "wearing a light-colored coat" around nine o'clock on the morning of the murder day. The mulatto was seated in Swing's workroom, reading a newspaper, while Swing sat smoking and talking with him. The boy's clue soon led to Thomas Murray, an acquaintance of Swing's who had also seen the mulatto in the light-colored coat. Murray had encountered him the previous night, when he came to call on Swing at 9 p.m. Murray had only stayed about 15 minutes, but he was sure that Swing and the mulatto were having hot words when he arrived, and he sensed that Swing was angry at the other man. Several hours later, the key breakthrough in the Swing case came when his friend Allen Williams stepped forward. Williams, it developed, had also seen the mulatto in the light-colored coat at Swing's shop, sometime during the middle of Monday afternoon. More importantly, Williams asked Superintendent Schmitt what had happened to Swing's gold watch.

Schmitt didn't know but he intended to find out, and by late Tuesday Cleveland detectives were checking all jewelry and watch repair shops in the area for anyone who could provide identifying details about Swing's missing timepiece. Sure enough, a man named Julius Koepler, in a Broadway Avenue jewelry shop, said the missing watch was one he had repaired several times over the previous 10 years. He told police its serial number (No. 45,006) and disclosed that he had scratched two identifying repair numbers on the inside of its case (1,100 and 1,157). Several hours later, Schmitt's men began distributing flyers with a description of the mysterious mulatto and the particulars of Swing's gold watch.

Now the case moved into high gear. In response to the flyer, an African-American man named Maxwell came forward. He told police that the mulatto was probably a man named John Cooper, with whom Maxwell had been living in a house on Newton Street (East 31st Street).

Early Tuesday morning, Maxwell related, Cooper had put all of this belongings into two trunks and hired a hack to take himself, his wife, and their luggage to the Union Depot on Bank Street. Maxwell didn't remember seeing any watch, but he did think that Cooper had said something about returning to Chillicothe, Ohio, where he had grown up.

Cooper seemed an improbable suspect at first. The police theory was that the murder had occurred sometime between 8 a.m. and noon on Tuesday—and Cooper's presumed southbound train had left at 6:50 a.m., at least an hour before Swing's death. But further investigation turned up witnesses who had seen Cooper at the Union Depot and at various other locations in Cleveland *after* the departure of the 6:50 train. Moreover, police learned, John Cooper had told several different stories to those he encountered after he left the Union Depot. One was that he was going uptown to retrieve his pocketbook from his home. The other was that he was going to drop by the Chamberlain block, where he had recently been employed as a laborer, to pick up his back pay. Inquiries confirmed that neither story was true. Even more interesting, it developed that Cooper, who at 6 a.m. had not been able to check his bags in at the Depot because he lacked the money for the train tickets, had returned there some time later with sufficient funds to book himself, his wife. and his luggage through to Xenia, Ohio, on the 3:50 p.m. Cleveland, Columbus, Cincinnati & Indianapolis (C.C.C.&I.) Railroad southbound train. Many of these details were confirmed by a hack driver, Jim Lantry, who had taken the Coopers to the Union Depot on the murder morning. Early on the morning of Friday, November 24, Detective Sam Rowe, acting on Superintendent Jacob Schmitt's demand that he capture "that nigger at all hazards," set off on the train to Xenia in hot pursuit.

Rowe's quest was almost aborted by his traveling companion, John T. Veney. Veney knew Cooper well, had served with him in the 5th Ohio Colored Infantry during the Civil War, and had been asked to accompany Rowe to help identify Cooper. But the indiscreet Veney insisted on telling everyone they met what they were about, so the exasperated Rowe sequestered Veney at a hotel when they arrived in Xenia. Late Friday afternoon, Rowe looked up United States deputy Marshall N. S. Tiffany and they decided to rent a rig and hunt for Cooper the next morning.

Saturday began well, with the discovery of Swing's watch at a nearby general store. Its proprietor, D. J. Fleming, told Tiffany that a mulatto calling himself G. C. Stewart had been there Thursday and had pawned the watch in return for a $14 stove. Fleming didn't know exactly where "Stewart" had gone, but he had the impression that he was setting up residence in the area. Hours later, after checking several miles of each of the major roads leading out of Xenia, Rowe and Tiffany stopped at a sawmill. Cooper wasn't there, but the owner told the lawmen he thought Cooper was working at the farm of L. P. Bonner, visible on a hill just a half mile away. Several minutes later, Rowe and Tiffany pulled into Bonner's barnyard to find John Cooper splitting wood with an ax. Walking up to him, Tiffany grabbed his arm, and Rowe said, "John Cooper, I arrest you for the murder of James Swing."

Cooper offered no resistance at all. In talking to L. P. Bonner, Rowe and Tiffany learned that Cooper had showed up Thursday, secured work with him as a tenant laborer, and purchased the stove for his living quarters. In the tenant house they found Cooper's thoroughly apprehensive wife, Sarah. She was sitting on top of one of her husband's trunks, and when Rowe opened it, he found a shirt and an undershirt heavily stained with blood. At first, Cooper blustered that the blood came from a nosebleed, but he soon broke down, confessed, and was carted off to the Xenia jail.

Even before they left Xenia, manacled together on the afternoon train, Rowe had extracted a confession from his seemingly impassive and emotionless prisoner. His story, with a few minor adjustments of chronology, confirmed the theory police had constructed for the Swing murder. Having exhausted his financial resources, John Cooper had decided in mid-November to return to the area where he had grown up in Chillicothe. His pregnant bride of 10 months, the former Sarah C. Newman, was loath to go; John had married her over the objections of his mother, and she felt she would be unwelcome in her husband's family. The couple finally compromised, agreeing to live in Xenia—but even that plan looked dubious when Cooper arrived at the Union Depot at 6 a.m. on November 21 and discovered that he didn't have enough money to check his bags, much less buy train tickets. Telling Sarah he was returning to his Newton Street house to retrieve his pocketbook, he left the Depot on foot. As would become notorious, he was wearing a light-colored coat.

His first stop, shortly after 7 a.m., was the Ontario Street Saloon near High Street, where he fortified himself with a dose of brandy. Then he walked up Prospect to Erie (East 9th Street) and breakfasted at a confectionery store. Turning east, he made his way to Cedar Avenue and Swing's shop. Cooper was well acquainted with the voluble tinsmith, and he probably told the truth when he swore that he only went to the shop to cadge a loan from the well-off Swing. Conveniently, the industrious tinsmith was already open for business and hard at work when the anxious Cooper walked in the door.

Their interview did not go smoothly, to say the least. When Cooper asked him for the loan of a few dollars, Swing curtly refused and started lecturing Cooper about not having saved his money, that he was like all these young fellows, and how he should have put some of his wages by for leaner times. Cooper explained that he hadn't been able to find steady work, but the older man was adamant. Finally, Cooper dropped the subject and picked up a newspaper and began reading it. It was sometime after 8 a.m., about the time the two men were seen together by the little neighbor boy.

Whatever his original intentions, Cooper, enraged by Swing's lecture, had now reached his fatal decision. He asked Swing what time it was, and his eyes strayed to a large tinsmith's hammer on the floor of the workshop. Shortly after Swing told him the time, Cooper picked up the hammer, walked up behind Swing, and hit him in the head as hard as he could with it. The surprised Swing turned around, looked up, said, "Hello! Are you going to murder me?" and fell unconscious to the floor.

Quickly fishing out Swing's pocketbook, Cooper extracted the $15 inside and removed Swing's gold watch from its chain on his vest. At this point, the stricken Swing made some kind of gurgling noise, so Cooper fetched the bloody hammer and hit him another three or four times—he could never remember how many—until Swing stopped gurgling. Then Cooper dragged the body into the bedroom and began tearing the house apart, virtually wrecking it, as he smashed and ripped open its contents in a desperate attempt to find more valuables. Once more, he was interrupted by some noise coming from Swing, and, again, he picked up the hammer and hit Swing until he ceased making a racket. Dr. William H. Carter, who performed Swing's autopsy, would find eleven wounds on Swing's pulverized head, any one of them sufficient to cause death, with four portions of the skull driven right into the brain. Just to make sure Swing didn't start up making noise again, Cooper took a soldering iron off a nearby shelf and crammed it as far as he could down Swing's throat. He then washed his bloody hands in a basin of water, neatly hung the stained hand towel on the back of a chair, locked the bedroom door, unlocked the front door, and left the bloody shambles behind him. It was about 8:30 a.m. Taking a circuitous route, he walked up Cedar to Case Avenue (East 40th Street), Case to Prospect Avenue, Prospect to Huntington (East 18th Street), Huntington to Superior Street, Superior to Erie Street (East 9th), Erie to St. Clair Street, and west on St. Clair to the Union Depot at Bank Street (West 6th). There he told the skeptical Sarah that he had collected his back pay, and they remained at the depot until the 3:50 p.m. southbound took them away to Xenia.

Cooper was an interesting contrast to the decidedly self-made, middle-class Swing. He was born Elias Stewart in 1844 to free parents. His father had died when he was very young, and he went to live at the age of eight with his uncle, William Cooper (whose surname he took), on a farm about 16 miles from Chillicothe. Enlisting in the 5th Colored Infantry for a 30-month stretch during the Civil War, Cooper had acquired a reputation among his fellow soldiers for viciousness and cruelty. Returning to Chillicothe, he had taken over his uncle's farm for a few years, a property he subsequently sold, criminally defrauding the rightful owners—his mother, grandmother, and aunt. Marrying Sarah, a light-colored mulatto, against his family's wishes, he drifted up to Cleveland about April of 1871. There he worked at various casual labors, including stints as a deckhand, construction laborer, and street paver. By early November he had run out of both money and work, and with his wife pregnant with their first child, he was desperate.

He had not meant to murder Swing, but he had needed the money, and his real motive, he insisted, was "my great love for my wife." Indeed, Cooper had nothing but good to say of the man he had butchered: "I never had no hard words with Swing. He always used me well."

Taken off the train at the Scranton Road station of the Atlantic & Great Western railroad (near the present-day intersection of Scranton and Girard, just north of the Lorain-Carnegie bridge) to avoid an ugly crowd at the Union Depot, Cooper was rushed to the Central Police Station and then taken to the county jail on Public Square. There, the next day, he dictated a full confession to fellow prisoner F. H. Bird, which confirmed everything he had already told Rowe on the train back to Cleveland. His wife Sarah remained in Chillicothe, as Sam Rowe had decided that her lack of money for a train ticket was not the responsibility of the Cleveland police.

What kind of man was John Cooper? His 1871 rap sheet in the Cleveland Police Department's register (a newfangled innovation of Superintendent Jacob Schmitt's) described him as American by birth, laborer by occupation, "colored," aged 28, 5 feet,10 inches, of yellow complexion; with black eyes, black, curly hair, good teeth, a straight nose, and weighing 173 pounds. Among truly distinguishing characteristics, it was noted that he was missing all the toes on his right foot, had scars on his left jaw and right ear, and that there was a bump on his left hand where a sixth digit had been amputated. Not that most of the white citizens of Cleveland were particularly interested. The prevailing social attitudes toward men like Cooper were revealingly expressed by the *Plain Dealer* article reporting his arrest:

> In appearance he does not differ particularly from hundreds of other colored men to be found in this city, so far as any expression of cruelty or malice is concerned. Indeed he would scarcely if ever be picked out from a crowd as a man likely to commit so inhuman a crime.

To say the least, Cooper's trial and execution were dispatched with a celerity that must have amazed participants in the drawn-out Skinner affair. (See "Shot in His Own Bed," in the author's *The Killer in the Attic*, 2002.) Taken to the police court for his preliminary examination 36 hours after he arrived in Cleveland, Cooper was indicted on a first-degree murder charge on November 29, only eight days after Swing was murdered. His trial, commencing on December 15, lasted exactly four hours. Held before common pleas judge Robert F. Paine, Cooper was defended by Isidore Roskoph and M. S. Castle and prosecuted by Edwin P. and A. T. Slade. It could not have struck Cooper as auspicious that his trial opened just 12 hours after the conviction of another African-American killer, William Jones, in the very same courtroom before Judge Paine. And the only family solace left to him was the presence of the long-suffering Sarah, who stayed tearfully by his side during the fateful day. In answer to M. S. Castle's plea for her help, Cooper's mother had written a reply that was made public that very morning:

> To M. S. Castle, Esq.
> There is no help for him here. As to the farm, he knows it has been sold, and the proceeds, belonging to myself, his grandmother and aunt, were stolen by him. He has made his bed and must lie in it.
> (Signed) Mary R. Cooper

It was truly a no-frills trial. After a jury was chosen in only 30 minutes, the state's witnesses testified briefly to the grisly details of the scene in Swing's shop, and Cooper's flight, pursuit, capture, and return to Cleveland. Then Cooper himself took the stand—and pounded the final nails in his own legal coffin. Repudiating the version of the murder retailed in his published confession, he now insisted that Swing had hit him first, trying to eject him from his shop. All Cooper could remember after that was knocking Swing down once with his fist—he had no memory at all of the murder, much less of shoving the soldering iron down Swing's throat. (The fact that Coroner J. C. Schenck was uncertain whether Swing was alive or dead when he swallowed the soldering iron probably neither helped nor hurt Swing's defense.) The jury's unambiguous reaction to Cooper's incredible testimony was vividly captured by a reporter for the *Cleveland Leader:*

> Frequent low ejaculations of incredulity were heard among his listeners as he continued in his account of the occurrences at the shop of his victim—a story contradictory of all his previous confessions made in jail and to some of the officers. These statements, which he was making under his solemn oath to the jury, seemed to be in such marked deviation from the truth that many expressed a regret that he had been allowed to go upon the stand at all.

After Cooper's foolish statement, there wasn't anything more for either side to say. Both the defense and prosecution rested without any rebuttal or final arguments, and, following Judge Paine's brief instructions, the case went to the jury at 5:30 p.m. They returned only 15 minutes later, after three quick ballots, with a unanimous verdict of guilty of murder in the first degree. (The first two ballots had been 11–1.) Consistent with his behavior since his arrest, Cooper showed no emotion as the verdict was read. The entire proceeds had taken exactly five hours of court time, still a record in a Cuyahoga County capital case. The next morning's *Plain Dealer* probably well expressed public opinion on the matter with its jocular headline: "A SWING FOR A SWING."

Remaining in character, Cooper exhibited no visible emotion on December 19, when Judge Paine sentenced him to hang. When asked if he had anything to say, Cooper replied, "No sir, I have not," and Paine let him have it with rhetorical gusto:

> The murder was discovered within two or three hours after it was committed and the mutilated body and its surroundings presented a spectacle so horrid and revolting as almost to lead to the belief that the wicked deed had not only been instigated by the Devil, but executed by him in person. . . . It is as difficult to satisfactorily comprehend and estimate as it is humiliating and

revolting to believe that depravity and malice necessary for such
a crime constitute elements in the human character. Fancied or
real necessity for a small sum of money and the hope that you
should by that means obtain it was made the occasion of thus
barbarously putting to death a man who had never given you just
cause of offense and whom you regarded as a friend. But it is not
proper that I should further remind you of the heinous nature of
your offense. . . .

Cooper remained erect during the judge's tirade, sometimes
with his thumbs in the pockets of his pantaloons or with his right
hand on the back of a chair, staring vacantly as if completely
unaware that his doom had been decided.

As the date for his April 25 hanging approached, Cooper showed
little change in his habitually stolid demeanor. Occasionally he
would laugh or sing, but most of the time he just stared off into
space. He had few visitors (his wife Sarah departed Cleveland in
March for her approaching confinement), except for the Rev. Dr.
Lathrop Cooley and the Rev. W. F. Jones. Cooley, a prominent
Protestant minister in Northeast Ohio, made something of a career
of inflicting himself on condemned prisoners. The Rev. W. F. Jones
was a well-known and beloved African-American minister in
Cleveland. In truth, Cooper showed little interest in their spiritual
ministrations as his days dwindled down to a precious few, being
far more preoccupied with the financial support of his wife. Two
hand-lettered signs on the bars of his cells beseeched visitors to
make donations to a small cardboard offering box, and it was
reported that it attracted an impressive amount of coin and scrip.
Even the hammering of the scaffold-builders during his last week
left him unfazed: to all visitors he simply announced, "I am first-
rate."

April 25 arrived, and, as expected, Sheriff John Frazee was
besieged with requests for invitations to the Cooper hanging.
Frazee eventually narrowed the lucky invitees down to about 150,
but hundreds of others crowded outside the jailyard, craning for a
view of the grim doings. After eating the traditionally "hearty"
breakfast, Cooper expressed a desire to see the scaffold, the same

used in all the previous Cleveland hangings except O'Mic's. Just before he left for his final walk, a delegation of prisoners led by forger Louis Brandt cheered him while Brandt read a short speech of sympathy. To them, Cooper said that he had no dread of hanging but he regretted the deed he had done.

At 11:48 a.m., John Cooper, wearing a dark sack coat, dark pants, a white shirt, a narrow black necktie, morocco slippers, and black gloves, was led out to the scaffold. With his hair parted neatly in the middle and his face an impassive mask, he was described by one witness as "undoubtedly the coolest man in the jail." Mounting the stairs to the gallows, he handed his last testament to Rev. Cooley and listened quietly while Cooley read from the 51st Psalm ("A broken and a contrite heart, O God, thou wilt not despise"). Then it was Cooper's turn:

> Well, I'm on the gallows, gentlemen, one and all. I've been told this will be the end of me but I don't know yet. Gentlemen, one and all, all I've got to say to you is that I have left a few lines which some of you may read in a few days and all I've got to say is not do as I have done . . . . Only a few minutes that I shall have on this earth, but that don't daunt me; that I can say to you all with a good heart. I hope the God above has pardoned me for all that I have ever done. In the sight of man and God, my heart beats, I must tell you gladly. . . I'm sorry for what I have done.

Following Cooper's speech, the Rev. Dr. Cooley, at his request, stated that Cooper wished everyone to know that the two leading causes of his crime were allowing himself to give in to his passions through physical violence and the frequent use of intoxicating liquors.

At 12 noon exactly, Cooper stepped to the drop. Taking off his necktie, coat, and vest, he laid them neatly on a chair, an observer noted, "as if he were just going to sleep in his bedroom." He bounced lightly on the trap, which some hanging purists present judged an unseemly levity. Then he shook hands with his executioners and submitted calmly while his hands were manacled, his arms and legs pinioned, and the black cap put over his head. The well-used hemp rope, which had taken off every condemned man since Dr. John Hughes, was placed around his neck. (For details on the Hughes hanging, see "In the Name of Violated Chastity," *The Corpse in the Cellar,* 1999.) Seconds later Cooper dropped like a stone through the trap at 12:03 p.m. The doctors couldn't decide later whether he died instantly from a broken neck or strangled to death at a more leisured pace, but they agreed that his sufferings had been slight. At 12:38 p.m. his body was cut down, put in a small, simple coffin, and shipped to his wife in Chillicothe.

COOPER'S CAREER CLOSED.

He Makes a Speech Upon the Scaffold —Is "Sorry for His Crime," and Hopes His Sins are Forgiven—The Trap Falls at Four Minutes Past Twelve, and He Dies Without a Struggle.

Plain Dealer, April 16, 1872.

In his final testament, published in Cleveland newspapers, Cooper expanded on his scaffold remarks but offered no additional particulars of how he came to murder James H. Swing. His last words were a warning to youngsters who might be tempted to embark on the same path that had brought him to a hangman's noose:

> Therefore, my young friends, wherever you may be, let these sayings of mine be a warning to you and all others, young or old, great or small, no matter what your station in life has been, it matters nothing about that. And if you have an evil habit, that is, in doing things "on the sly," if you have a habit of this kind, my friend, wherever you may be you had better throw it aside; if you don't it will be the ruination of you some day or other—may be you may be induced to do a deed like I have been led to do.

Chapter 19

"I'VE MURDERED MY MOTHER!"

The Krause Tragedy (1901)

Henry Krause's last days as a free man were not good ones. Long a devotee of books on magnetism, hypnotism, and mind-reading, the 27-year-old Henry had, by December of 1901, become convinced that he possessed supernatural powers. In mid-December he sent 10 dollars to a New York City company for a kit that would help him learn to read minds "in four easy lessons." Henry wasn't concerned that the kit would probably take a week to arrive, for he was convinced that he had already gained complete clairvoyant powers as soon as he dropped his order in the mail.

It was downhill for Henry from there. Henry had worked faithfully for the Sherwin-Williams Company for 14 years and had always been considered a sober, industrious employee. But on Friday, December 20, his increasingly eccentric behavior and wild speech caused his foreman to send him home. The foreman liked Henry and was sorry to dismiss him, but he felt he just couldn't have Henry working around dangerous machinery in his present state.

His dismissal from work didn't seem to bother Henry at all. He went to his home at 50 Rogers Street (now Rogers Avenue, running off East 65th Street in Slavic Village) and had supper with his mother, Matilda, aged 69, then left the house. He would later recall that he left home with the resolution to speak to no one, a resolve he kept. First walking down Broadway Avenue to Trumbull Avenue, he entered a house where he and his mother had once lived. There, he wordlessly took a little girl on his lap, and when the child's mother, who knew Henry, asked him why he wasn't

STRANGEST AND MOST HORRIBLE CRIME IN CITY'S HISTORY.

In a Nightmare Henry C. Krause, of Rogers-st, Saw a Writhing Reptile Crawling on His Mother's Face and About to Kill Her.

Cleveland Press, December 21, 1901.

speaking, he remained mute. Leaving the house, he went to the Young Men's Christian Association branch, where the muscular Henry often exercised. A similarly one-sided conversation passed there with the branch secretary, and then Henry wordlessly departed. As he walked down Broadway toward Willson Avenue (East 55th Street), he decided he would not move out of his determined path for anyone or anything. Inevitably, his uncompromising route led him straight into a large trolley pole on Willson Avenue. Convinced that he had supernatural strength, Henry tried for some time to pull the pole out of the ground. He didn't succeed, but he did manage to lose much of the skin on his hands, as they adhered firmly to the cold iron in the subzero temperatures. Eventually, Henry allowed himself to be led away from the pole to the office of Dr. N. E. Friedman at 1646 Broadway Avenue, where his badly lacerated and bleeding hands were dressed. He then returned home.

Whether Henry retailed his evening's peculiar adventures to his mother is not known. Apparently, however, she went to bed without incident shortly after he came home, and he followed her example at 11 p.m. About an hour later, he dreamed that he saw a brilliantly colored, star-shaped snake on the face of his mother. The enormous serpent was trying to kill her, and Henry rushed to her defense. Recalling the biblical example of Sampson's combat with a lion, Henry grabbed the jaws of the snake and began pulling them apart with all his strength. Somewhere far off he thought he heard a voice crying, "Henry, you are killing me!" but he only redoubled his desperate efforts. Finally, the snake fell dead, and the exhausted Henry stumbled back to his own bed.

Several hours went by. Henry awoke shortly before sunrise and, recalling the terrors of the night, went to check on his mother. One can imagine his consternation when he opened her bedroom door and found her dead in her bed, eyes staring lifelessly out of their sockets and clotted blood still oozing out of the jaws he had so powerfully wrenched apart. Indeed, Henry had pulled so hard on Matilda's jaws that he had strangled her. Her battered face, a mass of bruises and scratches, bore stark testimony to the struggle she had put up against her maniacal son.

Henry staggered from the scene of horror and began to roam the streets. As his hands began to hurt again, he went to Dr. Friedman's office and had them dressed once more. He didn't say anything to Friedman about his little domestic problem. But as he wandered by the home of his minister, the Rev. John H. Wefel of the St. Johannes Evangelical Lutheran Church, his conscience smote him sorely. Knocking on the door at 24 Cable Street, he roused Wefel and blurted out, "I have murdered my mother!"

Wefel was initially uncertain of what he should do. For a man who had just strangled his mother Henry seemed quite calm and rational. But he eventually accompanied Henry to the Cleveland police's 6th Precinct station at Willson and Broadway Avenues. There, without prelude, Henry dramatically announced to Lieutenant H. T. Felhaber, "I've murdered my mother! I've murdered my mother!"

Felhaber, like Wefel, was a little dubious at first. But as Henry's initially calm manner rapidly deteriorated into screaming mania, he decided to put Henry in a jail cell and send a squad to 50 Rogers Street. Felhaber's men soon returned with horrific news, and the next morning Henry was transferred to the Central Police Station on Champlain Street. The following day he was charged with murder in the first degree by Cleveland police court prosecutor George Schindler. Police court judge Thomas M. Kennedy scheduled a hearing for December 31 and appointed Edward Bushnell as his counsel.

Despite the gravity of the first-degree murder charge, no one really thought that Henry Krause would be prosecuted on a capital or even criminal charge. His background and previous conduct were exemplary, and he had been lauded as a model employee and son up until the moment of his horrific nightmare. The only survivor of Matilda Krause's 10 children, Henry had long been her sole means of support, and he had saved his modest wages for years so he could buy their house on Rogers Street. A regular and active churchgoer, Henry was also a frequent visitor to the Y.M.C.A., where he strenuously developed the powerful muscles that had crushed the life out of his beloved mother.

Henry's jailhouse demeanor increased the inclination of Cleveland authorities to treat his matricide compassionately. Sometimes placid, sometimes weeping and hysterical, Henry spent his first days in jail refusing to keep his clothing on and pacing the floor of his cell. Sometimes he seemed convinced that his mother was still alive, telling a visiting physician who insisted she was dead, "Oh, you can't fool me that way. I know I didn't hurt her as bad as that." Most of the time, however, he was only too aware of what he had done. He recalled his last evening in detail, remembering that at the time:

> I thought I was Jesus. I thought I had been nailed to a cross and someone was trying to freeze me. I was out of doors then and went inside. I thought I had to swing my hands and cry, "Praise to God!" I did so, but got no relief. I went to bed and my dream was horrible. . . .

It became clear to Cleveland officials, as Henry expostulated on his past and present delusions, that he was a very sick young man carrying an enormous psychological burden. It wasn't just that Henry had always been the reliable support of his widowed mother's sunset years. At a very early age he had become convinced that he was solely responsible for a large cataract on one of his mother's eyes. Every act he performed from that time on, he

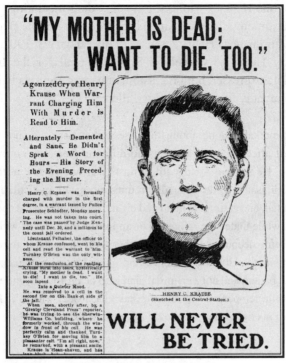

"MY MOTHER IS DEAD; I WANT TO DIE, TOO."

AgonizedCry of Henry Krause When Warrant Charging Him With Murder is Read to Him.

Alternately Demented and Sane, He Didn't Speak a Word for Hours — His Story of the Evening Preceding the Murder.

Henry C. Krause was formally charged with murder in the first degree, in a warrant issued by Police Prosecutor Schindler, Monday morning. He was not taken into court. The case was passed by Judge Kennedy until Dec. 30, and a mittimus to the count jail ordered.

Lieutenant Felhaber, the officer to whom Krause confessed, went to his cell and read the warrant to him. Turnkey O'Brien was the only witness.

At the conclusion of the reading, Krause burst into tears, hysterically crying, "My mother is dead. I want to die! I want to die, too." He soon lapsed

Into a quieter mood. He was removed to a cell in the second tier on the Bank-st side of the jail.

When seen, shortly after, by a "Greater Cleveland Press" reporter, he was trying to see the therwin-Williams Co. building, where he formerly worked, through the window in front of his cell. He was perfectly calm and thanked Turnkey O'Brien for moving him to a pleasanter cell. "I'm all right, now," he remarked, with a pleasant smile. Krause is clean-shaven, and has

HENRY C. KRAUSE.
(Sketched at the Central Station.)

WILL NEVER BE TRIED.

Cleveland Press, December 23, 1901.

told his interrogators, was "for the purpose of atoning for the injury he thought he had done his mother." Somehow, in the middle of his hallucinatory nightmare of December 21, Henry had confused that cataract with the vision of a deadly serpent.

Henry's hearing before probate judge Henry C. White was a careful but predictable formality. His neighbors and lifelong friends trumpeted his unblemished virtues, his hitherto spotless reputation, and the obvious love he had always exhibited for his mother. A Professor Fred Leutner, who had taught Henry in school, testified that Henry hadn't been quite right in the head since the day he was knocked unconscious by a snowball (containing a hefty chunk of coal) at the age of 12. Physicians J. R. Horton and Henry Upson detailed Henry's galloping delusional fantasies, emphasizing his beliefs that he was Jesus Christ returned to earth and that he possessed supernatural powers.

By the time Henry's witnesses finished their unstintingly sympathetic testimony, it was clear that prison was not the place for crazy (and orphaned) Henry Krause. In his January 3, 1902, order committing Henry to Cleveland State Hospital for the Insane, Judge White expressed both his astonishment at Henry's behavior and his sympathy for the unwitting killer:

> The remarkable thing about this case is that Krause comes to himself after the deed, and acts no different from any normal person. He seemed filled with utmost grief and sorrow at the deed. He is able to describe all circumstances with particularity and detail, and at times is lucid and clear. He committed the deed either while under the influence of an insane delusion or while in a semi-sleeping condition, together with an unstable mind, which smothered his conscience and made him an automaton. He is a patient and not a criminal, and is to be profoundly pitied, for, while temporarily insane, he has killed one, whom, if he were in his right mind, he would have protected with his life.

Chapter 20

BLOODY DOINGS AT OLMSTED

The Lonesome Death of Rosa Colvin (1866)

In the megalopolis that is today's Cleveland, it is difficult to grasp that the city was not always the physical core and psychological cynosure of Cuyahoga County. Indeed, the first five murderers executed in the city did not commit their crimes there but rather in the outlying, largely rural—even wilderness—townships. Olmsted Township was just such a wilderness area in 1866, and the terrible crime Alexander McConnell committed there affords an illuminating picture of the harsh lives and crude living conditions endured by the tough pioneers who lived beyond the relative sophistication of the Forest's City's muddy avenues and ramshackle commercial blocks.

William Colvin and his wife Rosa would not have been mistaken for one of Cleveland's First Families in any era. Arriving in the Western Reserve sometime in the mid-1860s, the Scotch-born Colvin and his American wife scratched out an uncertain existence in the wooded and sparsely inhabited area just southwest of the village of Olmsted Falls. The unskilled William, known to his neighbors as "Stuttering Bill," generally labored as a woodcutter or quarryman in the area, while Rosa kept house, such as it was, in a cabin in the woods, about three miles west of the Village. And it wasn't much: situated in a small clearing surrounded by a thousand acres of forest, the Colvin manse was variously described by contemporary observers as either a "hovel" or "shanty." Or, as one disgusted *Cleveland Leader* scribe limned the Colvins' domestic scene:

There was no hint of yard or garden. The open area was inexpressibly dreary, and the house seemed the picture of all that is wretched, dismal, and profane in life. But no conception of the squalor could be formed until the interior was inspected. There were but two rooms, lighted by one common and two very small-sized windows. No more were needed, since daylight flooded the house through the wide cracks between the upright boards. The floor was loose and full of fissures and chasms. In the front room were a bed, table, a broken cooking stove, two or three chairs, a cupboard in which were dirty dishes, bread, and crackers, besides several barrels, boxes, etc. A few comic pictures were pinned like a naturalist's insects to the siding. In the back room were two bunks, a box stove, and trumpery ad infinitum.

Of course, the reporter's impressions may have been prejudiced by the fact that almost everything he saw in the cabin was covered with blood—but let us not get ahead of our story.

The spring of 1866 found the Colvins living in imperfect amicability in the aforesaid woodland bower. When not working as a cordwood cutter for nearby landowner Robert Crawford, William Colvin cultivated local repute as a thick-witted, surly fellow, given to excessive drink and the physical abuse of his wife. Several of their perspicacious neighbors would later testify at Rosa's inquest that they had witnessed "Stuttering Bill" strike his wife, and others would recall seeing the marks of domestic violence on her face. Not that said neighbors had much sympathy for Rosa: she had married Bill about a year before, and it was whispered that the 28-year-old woman *had been married twice* before she sought lawful union with the unprepossessing Colvin. (The only certain fact ever proven about Rosa's past was that she was the mother of a previously deceased child, beside whom Rosa would be eventually be laid to rest in a Berea grave.) All of which would be remembered with lip-smacking relish when reports of ill-doings at the Colvin cabin electrified the talkative citizens of Northeast Ohio.

The first link in the chain of Rosa Colvin's doom was forged with the arrival of 35-year-old Alexander McConnell in Olmsted

Township at the beginning of March 1866. Originally hailing from County Tyrone in Ireland, the illiterate McConnell had emigrated to Canada in 1850. Settling in the town of Fitzroy, near Ottawa, McConnell married a widow with six children there, sired three more of his own, and prosecuted general farming without great success. But that prosaic life ended in the mid-1860s, when he was forced to flee to the United States after fracturing a man's skull in a dispute over a horse sale. The spring of 1866 found him drifting down from Buffalo to Olmsted Township, where he secured temporary work cutting wood for Robert Crawford.

OLMSTED FALLS MURDER.

Body of Mrs. Colvin Found.

Her Head More Frightful than Medusa

Cleveland Leader, March 28, 1866.

It suited both the convenience of McConnell and Crawford for the Canadian to board with the Colvins in their sylvan home, close as it was to the Crawford wood-lots. A thickset man, McConnell was about 5 feet, 5 inches, with light gray eyes, dark, sandy whiskers, brown hair, and a low brow. A possibly biased observer characterized his demeanor thus in the pages of the *Cleveland Leader*—on the day after he was hanged:

> [McConnell's eyes] are restless and sinister in their expression. When conversing he never looks you in the face; his lips wear a continual smirk and the corners of his mouth twitch nervously.

McConnell seemed to get along with his hosts; in the shadow of the scaffold he would recall the pleasure he took in helping them with household chores.

Saturday, March 24 dawned cold and clear. William and Alexander arose at 7 a.m., consumed a simple breakfast, and set out on foot for Berea. Both of them were intent on finding quarry work there, and McConnell hoped to arrange continued board at a house Colvin planned to rent there. But after only a quarter mile, near the Cleveland & Toledo railroad tracks, McConnell turned back, telling Colvin that his knee was hurting badly and that he was going to return home. Colvin continued on to Berea. Whether he concluded his intended business is unknown—but it is certain that he soon fell in there with a slow-witted acquaintance named Joe Miller, and that he and Miller spent the latter part of the day boozing it up at various drinking establishments in southwest Cuyahoga County.

Meanwhile, McConnell returned to the Colvin cabin. Picking up some of William's clothes (including an overcoat, a pair of fine boots, a pair of quarry boots, and a "pair of French gray pants"), Colvin put them under his arm and replaced them with his own shabby clothing. Then he broke open one of Colvin's trunks, abstracted several hundred dollars in bounty money Colvin had earned through various enlistments in the Union Army, and took his leave. McConnell's affairs had not prospered during his American sojourn, and he was determined to get back to Canada by whatever means necessary.

Not far from the cabin, however, he soon met Rosa Colvin in a lot owned by a man named Engler. She had learned that McConnell had returned to the cabin, become suspicious, and gone in search of him. Seeing her husband's clothing in McConnell's possession, Rosa demanded to know what the hell was going on. There was no problem, cooed McConnell, it was just that William had decided to stay in Berea and had sent McConnell back to fetch some of his clothing. Very well, replied the dubious Rosa, then I will go with you. No, riposted the increasingly frightened McConnell, your husband said he won't stay there if you come. The upshot of their tense dialogue was that they both returned to the Colvin cabin, probably about 11 a.m. that morning. There, Rosa soon found the rifled trunk and confirmed her original suspicions that McConnell intended to rob them and flee.

The only account we possess for what followed is McConnell's confession, but its details fit with the physical evidence of the murder. Seizing a poker, Rosa blocked the cabin door and told McConnell he wasn't leaving until her husband got home. As he tried to brush by her, she hit him on the arm with the poker. McConnell knocked her down with his fist, but she got up and hit him with the poker again. So he hit her with a stick of firewood—and she hit him with the poker again. The enraged McConnell had

had enough of this: grabbing an ax, he hit Rosa in the middle of her forehead, killing her instantly. The subsequent condition of the cabin supported McConnell's scenario: there was blood everywhere, giving unmistakable evidence that Rosa Colvin had put up an almost superhuman fight before falling before her murderer's ax. The fatal struggle had taken about 15 minutes.

It must have been a terrible scene that followed in that crimson-drenched shanty. McConnell later said that he just held Rosa's body for 20 or 30 minutes after his decisive blow, unable to believe that he had actually killed her. Then, coming to his senses, he soaked up some of the blood with a quilt and, wrapping Rosa's bloody body in a dress, carried it out of the cabin. At a woodpile about 430 feet away, he laid the corpse on the ground, covering it with the quilt and some loose pieces of wood. Then he fled, walking rapidly toward Elyria with two carpet sacks containing Colvin's clothes and money. From there he took a train to Sandusky, walked from there to Clyde, and from Clyde to Fremont. From Fremont he took the train to Detroit, crossed over to Windsor, and arrived back at his home in Fitzroy on Thursday, March 29, five days after Rosa Colvin's murder.

The simple brutality of the murder contrasted bizarrely with the byzantine confusion that followed its discovery. William Colvin and Joe Miller returned to the Colvin hovel about 8 p.m. that evening. It was already dark, a heavy snow was falling, and it is likely that Messrs. Colvin and Miller were feeling no pain from the day's copious libations. How else to explain that when they returned to the blood-spattered cabin *neither of them noticed anything untoward* at the scene? True, Miller later remembered that he had remarked on a broken window with a bloodstain and on the absence of Colvin's better half. But "Stuttering Bill" took it all in stride, merely remarking that Rosa must have "skedaddled" with his Canadian boarder.

Colvin's obtuse obliviousness continued into the next morning. Arising early, he and Miller were still enjoying their breakfast about 9 a.m., when a visit by Colvin's employer, Robert Crawford, and his brother James spoiled their quiet morning. Shocked by the blood all over the place—there were generous pools of it on the floor, and a mop head standing in a corner was stiff with encrusted gore—the Crawfords must have been further amazed by Colvin and Miller's assurances that they had not noticed the blood the previous night or when they arose in the morning. Nor, too, had they apparently noticed one of Rosa's bracelets and an earring on the floor, both of them caked with blood. Calling in neighbors to keep an eye on Colvin and Miller, Robert Crawford went to Olmsted Village for Constable Sabin. By nightfall, both Colvin and Miller were in jail, awaiting the outcome of the scheduled inquest on Monday morning.

Owing to the incredible demeanor of Colvin and Miller, the initial theory of the authorities was that Colvin, with or without the aid of Miller, had murdered his wife and hidden the body. The fact that his boarder McConnell, too, was missing inspired the further supposition that a jealous William had caught Alexander and Rosa in flagrante-something at the shanty and slain them together. Colvin's claim that his clothes and money were missing hardly argued for his innocence: everyone who saw the inarticulate Colvin that day noticed that he seemed more concerned about his missing clothes than the whereabouts or fate of his wife. Of course, he *would* say that he had been robbed, then as now, a convenient and all-too-transparent lie to cover a purely domestic killing. No one believed Colvin's assertion that the blood on his vest came from some freshly slaughtered beeves he had hauled on the day before the murder. And Joe Miller, a near-idiot, would not have helped anyone with his testimony, much less an unsympathetic, wife-beating, loutish sot such as William Colvin.

The discovery of Rosa's body on Sunday afternoon didn't improve the prisoners' prospects. Several hours of searching through the surrounding, snow-covered woods ended when a searcher's boot heel snagged on a bloody dress near the woodpile. Found next to the woodpile, Rosa's corpse was covered with snow, indicating that she had been killed sometime before 6 p.m. on Saturday. She was a horrible sight: her clothes were pulled up over her chest, her left arm thrown up to her cheek, her hair disheveled and clotted with blood, and the top of her left ear cut off, and she sported a large triangular wound in the middle of her forehead, shaped exactly like an ax-head. The discovery of his wife's body just a few hundred feet away from his cabin did not help Colvin's case, and few were surprised when the inquest ended on March 27 with the arraignment of the two suspects on a murder charge. Given local prejudice, however, it is probable that Colvin and Miller would have been held on far less evidence. Such prejudice was well expressed by Cleveland journalists, one of whom characterized Miller as "a pumpkiny-looking youth with fuzz on his face and apparently, a brain of mush," who sat stupefied before his accusers like "a piece of pig metal." The same scribe reserved even greater scorn for Colvin, whose supposed villainy he limned in columns that might have shocked the late Sam Sheppard:

> Colvin is a Scotchman and about forty years old. [He was actually 33]. He has a swarthy complexion and looks like a black snake. The eye is impenetrable and perfectly devilish. And this suits his nature. He is an essential brute, and has treated his murdered wife, whom he married a year ago, as only a fiend could, kicking and pounding her and threatening to take her life. He seems capable of committing any crime.

Fortunately for Colvin and Miller, there were several lawmen unswayed by popular prejudice. One was Cuyahoga County sheriff Felix Nicola, and the other was a detective named John Odell. From the beginning, they suspected that the missing McConnell was the guilty party, and, after consultation with county prosecutor M. S. Castle and county commissioner Randall Crawford, they began looking for him even before the inquest ended on March 27. Acting on a tip concerning the fugitive's original home, Odell arrived in Ottawa on Thursday, March 29. Securing a posse of Canadian detectives, Odell and his men knocked on Colvin's door in Fitzroy at 5 a.m. the next morning. His wife Ann answered the door and told the inquisitive officers that her husband was absent. It was obvious the worried woman was lying, and Odell's men began to search the house. As one of them mounted a ladder to a loft, McConnell, who was hiding above, hit him with a stick. Despite his protestations of innocence and repeated threats that he would be shot, McConnell refused to surrender himself until Odell's men began removing the floor beneath him. Taken back to Cleveland, he was arraigned and quickly indicted on a charge of first-degree murder. Released from jail, an estatic William Colvin shed tears of joy, in contrast to his noticeable lack of tears, censorious types noted, in his response to his wife's slaughter.

Opening on June 22, 1866, McConnell's trial consumed a week and was a cut-and-dried affair. With Judge Horace Foote presiding, McConnell was prosecuted by M. S. Castle and A. T. Slade and defended by C. W. Palmer and R. E. Knight. (It was an oddity remarked by all that these four lawyers reversed the roles they had played in the recent trial of John W. Hughes.) Not that it mattered much: McConnell had been captured with the stolen clothes, and much of the missing money in his possession. Not taking the stand in his own defense, he appeared emotionless and completely unmoved throughout his trial. Aside from vigorous cross-examination of the state's witnesses by Knight and Palmer, the only words offered in his defense were some depositions by Canadian character witnesses. Retiring on the evening of June 28, McConnell's jury returned a verdict of guilty of murder in the first degree the next morning. Twenty-four hours later, Judge Foote dismissed defense counsel's motion for a new trial without even bothering to listen to the state's brief, and pronounced sentence with these words:

> You have had a fair, patient, and impartial trial and you have no one to blame for the result but yourself, and no reasonable regrets therefore, save from your own misconduct. I abure you to prepare to meet the result of your trial, which I now announce to you. It is the sentence of the law that you, Alexander McConnell, be taken from this place to the jail of this county, that you be therein kept in close custody by the Sheriff thereof, until the 10th day of August, A.D., 1866, and that between the hours of 10 o'clock in the forenoon, and 2 o'clock of the afternoon of said day, you be hung by the neck until you be dead, and may God have mercy on your soul.

McConnell received his sentence with his habitual passivity.

Offered an opportunity to make a statement, he remained silent. Upon meeting his distraught sister outside the courtroom, however, he betrayed some uneasiness. Perhaps it was the knowledge that she had utterly impoverished herself, as did the rest of his family, to finance his hopeless defense. Courtroom buffs noted that the sentencing of the reliably histrionic Dr. Hughes had drawn a far larger crowd that of the stolid McConnell.

As Dr. Johnson might have predicted ("Depend upon it, sir, when a man knows he is to be hanged in a fortnight, it concentrates his mind wonderfully"), Alexander McConnell's disposition began to thaw and improve as his date with the scaffold drew nearer. Initially angry and bitter at the verdict, he fulminated death threats against his captors, especially Sheriff Nicola, and plotted an escape from the county jail. He almost made it: in late July, he and some other prisoners succeeded in blowing an adjoining cell lock off with some smuggled powder but were caught while trying to blast another hole through the jail roof.

After that, McConnell seemed to resign himself to his fate, or as he put it to a number of those with whom he conversed in his final days:

> It is useless to tremble at my fate; it must come and when it does come I will try to die like a man hoping Heaven will be merciful—for I deserve the Halter.

He began reading the Bible (he could read a little but could not write), and several weeks before his execution, on July 11, 1866, he dictated a full confession of his awful act in the presence of Sheriff Nicola, Prosecutor Castle, three of his jurymen, and two newspaper reporters. Averring that he never meant to harm Rosa, who had always treated him kindly, he swore that he only slew her because she barred his escape from the shanty. As for his flight to Canada, he admitted that he never thought he would be pursued there by lawmen; indeed, when Odell's posse came knocking on his door in Fitzroy he assumed they were bailiffs come to arrest him for a $12 debt. And he insisted that he had never taken any money from the cabin. Always the equivocator, though,

McConnell also hinted in some of his last conversations that William Colvin had once solicited him to help get Rosa "out of the way" so Colvin could go away to Canada with McConnell. McConnell's version of this improbable conversation ended with him piously responding, "I know what you mean, Colvin, but I would never do such a thing."

After McConnell's execution, a kindred story was related by one Henry Bislick. Bislick, who lived near the Colvins, claimed that he came upon William three days before the murder. There was a 16-year-old girl with Colvin, and he said to Bislick, "I'm going to marry this girl, as my wife will be dead in a day or two." When Bislick remonstrated that Rosa was still alive, Colvin allegedly replied, "I know that, but she's going to die in a day or two."

A small crowd of lawmen, invited spectators, and several newspaper reporters turned out for McConnell's hanging in the Cuyahoga County Jail on August 10. Early that morning, McConnell met with William Colvin for the last time. Asking his forgiveness, he begged Colvin to shake his hand. Colvin refused, muttering, "If God forgives you, I do," but he finally grudgingly clasped McConnell's hands when the latter fell to his knees in prayer and burst into tears. Then, after a final chat with his religious counselors, the Rev. Bush of the Methodist church in Berea and an Episcopalian minister, the Rev. Lathrop Cooley (who would make a career of ministering to the Cuyahoga County condemned), McDonnell was led to the scaffold at 12:18 p.m. by Sheriff Nicola and his deputies—the same scaffold used for James Parks, Dr. Hughes, and various other felons. (For details of the Parks hanging see the author's Internet-only "I Die an Innocent Man": The Gruesome Death of William Beatson," *By the Neck Until Dead: A History of Hangings in Cuyahoga County*, 2000, www.clevelandmemory.org/SpecColl/Bellamy). Deciding not to make an extended gallows oration, McConnell merely murmured, "I am ready to go—the sentence is just." His arms and legs were pinioned, the black cap put over his head, and the rope—a custom-made one-inch halter—adjusted around his neck. Just before Sheriff Nicola sprang the trap, McConnell turned toward his executioners and said, "Gentlemen, I trust in the Lord. I hope all men and women

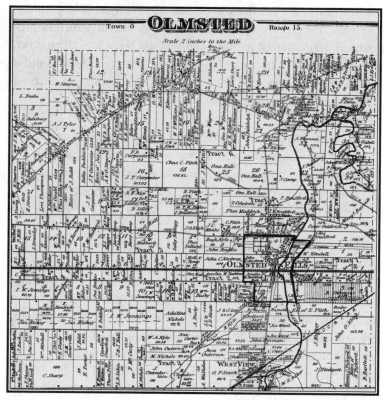

Scene of the crime: map of Olmsted Township. The Colvin home was located in Caroline Crawford's lot, lower left area, second tier. D.L.Lake, *An Atlas of Cuyahoga County* (1874).

will forgive me. I forgive all and hope to be done by the same. Goodbye." Then, turning to the press box, he said, "Goodbye—this is a dreadful hour."

He didn't know the half of it. A second later, Nicola triggered the drop, and McConnell fell through it. Apparently, McConnell turned his head slightly to the left a split-second before the drop opened. His movement allowed the rope to slip up under his chin just enough so that, instead of having his neck broken, Alexander McConnell began strangling in agony before the horrified spectators. Hanging buffs present concluded that McConnell's discomfiture was probably just an unfortunate combination of circumstances caused by his thick neck and light weight (140 pounds). The next day's newspapers noted that he was nonetheless pronounced dead after 14 minutes and that his body was taken down after a half hour. What *actually* happened was not reported until it leaked out 23 years later in a *Plain Dealer* Sunday feature on Cuyahoga County hangings:

> When the trap was sprung the noose slipped, the knot passed under his chin, he writhed for some minutes and strangled, the hangman [Sheriff Nicola] hastening the result by letting himself down by the rope until he stood on McConnell's shoulders, his weight drawing the noose tighter.

That, presumably, was the end of Alexander McConnell and the terrible Olmsted murder. One likes to think, however, that its enduring residue might be one still-haunted corner of Olmsted Township, about three miles southwest of Olmsted Falls. In the wake of the murder some felt the Colvin shanty should be burned, one journalist insisting, in his call for vigilante arson, that it had been "the abode of free fighters, prostitutes, and murderers" even before Alexander McConnell made it notorious. But the Colvin murder cabin was still standing six months later, now inhabited by a family named Miller. Preserving the high standards of Colvin housekeeping, the house was still marked with the stains of dried blood, with some of Rosa's bloody handprints even adorning the walls. Miller and his family also reported many poltergeist phenomena troubling the house at night: beds shaking, the sound of an ax chopping in the back room, and the chairs, doors, and windows acting in violent commotion. The author knows not the precise location of the Colvin murder cabin, but there are no doubt inquiring minds who might take up this matter.

Chapter 21

DON'T PLAY DOCTOR

Frenchy Balanescu's
Little Love Pills (1926)

"The Era of Wonderful Nonsense"
— Westbrook Pegler describing the 1920s

I love you as the bluebird loves the mellowness of May.
I loved you as the wild deer loved the coming of the day
I loved you as the sunshine loves the rain he makes his bride
And he girds her in a jeweled bow to signify his pride
I loved you as the blue sky loves the earth it brooks above
I love you as the lover loves the loving of his love
—from the love poems of Ermil ("Frenchy") Balanescu
to Miss Dorothy Kirk, c. summer 1926

By all accounts, Miss Dorothy Kirk was not at her best during her last 48 hours on earth. The comely 21-year-old stenographer spent most of rainy Friday, August 20, 1926, in bed at her 1041 East 141st Street lodgings. Her worried landlady, Ruby Larkin, couldn't even rouse Dorothy for supper. When Dorothy's boyfriend Ermil showed up at 6:30 p.m., he demanded to see her. Dorothy was so weak that she could barely get herself dressed, and when she came downstairs 30 minutes later, she must have been a terrible sight to see. Staggering, mumbling incoherently, Dorothy could barely stand up, and her complexion was a ghastly, sickly yellow. If Ermil was shocked by her appearance, he didn't let on to either Dorothy or Ruby Larkin. When Ruby told him that Dorothy needed to see a doctor, he pooh-poohed her anxieties, assuring her that Dorothy was already getting "the best care possible." Ermil then took Dorothy out on the porch, where the couple talked for awhile. When Ermil left an hour later, Dorothy went back inside and stumbled up to her bed. Ruby turned in about the same time herself, but when she awoke about 11:30 p.m. she found that Dorothy was gone. Lying on the victrola was a note: "Will be back as soon as possible—Dorothy."

Frenchy's trusting victim: Dorothy Kirk, 1926.

Dorothy was next seen at the duplex home of her friend Mrs. Anna Blackburn at 1439 East 66th Street. She showed up there with Ermil just about the time Ruby Larkin awoke and found her gone. Dorothy's demeanor had not improved during her trolley ride across the city in the rain. Almost blind, visibly yellowish, she babbled unintelligibly and writhed in intermittent and painful convulsions. When a concerned Anna told Ermil that Dorothy needed a doctor, he repeated his assurances about her having the "best care possible" and insisted, "Don't worry—I'll fix her up. She's going to get well."

Dorothy did not get well. On Saturday morning, after a restless night, she was worse, virtually blind, and unable even to get out of bed. When a worried Ruby Larkin finally tracked her down at Blackburn's house at 2 p.m., Dorothy couldn't recognize her and was "talking out of her head." An hour later, Anna Blackburn finally persuaded Ermil to go for a doctor. At 3:30 p.m. physician John D. Vitkus arrived. Quickly examining Dorothy, he found her delirious, her skin a vivid yellow, and with a high temperature and rapid, irregular pulse. His tentative diagnosis was inflammation of the liver, and he commanded Ermil to get her to a hospital. Ermil brought the now-unconscious Dorothy to St. John's Hospital about 5 p.m.—and promptly vanished.

Dorothy Kirk died early the next day, without ever regaining consciousness. In light of her alarming, unexplained symptoms and Ermil's suspicious disappearance, hospital authorities immediately contacted the Cleveland police.

After finding some questionable-looking pills in her purse, hospital doctors decided to analyze the contents of Dorothy's stomach. Their findings were reported to the police. After talking to Ruby Larkin and Dorothy's roommate, Hazel Davis, the cops went looking for the elusive Ermil.

They didn't find him until noon the next day, when he turned himself in at Central Police Station after reading newspaper accounts of the dragnet out for him. By that time detectives had already searched his home at 819 Woodland Avenue in the Haymarket district. What they found in Ermil's room and what he told them dur-

The man who played doctor: "Frenchy" Balanescu, 1926.

ing his interrogation quickly turned matters into Cleveland's sex crime of the decade: The Balanescu "Love Pills" Murder.

As is oft the case, the Cleveland police detectives who interrogated Ermil were disinclined to share with him what they already knew. Their cautious reticence encouraged Ermil to tell them a pack of lies he would come to regret. The police already knew that Dorothy's purse—and stomach—contained suspected aphrodisiac drugs. They had already seized a bushel basket's worth of similar drugs found in Ermil's room, so Ermil immediately blundered by denying that he either possessed or even knew of such wicked substances. Forced to constantly recant and revise his shaky story, he was quickly entrapped in a web that would hurtle him into prison at the age of only 20.

Ermil Balanescu's story was a common, if pathetic tale. Theodore Dreiser had written about a similar unfortunate wretch in his novel *An American Tragedy,* published just the previous year. Born in Bucharest in 1905, the adored and indulged eldest son of a Romanian Jewish couple (with a set of French grandparents on the maternal side), Ermil had emigrated with his parents and two siblings to the United States in 1920. Living in Warren, Ohio, the precociously bright Ermil had completed four years of courses in only two years at Warren High School. From his earliest youth, Ermil had wanted to be a doctor, an ambition, which—as we shall see—never slackened. So, after working as a drug store clerk, he enrolled in some premedical courses at Western Reserve University in the fall of 1923. Alas, there was not enough money for tuition, and his formal medical education was aborted after only two semesters. But Ermil, still working sporadically as a drug clerk, continued to dream of becoming a famous, skilled physician. Someday, he fantasized, he would be known as one of the most famous doctors in the world.

Sometime in the mid-1920s, Ermil's medical career fantasy crossed the line from unrealistic dream to dangerous delusion. By the time he met Dorothy Kirk in the spring of 1926, Ermil had ceased just wanting to be a doctor and decided that he *was*—in some sense—already a real and celebrated physician. We don't know how completely he believed it: whether he was just a particularly fervent wannabe or whether he actually believed that he had a medical license. But he certainly acted like it, and his delusive behavior led inexorably to Dorothy Kirk's death.

Ermil and Dorothy met at a church social, both of them being seemingly devout members of the First Methodist Church at the corner of East 30th Street and Euclid Avenue. It was no sham on Ermil's part; he had been involved for years with Methodist congregations in both Warren and Cleveland. He and Dorothy hit it off immediately. Within weeks they were seeing each other two or three times a week. They soon worked out a signal code, so that

Ermil could tell if Dorothy was available when he went by her East 141st Street home: two lighted lamps meant she was, one meant she wasn't. Several visits together to Dorothy's mother, May, in Canal Fulton followed, and it was clear by the summer of 1926 that Dorothy was totally besotted with the handsome, charming Ermil.

Dorothy was—but you couldn't say the same for her friends. Most of them, such as Ruby Larkin and Hazel Davis, disliked Ermil from the start. Their repugnance wasn't due to his olive complexion, indifferent ukulele playing, or the somewhat foreign manners that earned him the suggestive nickname "Frenchy." No, the fact, apparent to all except the smitten Dorothy, was that Frenchy Balanescu was a brazen and unrelenting liar. Although still working as a humble drug clerk and living in his mother's Haymarket tenement, Ermil nonetheless soon convinced Dorothy that he was a world-renowned physician, with a residency at Lakeside Hospital and a cosmopolitan clientele. When a distrustful Ruby Larkin called Lakeside and was told there was no Dr. Balanescu on its staff, a glib Ermil smoothly explained to the gullible Dorothy that he worked there in a "special" ward unknown even to many Lakeside physicians. Constantly embellishing his imaginary credentials, Ermil took to having acquaintances write bogus letters to Dorothy, in which they pretended to be eminent physicians and extolled Dr. Balanescu's incredible skill and medical feats. No fib was too great an imposture to the credulous Dorothy: she even believed him when he told her he had arranged a banquet in her honor and invited 20 prominent doctors and nurses to it. Imagine, he mourned to Dorothy, how mortified he was when he couldn't get in touch with her on the night of the banquet!

Many an insecure and enthusiastic wooer has presented himself to the object of his affection as an idealized version of his real self. The author himself has known susceptible persons, especially females of infinitesimal self-esteem, who repeatedly seek out ingratiating prevaricators—and end up merely sadder-but-wiser for the experiences. But pretending to be a physician wasn't enough for Ermil Balanescu. He wanted to *be* one—and he slipped into the role of Dorothy's personal physician almost as soon as he met her.

The later testimony of her friends was that Dorothy Kirk was in blooming health when she first met Ermil. Described by all as a hearty, active country girl, she suffered only the usual headaches and stomach pains that are the lot of the average young female. But soon after she met Ermil, he began dosing her with various "medicines" of his own choosing and procurement. What pills and potions Ermil actually gave her—and he gave her a great deal— was never clearly settled by the investigation of Dorothy's death or Ermil's subsequent trial. What remains indisputable is that Dorothy's health steadily deteriorated as her relationship with Ermil intensified during the summer of 1926. Her mother and her friends first noticed her losing her beautiful complexion; they then watched with alarm as it began turning a decided yellow tint in late summer. About the same time, Dorothy began complaining of severe fatigue, and when she and Ermil visited her mother, May, in Canal Fulton on August 15, she lay on a couch most of the time, complaining of weakness. By that time her mother and friends were beseeching her to see a doctor immediately, long before Ermil conceded the point as she lay in her death agony. Yet no matter how vociferous their pleas, Ermil assured them that Dorothy was already getting the best medical care in the world—from him. Dorothy's health continued to decline until the final crisis on the night of August 20.

Dorothy Kirk's death would have been an outstanding public sensation if only for the lurid element of the aphrodisiacs found in her purse and stomach. What elevated her tragedy into Cleveland's most delectable sex scandal of the Roaring Twenties were the pathologically complementary personalities of Dorothy Kirk and Ermil Balanescu. Dorothy was the perfect victim, a pitiable godsend to the sob-sister journalists of the age. She was no hardened flapper, and her naive trust and love for Ermil were documented on every page of her well-publicized diary. In its ardent pages, broadcast in Cleveland's three newspapers, readers could trace the progress of an affair that seemed the perfect cautionary tale of a girl who gave her heart away too soon. In the beginning, an infatuated Dorothy wrote of the flowers Ermil brought, pressing one of his carnations between the pages of her diary:

LOVELORN HEART SPEAKS IN LAST WORDS SHE WROTE

Cleveland Press, August 30, 1926.

> Ermil bought me flowers. You keep one for me, Diary, and I will
> look at it every day.

Just a few weeks later, Dorothy would write more passionately:

> I certainly do care a lot for him. Who wouldn't? I like him more
> than I ever did anyone else.

Several weeks more, and Dorothy's love was now in its full,
mature bloom. When Ermil gave her a necklace, she gushed:

> He is a dear. Really, I love him more and more. I know I would
> if he didn't bring me anything.

Then came the inevitable frost, as Ermil apparently began to
grow tired of his easy conquest. For newspaper readers of
Dorothy's diary, it was a delicious foreshadowing of the fate they
knew soon awaited her:

I felt terrible all day. What's the use of loving a person if they go out of your life so soon? Ermil may not be back. Cried all afternoon and prayed and prayed. Walked down past his house. [Interestingly, Dorothy was never inside his Haymarket home, and he never introduced her to his mother.] Someone was sitting in the window. Cried some more. Don't know what to think. I hope and pray I will hear from him in some way. Wondering where he is and what he is doing. And, I wish I'd get some word from him, for I love him so.

Then, the last entry in the diary, on July 31, an ominous prelude to her approaching doom:

Thought I might hear something from Ermil—but nothing.

If Dorothy Kirk was the perfect "love victim," Frenchy Balanescu was the consummate passion predator. A voluble fellow even when he wasn't lying, Ermil had developed the habit of writing perfervid love poetry long before he met Dorothy, and their encounter only stoked the furnace of his romantic muse. The modestly educated Dorothy was no judge of verse, and she must have been immensely flattered (à la Monica Lewinsky's reaction on being given a copy of Walt Whitman's *Leaves of Grass* by President Bill Clinton) by Frenchy's voluminous, if oft ill-metered strains. Found with her diary and her parcel of his letters were poetic gems like this:

Now she is dead—
You tell me to look in your eyes
Mine falter, you guess well why
For they cannot hold a disguise
That must always reflect your love

Not for nothing was Frenchy described by a Cleveland journalist as Cleveland's "pen love *de luxe*." How could the lovestruck Dorothy have resisted this:

If I can only love you for this hour
Just think how I love you and be sure
That while a fresh plucked rose may not endure
For me the earth not only holds this flower
But also you

Far more damning, if less sensational than Dorothy's diary and Frenchy's verse, were the "prescriptions" found with Dorothy's effects. Ever the conscientious "doctor," Frenchy had written frequent and lengthy dosage instructions to go with the pills and potions that he gave Dorothy. A typical "prescription" ran thus:

If your eyes continue yellow tomorrow night after supper, take blue pills. Take two of the others after meals daily. Leave a short note for me. I will consider your wish. I have no idea how long I will be away. I will hope you progress.

After Dorothy's death, city chemist Harold J. Knapp had a look at the contents of her stomach. Following his examination he stated to reporters:

If such a thing were possible I would say she had been existing on a drug diet. Her stomach was so loaded with opiates and hypnotics that it may be several days before we can aggregate them to determine definitely what caused death.

Cuyahoga County coroner A. P. Hammond then examined Dorothy's corpse and advised Cleveland police to hold Frenchy in custody, pending chemical analysis of her vital organs. After looking at the results, Hammond ruled that Dorothy's death had been caused by a poison, the nature of which he left unstated. A charge of manslaughter was filed against Frenchy on Friday, August 27. He engaged counsel from the firm of Day, Corrigan & Day, and both sides began to prepare for what promised to be a sensational trial.

Frenchy's trial in October did not disappoint its spectators, especially the standing-room-only crowds—mostly women—who jammed the Old Court House on Public Square to see it. It opened on Wednesday, October 13, in common pleas judge Carl V. Weygandt's courtroom on the fifth floor. Prosecuted by Assistant County Prosecutor James C. Connell, Frenchy was defended by brothers Arthur and Fred Day. Over the next eight days the jury of six men and six women heard several dozen witnesses and 70,000 words of testimony. Sob-sister columnist Nina Dornberg well captured the ambiance in Judge Weygandt's courtroom as the tawdry spectacle played itself out:

> It isn't a pleasant spectacle, this courtroom of hot-eyed men and women spectators, the ever-changing malicious feminine witnesses, the fighting, nagging attorneys who [spit] at each other like angry gnats, and the miserable nervous boy in the prisoner's chair. It is life at its ugliest, but to those who voluntarily give up their whole day to witness it, it is a good show.

Speaking to reporters at the opening of Frenchy's trial, canny county prosecutor Edward Stanton lowered expectations even before Judge Weygandt gaveled the trial to order on Wednesday morning. Vowing that Frenchy would get a fair trial despite the lurid publicity, Stanton emphasized that the verdict would be decided by medical experts rather than by any forensic showmanship on the prosecution's part:

> The state of Ohio has a very weak case against the boy. I say this in fairness and truth. I would not have voluntarily sought an indictment against him but the true bill was in line of duty when County Coroner Hammond reported to the grand jury that poison caused the girl's death. The case virtually rests with physicians whose expert testimony is to be given. On the surface of things we have not sufficient facts to convict.

Later that afternoon, as Prosecutor Connell made his opening statement, Frenchy's lawyers finally learned exactly how their client was accused of causing Dorothy Kirk's death. Coroner Hammond's ruling had not stated the specific cause of death, and the manslaughter indictment had relied on the usual, vague legal phrase "force and arms" in naming the agency of Dorothy's death. Prosecutor Connell now spelled it out: it was quantities of "yellow phosphorus" contained in the aphrodisiac pills and potions administered to Dorothy. It was that simple, Connell stated, and as it was a charge of manslaughter—instead of first- or second-degree murder—the state didn't have to prove malice or intent, only that Frenchy had administered the poison and that it had caused or hastened Dorothy's death.

That afternoon and the following day were the worst hours for Frenchy and his beleaguered lawyers. Attorney Arthur Day had maintained a stance of confident bravado from the outset, proclaiming from the moment of Frenchy's indictment that he was a "pure" young man and guiltless of any wrong in his "clean" relations with Dorothy Kirk. But a parade of witnesses, beginning with Dorothy's grieving mother, May, quickly demolished that character fiction. A weeping May Kirk described the physical deterioration of her daughter during the previous summer and Ermil's bland assurances that she was getting the best medical help possible. Ruby Larkin, Hazel Davis, and Anna Blackburn followed May, providing the horrific details of Dorothy's final illness and Ermil's stubborn and prolonged reluctance to get a real doctor. Anna recalled hearing Dorothy's agonized scream, "God only knows how I suffered!" More significantly for Frenchy's fate, she also remembered how the writhing Dorothy had reached for Ermil's hand and how he tried to pull it away. And how Dorothy grabbed his hand again and hissed, "You put me here; now you stay with me!" All three of the women told of how Ermil had consistently lied about himself from the moment he met Dorothy. The repugnance Hazel Davis and Ruby Larkin shared for Ermil was almost palpable in the courtroom as they told of their repeated but vain attempts to make Dorothy realize the truth about her mendacious beau. Cleveland police detectives Patrick J. Ryan and Bernard Wolf followed, describing the tissue of lies Ermil had told them before being confronted with Dorothy's diary, his letters, and the bushel basket of drugs found at his home.

Then it was the turn of the medical experts. Legally speaking, the burden should have been on the prosecution: Connell and his experts had to prove that yellow phosphorus—and only yellow phosphorus—had caused or hastened Dorothy Kirk's death. The defense, in theory, didn't have to prove anything. But the practical reality for defense lawyers Arthur and Fred Day was that they had to provide an alternative explanation for Dorothy Kirk's sudden degeneration and death. Absent a clearly diagnosed organic disease, blooming country girls generally don't sicken and die in such fashion, and the defense mustered experts to fashion an alternative theory of her fatal malady.

They didn't quite succeed, although the state didn't do a bang-up job in proving its case. Federal narcotics agent John T. Wall was the opening witness at the Friday morning session on October 15. Although he testified that he found samples of the aphrodisiac drug papine, the sedative veronal, and divers "love drugs" at Frenchy's house and in Dorothy's purse, his findings were irrelevant to the question of yellow phosphorus. City chemist George H. Voerg, considered a key state witness, was forced to admit that he had found no trace of yellow phosphorus in Dorothy's stomach. He did, however, give an unexpected thrill to his courtroom audience when he suddenly lit a chunk of phosphorus in the witness box. As the stunned courtroom crowd watched it flare, he waited until it began burning some papers under it, and then he hurled the flaming mass out the fifth-floor window. Voerg's purpose here was to demonstrate that the absence of yellow phosphorus in Dorothy's stomach could be due to oxidation—but neither his theatrics nor his testimony buttressed the prosecution's case. When Voerg returned as a rebuttal witness on Monday, October 18, he explained that the oxidation of the supposed phosphorus could have been accelerated by the chemical effect of a stomach tablet that Frenchy gave to Dorothy. Arthur Day scored an important point that afternoon, however, when he forced Voerg to admit he had found no strychnine in Dorothy's stomach.

As the prosecution's theory was that the yellow phosphorus might have been contained in some pink pills that also contained strychnine, Voerg's admission was a heavy blow to the prosecution's theory about Dorothy's death. If there was no strychnine in her stomach, then there had likely been no yellow phosphorus. After Voerg finished testifying, a newly optimistic Arthur Day crowed, "No certain evidence showing that Miss Kirk's death was caused by any kind of drug has been produced." Just before the trial resumed on Monday, Day flatly predicted: "Frenchy will be acquitted. The case will probably be dismissed before it reaches the jury."

Day spoke too soon. Coroner A. P. Hammond, a most fervent advocate for Frenchy's prosecution from the beginning, testified on Monday afternoon. He stated that he had examined Dorothy's vital organs and concluded there were only three possible explanations for the acute fatty degeneration of Dorothy Kirk's liver: 1) yellow phosphorus poisoning; 2) acute yellow atrophy of the liver; or 3) some other organic disease. As he found no evidence of yellow atrophy (a disease that generally kills rapidly within several weeks) or any other organic disorder, he concluded that the agent of death was yellow phosphorus. Moreover, Hammond added, Dorothy's symptoms during her final death agony were perfectly consistent with phosphorus poisoning: acute stomach inflammation, abdominal pains, a sharp rise in temperature followed by an abrupt decline, and yellowed skin. Defending his conclusions against Arthur Day's persistent suggestion that Dorothy's deterioration was due to acute yellow atrophy, Hammond noted that he had only found that disease three times in the 10,000-plus autopsies he had performed. He explained the absence of yellow phosphorus in Dorothy's stomach by citing possible oxidation and the probability that Frenchy had administered it to Dorothy over an extended period of time. Dr. Otto Spahir, City Hospital pathologist and Hammond's successor on the witness stand, gave less emphatic testimony for the state. While he conceded that Dorothy's death *could* have been caused by yellow phosphorus poisoning, he admitted that he found no direct evidence of it.

The turn of the defense came the next day. Arthur Day began the Tuesday morning session by making a motion to Judge Weygandt for a directed acquittal. It was immediately rejected, and the defense brought its witnesses forward. First came Mrs. Anna Balanescu, Ermil's adoring mother. Speaking in broken English, she was visibly upset, difficult to understand, and had nothing to say

Cleveland News, October 15, 1926.

except that she uncritically worshipped her son. Then came the moment the 300-plus spectators had been waiting for, as Arthur Day called his client, Ermil "Frenchy" Balanescu to the stand.

Nattily attired in a freshly pressed blue suit, black shoes and socks, a gray- and green-striped necktie, and sporting a white silk handkerchief in his breast coat pocket, Ermil testified in a low, calm voice for most of the afternoon. He may have convinced his jury he was not a deliberate poisoner; he certainly persuaded them that he was a cad and a first-class louse. Under Prosecutor James Connell's prodding, he admitted posing as a physician to Dorothy and others, he admitted writing and soliciting letters from fictitious persons, and he admitted lying to Dorothy about almost every aspect of his life and character. The more florid passages of his love letters and poetry were read aloud, and he was forced to try to explain the meaning of such ominous passages as:

> Life can't last forever. So let's enjoy it before the angry years of age destroy it.

And:

When a man can neither have the one he loves and worships, nor stop loving her, the end of one or both of them is almost certainly tragedy.

And, even more cryptically:

How can I save myself from the doom that threatens us both?

Worse yet:

Probably you have taken the tablets as I directed. Tomorrow do not take anything at all. Tomorrow night you will receive another final dose (I hope) with final directions how to take them.

A flustered Frenchy, at times barely audible, had a terrible three hours on the stand, as Connell pressed him severely on the meaning of phrases like "final dose" and "the doom that threatens us both." For all of Connell's invidious interpretations of Frenchy's words, it's likely that the prolonged airing of Frenchy's overwrought writings didn't hurt him much with the jury. Indeed, it was emphatically clear to everyone even before Connell finished his brutal parsing of French's literary vapourings that Frenchy himself had never understood the faux-romantic nonsense he uttered. His prose and poetry were replete with mendacity, posing, and pretentious rot—but they were no evidence of a motive to manslaughter.

What hurt Frenchy much more with the jury was his implausible explanation for the drugs consumed by Dorothy Kirk. He claimed that he had only given Dorothy innocuous over-the-counter remedies, not the lurid "love drugs" cataloged by the prosecution. "I only wanted to test her love," he told his courtroom audience, "and I gave her the medicines because I loved her so very much I wanted her to get well." But Frenchy did have to admit, thanks to the previously incriminating testimony of Marshall Drug Store pharmacist W. H. Timmons, that he had, in fact, obtained a supply of tablets containing the aphrodisiac johimbin on at least one occasion during the summer of 1926. Frenchy swore on the stand that he had only done so because a man named "McIntyre," whom he met at the East 140th Street/St. Clair Avenue trolley stop, had asked him to procure it for him. When Frenchy later returned to the trolley stop, he couldn't find McIntyre, so he just kept the aphrodisiac tablets in his pocket. Later that evening, when he saw Dorothy, she playfully went through his pockets and apparently, without his knowledge, took the tablets.

Ermil's moral character lay in utter ruins by the time Connell was finished with him. The crowning touch in his demolition came with Connell's sarcastic elucidation of Ermil's behavior on the day Dorothy died. Realizing that he was wanted by the police, Ermil had deserted his usual Sunday haunt at the First Methodist Church to spend the entire day at St. John's Cathedral at East 9th Street and Superior Avenue. Connell's inference was plain to the jury: the cowardly Ermil had taken refuge there because he knew no one would look for him in a Catholic church. As Connell put it later in his summation:

> If he had really loved her—if he had been honest—would he have gone to a church other than his own and stayed there most of the day when she died without trying to learn what her condition was? If I ever do anything out of the way, I doubt if I'll be smart enough to hide in a church, as he did while her body was being sliced up at the County Morgue.

A clutch of character witnesses followed Ermil, all of them testifying that Ermil was an exemplary young Methodist of churchgoing habits and irreproachable behavior. Then came Dr. Marion Blakenhorn, the defense's last hope in countering Coroner Hammond's unequivocal and damning testimony. Blakenhorn, a Lakeside Hospital physician and Western Reserve University instructor, didn't help Ermil much. Blakenhorn gave his opinion that Dorothy had died of acute yellow atrophy, not yellow phosphorus poisoning. But Connell forced him to admit that he had not examined Dorothy Kirk's stomach or its contents.

The final arguments began on the afternoon of October 20, the eighth day of the trial. Both the defense and the prosecution largely eschewed the medical aspects of the case and focused on Ermil's moral character—or lack thereof. Arthur Day, for the umpteenth time, characterized Ermil's feelings for Dorothy as "clean" and "pure, moral love." Emphasizing his client's modest social origins, he painted a poignant picture of Frenchy that Theodore Dreiser would have been proud to call his own:

> Ermil Balanescu represents to me a pathetic figure. He tried his best to conquer, to rise socially. He lived in the Haymarket district. Is it any wonder he fabricated such stories? As a matter of fact, he was the only real friend that Dorothy had. The only poison in this case is that injected by the state.

His voice rising with emotion, Day warned the jury, "If you convict him you will be ruining the life of just a little, insignificant boy, doing the best he knows how, trying to prepare for an ambitious future, guiltless of any wrongdoing." The whole case, Day thundered, was one of sheer, spiteful prejudice, not cold, hard fact. He blamed a vengeful Ruby Larkin and Hazel Davis for what had happened to his persecuted client.

As always, the prosecution had the last word—and James Connell made the most of his advantage. Simply asserting that Dorothy's death had been caused by Frenchy's drugs, he proceeded to further blacken Frenchy's battered character. Portraying him as a fakir and impostor, Connell jeered at Arthur Day's portrait of Ermil as a poor boy harboring laudable dreams of success:

> Yes, a poor little boy with an aphrodisiac complex; whose mind stooped to sex and loved pills, who wore nice clothes and posed as a prominent physician while his mother went out and worked for her family. . . . How ridiculous to claim he is a typical American boy. Something else besides sex and aphrodisiacs dominates the mind of the average American boy, who is far less of a sneak and fakir. . . . . Waste no sympathy on Balanescu. Give it to the mother of the dead girl and help keep other girls from the same fate. . . . Let him go free and he will be the city's "sheik hero" to the adoring maudlin mob which seizes with gusto on just such characters. You will be releasing him with permission to go out and ruin the lives of others. . . . There has been an

Cleveland News, October 21, 1926.

intense interest in this case. It is the second poison offense in this county in six years. . . . The result of this trial will have a universal effect. If you find him guilty your action will serve as a deterrent to other young men who may be on the verge of committing similar offenses.

Turning dramatically to Hazel Davis, Connell pointed to her face and said, "See the bloom in her cheeks? She took no aphrodisiacs from Balanescu. Dorothy once had rosy cheeks, too. Now she is dead!"

After Judge Weygandt's careful instructions on the law covering manslaughter, the case went to the jury at 10 on Thursday morning, October 21. As an anxious Arthur Day waited, the jurors filed out of the courtroom. He commented, "We hope they will be back in ten minutes." He must have been doubly disappointed when they returned at 2:30 that afternoon—with a verdict of guilty. Within 15 minutes the verdict was read, Arthur Day's motion for a retrial was denied, and Ermil was sentenced to one to 20 years in the Mansfield Reformatory and escorted back to his county jail cell. Anna Balanescu went into hysterics and collapsed as the verdict was read to the largest crowd ever assembled in the Old County Courthouse.

Judge Weygandt made it clear in his sentencing remarks that he had some doubts about the evidence in the case. But, like Prosecutor Connell, he seemed more interested in Ermil's moral depravity than in technical questions about his guilt. Addressing Ermil, he lectured him sternly:

Without attempting to infringe on the rights of the jury, let me
say to you, Ermil: There isn't any question but that the jury
reached the conclusion very soon after you took the stand that
you had led a life of deception. As you say, you may not have
given Dorothy those substances. If so, you have learned a terrible lesson. When you come out of the reformatory, make up your
mind that your life is going to be lived as a result of that lesson.
Don't be vindictive. We all hope you have learned your lesson. .
. . You may think that the ways of the machinery of justice are
severe but I want you to know that we all have admired your
ambition to be somebody. You are to be commended for that. But
from some source you have got the idea that living a life of
deceit is the way to attain your ambition. For that you must be
punished.

Ermil's only response, when asked if he had anything to say, was
to insist anew, "I am not guilty of the crime charged. That is all I
have to say."

That was Ermil Balanescu's story—and, whatever else you may
say about him, he certainly stuck to it. From the moment of his conviction, he never wavered from his protestations of innocence.
Finally removed from the Cuyahoga County Jail on April 1, 1927,
he comported himself as a model prisoner at the Mansfield Reformatory from day one. He insisted that Dorothy Kirk was the only
sweetheart he had ever had, and his cell became a shrine to her
memory, her photograph always flanked with flowers and illuminated by a blue-shaded electric light.

Ermil's health declined until he was transferred to the prison
greenhouse, where he developed into a skilled florist, designing
and maintaining the prison's impressive rock garden. His interest
in art, too, eventually revived, and he began to sketch and paint in
his idle hours. He became eligible for parole in 1930, after serving
only three years. Astonishing even his partisans, however (who by
now included both Judge Weygandt and Prosecutor Connell), he
refused to accept a parole, stating that to accept anything less than
a full pardon would be interpreted as a tacit admission of guilt.
Frenchy declared, "I know that I am innocent and would stay here

20 years before I gain my freedom by admitting that I killed the girl I love, and still love." He refused another parole in 1931 (melodramatically overshadowed by his mother Anna's attempted suicide), and yet another in 1932. On the latter occasion Frenchy philosophized, lest anyone doubt his perseverance: "Liberty is a state of mind and a man, by keeping faith with himself, may be free even though he is shut away from the world." Finally, in December 1933, a weary Mansfield Reformatory superintendent T. C. Andrews told Frenchy he had to leave whether he wanted to or not. In the end, however, stubborn Frenchy got his way: when he left at Christmastime it was with a full and unconditional pardon from Governor George White. Frenchy then returned to his family's home in Cleveland, virtually forgotten by the thousands of Clevelanders who once abhorred or admired him. He had continued to pursue his medical studies while in prison, and he said he hoped to become a doctor someday . . .

From the enlightened (or perhaps degraded) perspective of the 21st century, the manslaughter conviction of Frenchy Balanescu seems absurd. As far as the medical evidence was concerned, the state never came close to proving its case. But Cleveland juries of the 1920s took a dim view of aphrodisiacs and the kind of slick young sheiks like Frenchy who dabbled in them. His prosecutor, judge, and jury all agreed that, whatever killed Dorothy Kirk, Frenchy should be punished for his pathological lying, his casual attitude toward taboo sexual stimulants, and for "ruining" a presumably innocent young girl. Maybe it wasn't yellow phosphorus that killed Dorothy, but it was a truth self-evident to Frenchy's jurors that she would have remained alive but for meeting the young man with pills who liked to play doctor.

Chapter 22

DEATH OF A DETECTIVE

The Killing of
William Foulks (1900)

A tough labor town. Back when organized American labor had serious clout, that was a reputation that Cleveland long maintained. There are still many Clevelanders alive who remember the prolonged disturbances of the 1937 "Little Steel" strike at the Corrigan-McKinney plant, an orgy of tear gas and mob violence ultimately suppressed by the Ohio National Guard. But that was only the last chapter in a tradition of labor feistiness stretching back three score years.

Although Cleveland was spared the worst excesses of the labor violence that swept many cities in 1877, it did furnish a first-class melee when militant strikers' wives attacked hostile Cleveland policemen. The succeeding years brought more violent conflict. The 1892 East Cleveland railway strike featured considerable mayhem, with imported Pinkertons and strikebreakers repeatedly mauled by enraged strikers. Disturbances by the masses of unemployed thrown out of work by the Panic of 1893 brought Cleveland to the edge of anarchy in May of 1894, with several pitched battles between mobs and police fought in the streets of the city. Two years later, Forest City civic life was enlivened by concurrent strikes at the Berea quarries and the Brown Hoisting Company. The latter contest featured intermittent gunfire, with one striker shot dead by a strikebreaker in alleged self-defense, while the Berea strike included vindictive episodes of arson and firebombing. Such unpleasantnesses, however, were but gentle prelude to the mass violence of the "Big Con" streetcar strike of 1899, which featured the usual mob violence and the spectacular dynamiting of several streetcars.

When labor violence occurs, no one has a more thankless or hapless role than a policeman. Whatever his private sympathies, his sworn duty is to maintain public order—and all too often in the late 19th and early 20th centuries, "public order" was an official

euphemism for government protection of strikebreakers. This was always a rough job for a cop, and it inevitably and invariably led to bad feelings between strikers and policemen. Sometimes it led to worse, with both strikers and strikebreakers lashing out at the Cleveland police in the turmoil and confusion of their mutual combats. On September 29, 1900, such labor violence led to something much worse: the death of Cleveland police detective William L. Foulks.

The roots of the Foulks tragedy lay in a prolonged iron moulders, strike that had begun on June 25 of that year. On May 1, the moulders of Local 218 of the Moulders International Union demanded an increase of 25 cents a day from the foundry employers of Cleveland. Acting through their corporate mouthpiece, the National Founders Association, the foundry owners refused to grant the increase but agreed to negotiate with the moulders and to initiate a 10-cent-per-day increase while the talks went on. Eventually, however, negotiations broke down, and when the foundry owners rescinded the temporary 10-cent increase, the moulders walked out on June 25.

The foundry owners had prepared well for this event. Through the National Founders Association, they had amassed a war chest

Cleveland police detective William L. Foulks.
Plain Dealer, September 30, 1900.

of $100,000 for strikebreakings expenses, and they gave a free hand to association secretary John Penton to spend the money as he saw fit. Within days, thanks to Penton's generous expenditures, scores of professional strikebreakers began pouring into Cleveland, where they were methodically farmed out to local foundries at the going rate of $7 per day. Like their striking counterparts, Penton's imported scabs were tough men and not averse to carrying concealed weapons in the streets of Cleveland. Tensions began to build from the moment the first strikebreaker alighted from a train at the Union Depot on Water Street (West 9th Street) in late June, and ratcheted up in the weeks that followed. By September, both sides were itching for a fight, and there were frequent incidents of threats, menacing, and pushing and shoving as the increasingly desperate strikers tried to intimidate their replacements.

The accused killer: Charles Peck
Plain Dealer, October 1, 1900.

Tensions finally boiled over on the evening of Saturday, September 29, 13 weeks into the strike. Early that evening, Charles Peck and Edgar McIntyre, two scabs employed at the Kilby foundry at Lake and Kirtland Street (East 49th Street) fell in with three strikebreakers from the Riverside foundry on Carter Road: Thomas Jennings, Frank Irving, and Willis Webster. After dining at the Wright House on Ontario Street, they paid a call on Secretary Penton at his sixth-floor suite in the Hollenden Hotel. What was said at that meeting is unknown, but the five men soon departed and walked to the Hawley House Hotel at St. Clair and Seneca Streets (West 3rd Street), where three of the men intended to spend the night.

At this juncture the story starts to get murky. Likely no one

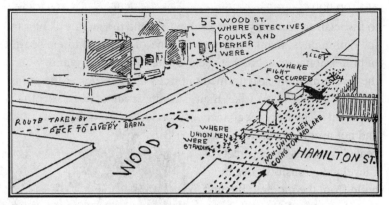

Another view of the scene. *Plain Dealer*, October 1, 1900.

involved in that evening's fatal mayhem at Wood (East 3rd) and Hamilton Streets ever told the complete truth about what happened. The five strikebreakers later testified they intended to escort Webster to the Union Depot on Water Street, where he was to board a train bound for Chicago. Why, then, did the quintet leave the Hawley House on Seneca Street and proceed as far east as Wood Street—an odd route to take if you were going to the Union Depot? And just who else was with them as they turned north on Wood Street from Superior Street and began walking toward Lake Avenue (now Lakeside Avenue)? Many men were at Wood and Hamilton that night—both strikers and strikebreakers—and it is unlikely they all arrived there at 8:30 p.m. just by coincidence. Ergo, it's quite possible the five strikebreakers and their unknown allies deliberately went to Wood and Hamilton to provoke a fight with the strikers who had baited and menaced them during the long summer months of the foundry lockout.

If they were looking for a fight, they certainly got it. Peck and his companions noticed they were being followed as they walked north on Wood Street. Their pursuers, at least a half-dozen strikers, caught up with them just north of Hamilton on the east side of Wood Street. Surrounding them on the badly lit sidewalk in front of the Giles Bernard residence, one of the strikers shouted, "Let's kill the scabs!"—and they moved in.

The assault was led—most probably—by striker Jacob J.

SCENE OF THE SHOOTING ON WOOD STREET.
(From a description by an eye-witness.)

Cleveland World, September 30, 1900.

Adams. Grabbing Peck by the neck, he cried, "Now Peck, we will finish you, you _____, _____, _____!" Adams and his men, including moulders Henry Cronenberger, and Patrick McCabe, and at least two other unidentified men, began to kick, punch, and beat Peck and his companions. As virtually everyone on the street was armed, it was only a question of time before guns came into play. Peck would later claim that he tried to pull his gun out only after Adams and his companions started beating him. Indeed, Peck claimed they took his gun away from him before he could use it. But his assertion is undermined by his admission that one of the strikers screamed, "Peck, don't pull your gun out!" just before the gunfire erupted. Peck had recently boasted to a Cleveland police-man that he would fire first at anyone threatening him, and it seems likely that he beat Adams and his men to the draw on the darkened corner of Wood Street. Within seconds, the entire block erupted in gunfire, as both sides opened up a fusillade of bullets.

It is probable but not proven that the badly beaten and justifiably

terrified Peck drew first blood. It may have been bullets from his
.32-caliber revolver that mortally wounded striker Henry Cronenberger. More bullets soon hit scabs Thomas Jennings and Frank
Irving, wounding them slightly. Just how many casualties occurred
in the Wood Street battle will never be known; there may have been
many others wounded who fled or were carried from the scene
before the law arrived. A number of eyewitnesses later testified to
seeing several wounded men crawling away, none of whom were
ever accounted for or even acknowledged by the warring sides.

It was an unlucky night for Cleveland police detective William
L. Foulks. At the time the gun battle unexpectedly started, he and
Detective Charles E. Parker were across the street in Hulda
Farmer's saloon. They were searching for a fugitive wanted on an
assault charge, when their conversation was interrupted by gunfire.
Without hesitation, both men rushed out the door onto Wood
Street. Parker saw two men running south down Wood Street and
began running after them. He was soon winded and outdistanced
and was about to give up when a little boy stepped forward and volunteered to chase the fleeing men and report back to Parker. Several minutes later, the boy returned and told Parker the fugitives
had entered the western entrance of the Hollenden Hotel on Bond
Street (East 6th). When Parker got there, he encountered private
detective Jake Mintz and Cleveland police detective John ("Jack")
Reeves. They traced the fugitives to Secretary Penton's sixth-floor
suite, where they found Thomas Jennings and Frank Irving bleeding from minor wounds. They were immediately arrested on suspicion and carted off to cells in the Central Police Station on
Champlain Street.

Meanwhile, William Foulks had met his doom. There were no
willing or even reliable eyewitnesses to his death, but the most
likely scenario is this: as he ran out of Farmer's saloon he saw
Charles Peck standing in the street. Peck may or may not have had
a gun in his hand, but he looked suspicious enough to Detective
Foulks. Running up to him, the beefy (270 pounds) Foulks
knocked Peck to the ground and began beating him with his night-
stick. Unfortunately for Foulks, however, he was wearing civilian
clothes, and Charles Peck had no way of knowing that his assailant

was a policeman. So when Foulks's .32-caliber Smith & Wesson service revolver fell out of his pocket and onto Peck's chest, it seemed like a providential gift to the hard-pressed Peck. He seized the revolver, pointed upward, and fired once.

Peck's shot was a mortal wound. The bullet smashed into Foulks's chest just three inches to the left and below the right nipple and drilled through his heart before lodging near the spinal column. He managed to stand up for a second but then fell to the ground, blood spurting out of his mouth. Eyewitness Joseph Stotter tried to give him aid, but Foulks could not speak and was obviously near death. So was William Staffield, lying in the street near Foulks. Staffield had apparently been an innocent bystander on Wood Street when the shooting broke out. He was killed by an unknown gunman while attempting to come to the aid of the downed Foulks. It was charged—but never proven—that Charles Peck also fired the shot that killed Staffield.

Minutes after the shooting ceased, policemen and curious bystanders swarmed onto the murder scene. Charles Peck had fled the area but was soon arrested by Patrolman William Thorpe, who found him in a barn near Hamilton and Ontario. Found on him was Foulks's police revolver, obviously recently fired and with four empty chambers. Peck was taken to join Irving and Jennings in jail, and shortly thereafter so were Willis Webster and Frank McIntyre. They were all initially charged with "suspicion," but the charges were boosted to first-degree murder within 24 hours of their incarceration. Cronenberger died at 1:30 on Sunday morning, and Staffield succumbed to his wounds that afternoon at 3:30.

As the identities of the dead men became known, the terrible human toll of the Wood Street shootout became clear to shocked Clevelanders. At his modest home on Marcy Avenue (East 86th Street), Foulks left a widow, Alpha, and six children: Daisy, 16; Shannon, 13; Lee, 11; Roy, 6; Lucille, 2; and an infant of two months. Born in 1862, the 38-year-old Foulks had joined the Cleveland police force on January 7, 1897, after a career as a trolley conductor on the "Big Consolidated" streetcar line. His merits quickly brought him to the attention of his superiors, and he was promoted to sergeant on January 1, 1898, and to the detective squad with the rank of lieutenant in the spring of 1899. He was known as a brave and capable officer, and the manner of his death testified to his courage in confronting danger. He left no insurance and was not a member of the voluntary police pension funds.

Henry Cronenberger, the only known union man killed in the fray, likewise left a house of mourners behind him, including his wife Jennie and children Maud, 15; Earl, 11; and Frank, 9. Ironically, he had only been a moulder for a few months; his original career as the Center Street bridge tender ended when newly elected mayor John Farley dismissed him from that post in 1899. Bricklayer William Staffield, whose courage in coming to the aid of Foulks probably cost him his life, left a wife, Maud, and sons Harold, 3, and William, 2. In all, the Wood Street tragedy created three widows and eleven orphans, all of whom were left without substantial financial resources. Perhaps the most poignant spectacle of grief was the sorrow of Maud Cronenberger. She had long been afflicted with a life-threatening heart condition, and it was feared that the shock of her father's death would kill her.

The official reactions from both sides in the labor fight were pious and predictable appeals to public sentiment. Secretary Penton painted an admirable portrait of his strikebreakers involved in the fight, warbling at length about their personal virtues, and demanded stern measures against the striking moulders:

> They were all quiet, inoffensive, thoroughly sober and industrious men. Three of the men were total abstainers and one [or] two of them were unusually well read and well informed and seemed to command the esteem of their employers to a very remarkable and unusual degree. . . . This should teach the people the only way to restrain these men from interfering with and injuring the men who wish to work is by the power of an injunction. Our men were molesting nobody. They were ambushed and only defended themselves when their lives were in danger.

More offensively, Penton wrote a note to Charles Peck in jail, promising every effort to free him and assuring him that he would soon receive the "congratulations" of his many friends and sympathizers. The latter phrase provoked an outraged Cleveland police chief George Corner to complain to a newspaper reporter that it seemed "rather odd to congratulate a man for having killed a detective and two others."

Penton's opinions, of course, were hardly the sentiments of the striking moulders, as vigorously expressed by the first vice-president of their union, Joseph F. Valentine:

> This was a very unfortunate affair and we regret it very much. It seems to us that even if clashes are unavoidable, it is not necessary for either side to resort to the use of knives or pistols. . . . I cannot account for Cronenberger's being mixed up in the trouble. He was a quiet, inoffensive fellow, never known to carry a gun and in my opinion too kind hearted to do anyone any harm . . . He was one of the best citizens of Cleveland. We are not accountable for the actions of men on the streets. . . .

On the morning after the Wood Street killings, Clevelanders learned that another labor tragedy had been narrowly averted just an hour before the Wood Street affair. About 7 that Saturday night, Joseph Parker and John Smith, two African-American strikebreakers working at the Palmer & DeMooy foundry, were walking near the Erie Railroad depot on South Water Street (West 9th), when they were accosted by hostile strikers. When they refused to promise to quit working, they were set upon and beaten by the angry crowd. They managed to escape from the mob and ran through the Erie depot, only to be caught and pummeled anew outside. Smith managed to escape again, but Parker tried to pull out his revolver. It was taken from him, and the crowd was just beginning to holler, "Lynch him! Lynch him!" when Patrolman Frank Kulas happened upon the scene. Kulas managed to rescue Parker from the mob and escorted him to Central Police Station.

Unsurprisingly, the editorial voices of the Cleveland newspapers echoed the predictable biases of their owners. The *Cleveland Leader,* forever a bastion of Republican business rectitude, sought to persuade its readers that the matter was simply a question of public safety, ignoring the equivocal role of the police in confrontations between capital and labor:

So long as strikers and the men who are employed in their places are allowed to carry arms, such scenes of violence and bloodshed as disgraced Cleveland last Saturday evening are likely to occur whenever labor troubles come. . . . The laws, if properly enforced, will give protection to all in their rights, strikers as well as the men who take their places. . . . If it is necessary, the city can detail a policeman, special or regular, to guard every man implicated on each side in any strike . . . Search every suspected man and if he has violated the law, arrest him and punish him.

The *Plain Dealer* took an even stronger anti-union line. While admitting that the laws against carrying concealed weapons should have been uniformly enforced, it insisted that the tragedy could have been avoided if only the police had properly protected the rights of the strikebreakers:

Had the right of the working man to work on terms satisfactory to himself and to his employers been respected by other working-men who were not satisfied with the same terms, there would have been no assault. . . . It is no justification for annoying and assaulting peaceable workingmen who are earning an honest living, that they are doing work which other men refused to do. The strikers should understand that without being reminded of it, and if the affair of Saturday night began with an assault of this character, the strikers should, in their own interest, give every assistance in their power to discovering the guilty parties and giving them up to justice.

The *Cleveland World,* while taking no official editorial stance, gave oblique support to the strikers' side by fulsomely broadcasting police suspicions that Peck and his comrades had deliberately provoked the Wood Street battle:

First, the police ask, why did Peck and his companions select the "tenderloin" to walk in, and why did they deliberately walk to the very darkest portion of Wood Street, if they knew they were being followed? . . . Detective Parker further says, "Why did

Detective Foulks run directly across the street and take hold of Peck? He must have seen him shooting, and seeing this believed that he was the man who was causing the trouble."

From the outset it was clear to savvy Cleveland policeman and judicial officials that it was going to be difficult, if not impossible, to secure convictions of the accused. Peck was charged with first-degree murder several hours after he was jailed, and the shooting-to-kill charges against Jennings, Webster, Irving, and McIntyre were augmented to the same level on Sunday, September 30. But by the time they all appeared in Judge Thomas M. Kennedy's Cleveland police court on Monday morning, October 1, the charges had been reduced to second-degree murder for all five men. They were immediately admitted to bail at a gross figure of $60,000 and released from jail when Secretary Penton posted the required sum. The bail money, supplied from the coffers of the Cleveland Trust Bank, was underwritten, naturally, by the National Founders Association, which had already shown its support for the accused by having their jail meals catered out of the Hollenden Hotel kitchen.

The outlook for the prosecution was bleak. Most of the witnesses to the Wood Street fight were unknown, unwilling, or unavailable, and none of the captive witnesses was likely to tell the whole truth. As the inquest testimony made clear, there were no reliable eyewitnesses or confessions to the shootings of Cronenberger or Staffield, and even the killing of Foulks made for a flimsy case. As Lieutenant (and future Chief of Police) Fred Kohler opined to a *Plain Dealer* reporter, Charles Peck had a very plausible plea of self-defense:

> Peck had no means of knowing that Foulks was an officer, he being dressed in citizen's clothes. It is argued that Peck was looking for protection from his assailants and that had he known Foulks was an officer he would have readily submitted . . . under those circumstances, the non-union men certainly had the right to defend themselves, the same right possessed by any law-abiding citizen when he [is] assaulted.

Funeral services for William Foulks were held at his Marcy Avenue home at 2 p.m. on Tuesday, October 2. A large contingent of policemen was present, and their striking floral tribute was an enormous wreath of flowers spelling out "Our Comrade." After the services, conducted by the Reverend Frank L. Chalker of the Wade Park Avenue Methodist Episcopal Church, the body was shipped to Moultrie in Columbiana County for burial.

"NOT GUILTY," SAID JURY IN PECK'S CASE

___

NON-UNION MOLDER, ACCUSED OF MURDERING DETECTIVE FOULKS, ACQUITTED.

Cleveland World, April 28, 1901.

Henry Cronenberger's funeral was held at the Old Stone Church. The services were conducted by the Reverends Paul Hickok and H. W. Hulbert of that congregation, and his body was escorted to Woodland Cemetery by contingents of the Odd Fellows and his fellow moulders. After an autopsy, the body of William Staffield was shipped by boat to Buffalo for burial by his family there.

Probably no one except Charles Peck and his strikebreaking comrades was satisfied by the denouement of the Wood Street shootout. The charges against all but Peck were eventually dropped for lack of evidence. Peck's trial in April 1901 was a brief and passionless affair. After hearing the fragmentary and inconclusive testimony of several witnesses, the jury listened to Peck repeat his story that he had not known he was struggling with an officer of the law when he shot Foulks. His jury unanimously agreed on April 27 and freed him after only a few hours of deliberation. Apparently, they were not convinced beyond a reasonable doubt that it was Peck's bullet that had killed Foulks, or, even if it was, that he had known he was shooting at a cop.

So who killed William Foulks—not to mention Henry Cronenberger and William Staffield? No one will ever really know, but it seems likely that the badly beaten and panicky Charles Peck was the guilty gunman. There were four empty chambers in Foulks's revolver when Patrolman Thorpe took it away from Peck, and several of the eyewitnesses identified him as the most prominent shooter at the chaotic scene. Both Staffield and Cronenberger made death-bed statements that they had been shot by a "curly-haired man"—and the only one of the identified combatants who fit that description was Charles Peck. Eyewitness Joseph Mulcahy was probably mistaken in his vivid recollection that he saw Peck exchange shots with Foulks in classic Western fashion as they stood facing each other on Wood Street. But even if Mulcahy's testimony was accurate, Peck was probably guilty of no more than manslaughter, as he did not know Foulks was a policeman. Under the confused circumstances, he might well have been exonerated by the jury on even that charge.

About the same time the Peck verdict was handed down, the moulders' strike was finally settled, on terms mildly advantageous to the union. Everyone except the grieving families forgot about the dead and injured and the issues raised by the Wood Street shootout. Which is probably why the tragedy was repeated twice within the next dozen or so years. On August 22, 1911, Patrolman Walter Chapman was shot to death by an unknown gunman while guarding the Decatur Alley homes of strikebreakers involved in a dispute with Cleveland cloakmaking establishments. Less than a year after that, Patrolman Edward Parker was shot to death during a melee with striking railroad construction workers at East 26th Street and the Pennsylvania Railroad tracks. No one was ever prosecuted for either slaying. But the deaths of Foulks, Chapman, and Parker provide powerful, if forgotten, proof that Cleveland was once a tough labor town.

William Foulks's name can be found on the National Law Enforcement Officers Memorial Wall, Judiciary Square, Washington, D. C.: Panel 54, West Wall, Line 5.

Chapter 23

A SECOND SHOT AT LIFE

The Gothic Tale of Eula Dortch (1965)

Are some people just no damn good? Are some persons rotten to the core, incapable of redemption or rehabilitation? Mankind has struggled with this question for all of recorded history without coming to a final conclusion. Most correctional institutions have struggled too, alternating between sheer punishment and hopeful rehabilitation. Various cultural voices have argued for the redemptive outlook, as in the sublime figure of Victor Hugo's Jean Valjean or the sentimental melodrama of Jimmy Valentine. But a skeptical public has, more often than not, put little faith in giving criminals a second chance. The author's own annals of Cleveland woe offer instances of persons who committed terrible crimes and lived to regret them in later lives of repentance: Joe Filkowski, Velma West, and "Big Jim" Morton come to mind. (The Joe Filkowski saga is recounted in the author's "Stand by Your Man," *The Corpse in the Cellar*, 1999; the Velma West tragedy is told in "Twelve O'Clock Girl in a Nine O'Clock Town," *The Maniac in the Bushes*, 1997; the "Big Jim Morton" story is told in "Gangster's Gangster," *The Killer in the Attic*, 2002.) Those same annals, however, also furnish tales of thorough evildoers who never learned their lessons, pursuing wickedness right up to their unlamented deaths: monsters like Jiggs Losteiner, Henry Hagert, and John Leonard Whitfield. (For the Jiggs Losteiner saga see the author's "High Noon at Bedford," *They Died Crawling*, 1995; for the Hagert saga see "When Monsters Walk," *The Killer in the Attic*, 2002.) No one seems able to predict the fates of once fallen souls. It is with these suitably sobering thoughts in mind, therefore, that we begin the cautionary tale of Eula Mae Dortch.

Many and many a year ago . . . and in a galaxy far, far away . . . lived a woman named Eula Dortch. Actually, it was 1965, and the place was the East Side of Cleveland, 927 East 129th Street, to be

A formidable female:
Eula Dortch, 1965.

exact. It was a three-story frame house, and it was there that Eula dwelt with her husband John, 34, and their seven children. They lived in imperfect amicability, sorry to say, for the word in the neighborhood was that John Wesley Dortch beat his wife during their not infrequent quarrels. She would later claim that he used both his hands and feet in assaulting her during their bouts of domestic infelicity.

Perhaps it was the stress of their hard lives: Eula toiled at Lutheran Hospital as a nurse's aide for only $45 a week, while John labored as a machinist at Wood, Spencer & Co. and took other jobs on the side. Or maybe it was just the pressure of too many children and too many bills to meet over the 13 years Eula and John had been wed, not to mention their hard journey from Jackson, Mississippi, to the mean streets of Cleveland in 1954.

Perhaps, too, it was the times. The 1960s were tumultuous and unprecedented times for African-American Clevelanders like the Dortches. As with many of their Glenville neighbors, they were involved in the struggle to obtain better and unsegregated schools

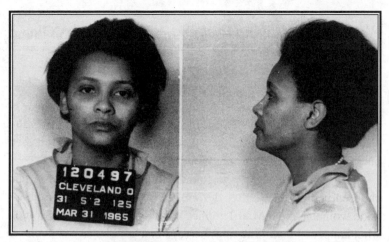

Cleveland Police Department mug shots of Eula Dortch, 1965.

for their children. In the fall of 1964, Eula jumped into the fight over the new Stephen E. Howe Elementary School. It was a complex controversy, but the crux of it was that many Glenville African-Americans like Eula believed the new school was too far away for their children to walk to and had been sited to perpetuate segregated schools for the black residents of Glenville. (The United States Supreme Court would eventually validate that interpretation in its historic 1976 ruling ordering the desegregation of Cleveland schools.) In September of 1964, Eula and like-minded neighbors organized the Hazeldell Parents Association (Hazeldell was the former neighborhood elementary school) and boycotted Howe Elementary. There is no reason to doubt Eula's idealism or sincerity in that cause: the Cleveland *Call & Post* would subsequently dub Eula a "Joan-of-Arc" in the fight against inconvenient, inferior, and segregated Cleveland schools. But by January 1965, Eula had given up on the public schools and transferred her children to a Catholic parochial school.

In retrospect, she had also given up on her husband John. On the morning of January 7, Eula was working at a little business called the Hazeldell Variety Shop, a small shop she operated with a friend at 805 East 125th Street. The friend's husband had left a handgun at the store, a .35-caliber Walther automatic pistol. Eula asked her

Wife Admits Slaying Husband, Hiding Body in Cellar

Cleveland Press, April 1, 1965.

friend if she could borrow the gun, saying her husband John was going to drive to Detroit and needed it for protection on the highway. The friend agreed to loan her the gun, and Eula put it in her purse and left the store sometime that afternoon.

When Eula got home, she found John alone in the house, her children being looked after during her work days by a neighborhood woman named Mrs. Thomas. We only have Eula's version of what happened next. She told the cops that as soon as she came in the side door of the house, John started arguing with her. She didn't remember later what it was all about, but she did recall that he threatened to kill her. She drew the gun from her purse and pointed it at him. Then he sat down on the couch in the living room, repeating several times his threat to kill her as soon as she fell asleep. Suddenly, he got up from the couch, and she thought she saw something in his hand. She fired one shot. It hit him in the chest and he went down. He lay there moaning for 45 minutes until he died.

At this juncture the Dortch tragedy evolved from a mundane domestic killing into a tale of unique gothic freakishness. Many women are mistreated by their husbands, and some of them eventually turn on and even kill their tormentors. But Eula Dortch was no common woman, and what she did now was breathtakingly bizarre. After calming down for about an hour, she decided that she just couldn't face the disgrace to herself and her family potentially ensuing from John's death. So she decided not to tell anyone about it and to hide the evidence.

Laboriously hauling the late John down to the basement, Eula dragged him into the fruit cellar, a 10-foot by 5-foot concrete-floored room in the southeast corner of the basement. Then she brought in a posthole digger and a sledgehammer and went to work. All that afternoon and part of the next day, she hammered away at the four-inch-thick concrete. Her plan was to bury John underneath it, but by the time she got through the four inches she was tired.

Not just tired of pounding at the concrete, but tired of the sight and smell of John Wesley Dortch. So, sometime on the morning of January 8, she decided to forget about it. There was already a hasp on the fruit cellar door, so she walked over to the Eddy Road Hardware store at 12424 Arlington Avenue and purchased a Slaymaker padlock from owner Ben Asnien. Returning home, she placed a beige bedspread over John's corpse and padlocked the door.

It's quite possible that if Eula Dortch had stayed out of other kinds of trouble, no one would ever have known what happened to John Dortch. She told her children and relatives that John had gone to Detroit to take another job. They believed her story, as did Henry Berghaus, the Wood, Spencer & Co. manager she called right after killing John to tell him about the Detroit job. Everyone believed Eula, even her sister Elizabeth Cobb and Elizabeth's husband Joseph. Week by week, Eula kept up the fiction of John's life in Detroit, telling everyone of his telephone calls and the support money he faithfully sent back. (Sometimes Eula varied the fiction, boasting that John had inherited a legacy from an aunt.) As January passed into February, February gave way to March, and March waned toward April, Eula's daring and improvised murder cover-up plan seemed to be working on every front. As Cleveland police homicide bureau chief Lieutenant Carl Delau, not a Eula Dortch admirer, later put it: "It could have been a perfect crime. I wonder how many persons have disappeared like this before, and were never heard of again."

But, as Bob Dylan once astutely remarked, "To live outside the law, you must be honest." Eula had not quite thought out the long-term aspects of killing her husband, and her lack of foresight now led to her downfall. If she didn't miss the personality or the physical abuse of the late John Wesley, she certainly did miss his weekly paycheck from Wood, Spencer & Co. Her $45 per week wage at Lutheran Hospital didn't go very far in covering the demands of seven kids and a mortgage. So Eula Dortch decided to steal.

For the hard-pressed Eula, it must have seemed an irresistible opportunity. Back in the fall of 1964, when she was involved in the boycott of Howe Elementary, she had been elected second vice-president of the Hazeldell Parents Association. With the responsibilities of that office came access to the organization's checking account. Sometime later that fall, the Association officers were told to transfer any checking funds left into a savings account. This they duly did, but Eula hung on to some of the blank checks from the defunct account. After the money from John's paychecks ceased in January, she began forging and cashing the checks at local stores. By the end of March, she had cashed checks worth $1,000 on the nonexistent account.

The end came at the close of March. Following a parade of bouncing checks, local businesses and banks contacted the Cleveland police. They arrested Eula Dortch on the evening of Tuesday, March 29, 1965. She was arrested at her home and taken away to the city jail, pending a charge of forgery. Some years ago the author talked with one of the Cleveland detectives who arrested Eula that evening. He regrets to this day the fact that he and his partner did not search Eula's home when they arrested her. It could have been the crime scoop of their career. Later investigators of matters at the Dortch house would be praised and promoted for what they found; for the arresting officers, it was simply a case of might-have-been.

Actually, it was hardly brilliant police work that broke the Dortch case. Eula had left home in haste, and Mrs. Thomas, who normally minded the Dortch children, became aware that the seven kids were now left completely unsupervised in their East 129th Street home. She called Elizabeth Cobb, Eula's sister, the next day and shared her concern. That evening, Elizabeth and her husband Joseph went over to Eula's house to search for John Dortch's address or telephone number in Detroit.

When they didn't find any information about John after several hours of searching, they decided to try the only unsearched area— the basement. Eventually, having run out of options, Joseph Cobb got a screwdriver and took the hasp off the fruit cellar door. They opened it . . . and found what was left of John Wesley Dortch. Undisturbed by anyone since January 7, his corpse was in an advanced state of decomposition. His eyes were gone, as were his penis and testicles. He was still wearing black shoes, black-and-white socks, gray Oxford pants, a red, white, and black sport shirt, a white tee shirt, and white jockey shorts. There were two dried bloodstains underneath the body.

Initial public shock over the grisly find in Eula's fruit cellar was soon displaced by disagreement over the character of Eula Dortch and her deserved fate. Surprisingly, it was only the minority opinion that Eula Dortch was an inhuman monster deserving harsh judicial treatment. Lieutenant Carl Delau succinctly voiced that judgment soon after he toured the crime scene and interviewed Eula in jail:

> This woman was calm, cool, scheming, and cunning. She showed no signs of regret in this killing. She kept a dirty, filthy house, and it's unbelievable that nobody smelled the foul odors outside of her house at 927 East 129th Street. She told of frequent beatings, but she never went to the prosecutor's office and she never went to a hospital. They quarreled that night while he was sitting down, and when he stood up she shot him . . . she just didn't like her husband. She called his job right away—he was getting ready to go to work, and told them he was gone to Detroit. Then she went down and picked up his pay check. She smashed up the concrete but never got to dig the grave.

Delau's skeptical opinion was hardly the majority view. From the moment Eula's arrest was blazoned forth by the Cleveland media, her version of the crime dominated interpretations of the crime. They didn't used the term "battered woman syndrome" or talk about traumatic stress disorders in the 1960s, but the times they were a-changing toward those kinds of things. Eula herself was the most forceful and articulate analyst in explaining her seemingly unbelievable behavior. Describing her 13 years of marriage as "hell," she justified her actions by invoking notions of self-defense, motherly love, and idealistic visions of a better, higher life:

> You wonder why? For myself I could stand anything, any physical harm. For my children I could not. . . . John had a different philosophy in life. It was for material things. I wanted more from life, more from my children. . . I have no self-pity for myself, but I could not stand to hurt my children more.

Referring to John's murder and macabre burial only as the "incident," she told *Plain Dealer* reporter Doris O'Donnell that she hid the body to avoid disgracing her family:

> I realized and knew what I had destroyed, and I thought of John's family and mine and the children, and I could not face reality. But I was relieved when everything ended.

Following her arrest, Eula was charged with forgery on April 1. The next day she was charged with second-degree murder. On April 4, accompanied by her attorney, Glenville councilman George Forbes, she waived preliminary examination before municipal judge Hugh P. Brennan and was bound over to the grand jury. Bond was set at $5,000 and she remained in jail.

By the time Eula Dortch came to trial in late June, the groundswell of support for this supposed abused wife and struggling mother was almost universal throughout the Cleveland community. Many Clevelanders had decided it was a shame about Eula Dortch and that maybe the late John Dortch had deserved what he got. *Plain Dealer* columnist J. F. Saunders spoke for all of Eula's pitying champions in a column published just before her case came to trial:

> In 1952, Eula Dortch was the radiant bride of a young man she had known through all of her teen years and had grown to love with deepening affection. She was then 19. . . . She had seven children and they were her life. She involved herself in all of their interests, gave freely of her time to helping solve community problems [no mention of check forging here!] and became an officer in an association seeking to improve the educational environment of neighborhood children. All this time Eula Dortch was aware that her marriage was a mistake but she could not bring herself to concede defeat. She had seven compelling reasons for her resolve to maintain the struggle even after the battle had been lost. And then in a sudden climax of supreme despair and distraught tension Eula Dortch picked up a small gun and shot her husband of 13 years, killing him with a single

squeeze of the trigger. The castle came tumbling down. The dream exploded. . . .

Warming to his theme, Saunders pleaded that Eula deserved a second shot at a decent life:

Society has treated Eula Dortch cruelly and is not through with her. A year in prison can destroy this sensitive, patient, and devoted mother who withstood as long as she could the tortures of a married hell to give her children a chance at a normal life. Her crime was an impulsive act of passion committed in a moment when endurance had run out and reason had deserted a mind that could absorb no more of the punishment that astonished her attorney in its magnitude and terror. Eula Dortch is not a criminal and no imprisonment can inflict upon her suffering that could match the agony that was hers in seeing her children's world collapse. A way must be found to restore her to those children. . . .

The pleas of J. F. Saunders and many other voices were not in vain. On June 18, 1965, Eula Dortch stood trial before Judge Hugh A. Corrigan in Cuyahoga County Common Pleas Court. After listening to her version of her unhappy marriage, Prosecutor Lloyd Brown accepted her plea of guilty to a reduced charge of first-degree manslaughter. Judge Corrigan then sentenced her to a term of 1 to 20 years in Marysville Reformatory. He also sentenced her to 1 to 20 years on the check forging charge, to be served concurrently. Giving thanks that her seven children were being reared properly by her sister, Eula Dortch vowed to get an education while she was in Marysville. And, as J. F. Saunders had so passionately hoped, a way was found to restore Eula Dortch to her seven children. In 1967, Ohio authorities decided to give her a second shot at life and released her after only two years. Three years went silently by. . . .

Early on the morning of January 7, 1970—five years to the day after John Dortch died—police got a call to come to the Montgomery Brothers Market, a grocery at 8425 Euclid Avenue. What they found when they got there wasn't pleasant. Entering through the east door, they found the body of a young black male about five feet from the door. He was lying on his stomach, and on the other side of the door was the body of a middle-aged black female. In the rear of the store, by the beer cooler, lay the body of another young black male. They were all dead from recent gunshot wounds.

The story told by brothers Robert and Jack Montgomery was a straightforward and blunt narrative. An hour earlier, they had been working in the store with clerk Calvin Hill. Robert was behind the meat counter by the entrance when a black female entered the store. As she walked past the meat counter, he noticed a large .38 Colt revolver sticking out of the woman's waistband. She browsed around the store for a few minutes and then asked Robert what time the store closed. He told her in about 15 minutes and she went out the front door. She returned to the store several minutes later, accompanied by two young black males. One of them headed for the beer cooler, and the other one stood by the door. The black female walked up to Robert at the meat counter, pulled out her gun, and said, "Don't move!"

Robert and Jack Montgomery had worked very hard to open their business in the heart of one of Cleveland's ghettoes. The two brothers worked 12-hour days, seven days a week, and were still paying off the Small Business Administration loan that had helped them start up the business. So when Robert heard the woman and saw the gun, he knew what to do. Ducking behind the counter, he ran to the rear of the store. Picking up a shotgun he kept there for such conversations, he sprinted back to the meat counter as the woman tried to run out of the store. Even as Robert's Ithaca Model 37 shotgun roared, Jack's .38 Iver-Johnson revolver thundered from over by the beer cooler.

She never had a chance. As Jack Montgomery later remarked, "It's suicide to try and rob this store." The black female robber and her two accomplices didn't know that both Montgomery brothers were armed. More importantly, they didn't know that the store was equipped with a special antitheft device that allowed the brothers to lock the exit door from the inside by pressing a button. Even if the trio had made it to the door, they would have been cut down by the six shots and two shotgun loads fired, respectively, by Jack and

Two tough businessmen: Robert and Jack Montgomery, 1965.

Robert Montgomery. By the time the brothers stopped firing, there was nothing for the police to do but pick up the bodies and identify them.

It wasn't difficult to discover who they were. One of the black males was 18-year-old Joseph Moore, address unknown; the other black male was Tommy Lee Perkins, 20, of 20103 Longbrook Road in Warrensville Heights. The families of the two young men were outraged at the celerity with which police prosecutor Clarence Rogers ruled the killings "justifiable homicide." They pointed out that neither of the two men were armed and that it couldn't be proven that they were acting in concert with the black female when she pulled the gun at 12:55 a.m. According to their grieving relatives, Joseph and Tommy Lee were just innocent bystanders, caught in the wrong place at the wrong time.

It's possible—but not too likely—that such assertions were true. Yet no one ever entertained any doubts about the female gunman of the supposed robber trio. The woman lying dead on the floor of the Montgomery Brothers meat market was, of course, our old friend Eula Dortch. Whatever the truth about the death of her husband, it remains an indisputable fact that Eula Dortch hadn't made much of her second shot at a decent life. Many people don't—and it would be well to remember Eula's cautionary tale the next time you hear someone whining about letting "reformed" killers out of prison because they have "paid their debt to society." As my brother's astute sister-in-law Laurie has oft remarked, "with some people, *once* is a pattern." So it proved with Eula Dortch, truly one of the most cold-blooded and gothic killers in the annals of Forest City woe.

Chapter 24

"A LIVING TOMB"

Ellen Hunt's Crusade (1897-1935)

The laws governing insanity were notoriously unfriendly to 19th-century women. The institutionalization of Mary Todd Lincoln was only the most publicized instance of a woman "put away" against her will. The case of Elizabeth Packard, an Illinois minister's wife, was an object lesson in what could happen to even a "respectable" middle-class woman caught in the toils of discriminatory justice. Committed to an insane asylum merely on her husband's insistence that she was insane (i.e., demonstrating too much independence), Elizabeth spent three years in that Illinois snake pit. When she returned home, her husband locked her in the nursery and nailed all the windows shut. Elizabeth eventually escaped his clutches, vindicated herself, and won her freedom in a sensational trial at which the jury only deliberated seven minutes before deciding in her favor. (She returned to her husband, but that's another story.)

The legal pitfalls for women of lower social rank than Mrs. Packard or Mary Todd Lincoln were even dicier. An 1856 survey of the diagnoses made of female patients in Ohio state insane asylums affords glimpses of the flimsy grounds on which some of them became involuntary guests of the state. What of Mary Purd, incarcerated for "bad disposition"? What of Loretta Plymton, committed for 20 years, deranged by "disappointment"? What of Elizabeth Swisler, institutionalized because of "difficulty with husband"? Or Sarah Brower, "abused by husband"; Christiania Geistivite, demented from "turn of life"; or Lydia Rhodes, driven to the madhouse by "smoking and snuff"? Not to mention Adelaid Countryman of Ashtabula, diagnosed as congenitally doomed by "masturbation of parents." There were many insidious roads to the

19th-century crazy house, and it is clear that a woman couldn't be too careful back then, lest she end up in some local bedlam. Which leads us to the sad but oddly uplifting story of poor Ellen Hunt.

Except for her suffering and struggle, we actually know little of Ellen Hunt. Born about 1867 in Ireland to Irish parents, she emigrated to the United States sometime in the 1890s. The year 1897 found her working as a dressmaker and living in a rooming house at 391 Detroit Street. There, in some evil hour, some malign fate led her into a conversation she would regret for the rest of her life.

We don't even know what the conversation was about. It was vaguely stated in later years that Ellen heard someone had misappropriated some funds—stolen some money, to be blunt—and she indiscreetly babbled about it to persons with whom she lived and worked. So casually and simply did the road to the insane asylum open up before Ellen Hunt.

ELLEN
HUNT

Sketch of Ellen Hunt.
Cleveland Press, March 10, 1923.

Whoever the misappropriating miscreant was, it's clear that he was a more powerful individual than humble seamstress Ellen Hunt. Before she knew what had hit her, she was emphatically denounced as insane and hauled before Cuyahoga County judge Henry C. White. Her first sanity hearing before White was inconsequential, perhaps because a Dr. John M. Fraser was willing to testify that she was not insane. Her unknown persecutor, however, did not give up. She had no powerful friends and no attorney to defend herself against such a charge. After a second complaint against her made in September of 1897 was heard by Judge White, he committed her to the state hospital for the insane in Newburg.

Like most facilities for the mentally ill in that era, the Newburg hospital on Turney Road (known derisively to generations of Clevelanders as "Turney Tech") was an inhumane and barbaric institution. A series of newspaper exposes in the Cleveland Press during the first decade of the 1900s would exhaustively expose and document the scandalous living conditions and brutal treatment accorded the patients there. And there is every reason to believe that Ellen Hunt experienced the worst of such treatment and conditions during her two years there. In later life she would sadly recount the numberless and repetitive beatings, humiliations, and indignities she suffered there. Whatever her mental and physical condition when committed, it is clear she was a physically unhealthy and psychologically broken woman by the time she was pronounced "sane" and released in 1899. Although she was only in her early thirties, Ellen's hair had turned white from the rigors of

IN ASYLUM BUT NEVER INSANE.

Woman and Doctor Declared Her Sane Before She Was Locked Up.

Cleveland Press, November 12, 1905.

her ordeal. She was also missing most of her teeth, knocked out during various mistreatments in the asylum. She had no friends, no resources, and a hard living to make. Her grim comment on exiting Newburg was a weary, "I have been in a living tomb."

Such a plight might have been the end for many persons, but not for one made of such stern stuff as Ellen Hunt. The moment she got out of Newburg, she began working to clear her name and obtain compensation for her wrongful imprisonment. In 1902, working in concert with attorney Alexander Hadden, she petitioned the Cuyahoga County Common Pleas Court to expunge the record of her insanity committal. While that suit was under way she contacted Judge White the following year and submitted the testimony of three physicians, including Dr. Fraser, who found her perfectly sane. Judge White refused to expunge the record of her hearing, but he did make an additional—and very unusual—entry in the probate record. Setting aside his original finding, he wrote, "Ellen Hunt was in a condition of physical and nervous weakness, but the question of whether she was insane is in doubt." More unusual still, it was now discovered that most of the original records of Ellen's commitment were missing. That same year, Ohio governor Myron Herrick refused to intervene in Ellen's case. Finally, in 1907, after several years of work by attorneys Thomas Dissette, Edward Dissette, and Wilbur D. Wilkin, the common pleas court reheard Ellen's lawsuit and reversed itself. Deciding that Ellen Hunt was not insane at the time of her original hearing, it ruled that she had been wrongfully incarcerated.

It had taken eight years to win this legal victory—but it wasn't enough for Ellen Hunt. Toiling as a clerk at Bailey's Department Store, she refused to give up her dreams of total vindication and financial compensation. About 1910, she began to lobby state legislators, asking them to introduce a legislative bill in Columbus for the purpose of compensating her for her two-year ordeal. For 20 years, sympathetic lawmakers brought up such legislation to 10 different Ohio legislatures. All such efforts but one died in committee, including a 1923 Cleveland Press campaign complete with front-page headlines and a drive for thousands of signatures to Ellen Hunt's petition. The Ohio Legislature did pass an Ellen Hunt compensation bill in 1927, only to have her reject its $1,000 offer as inadequate. Still, she refused to give up, always saying in the teeth of some fresh defeat, "Someday I'll get my just desserts."

The years passed fast, and then faster, and soon Ellen Hunt found herself in the hardscrabble 1930s, three decades into her personal crusade for justice. She was truly old now, in declining health, and a pitiable figure as she wrote endless letters and haunted newspaper offices for publicity and legislative chambers for support. *Cleveland News* reporter Howard Beaufait would later recall the frequent sight of this lonely, stubborn, and indomitable woman:

I can still see her in the last days of her life, hurrying against

Northern Ohio Insane Asylum (later Cleveland State Hospital).

time, her old-fashioned black hat set squarely on her small head,
the pinched cheeks, the zealous fire in her watery eyes . . . .

Another observer described her this way:

Her name, her history, her appearance—all lent themselves to
the aura of mystery which clung to her. In appearance she was
unforgettable—a thin, fragile wraith in black, ancient high-top
shoes, an ancient black bonnet on her head, her face angular,
birdlike, white as chalk and infinitely wrinkled.

Ellen Hunt's lonely quest finally began to pay real dividends in
1931, 34 years after her ordeal began. On April 9, 1931, a com-
pensatory bill to pay Ellen Hunt $15,000, offered by State Repre-
sentative A. B. Harding, passed the Ohio House of Representatives
97 to 1. (The money actually came out of the coffers of Cuyahoga
County but had to be authorized by the state legislature.) The next
day it passed the Ohio Senate by a vote of 29 to 2 and headed to
Governor George White's desk for his promised signature.

Ellen, who was in Columbus when her bill passed, was too over-
come by emotion to speak to reporters. It seemed like her ordeal
was finally over.

Nothing, of course, was ever really "over" in the Ellen Hunt
saga. Following the monetary award, six months of bickering
between Cuyahoga County probate court judge George S. Addams

Ellen Hunt Wins 35-Year Fight to Obtain Vindication

Senate Votes Trust Fund to Repay Seamstress for Having Wrongfully Been Sent to Asylum.

Cleveland News, April 11, 1931.

and Cuyahoga County commissioners J. H. Harris, Joseph T. Gorman, and Walter E. Cook ensued. They were the authorities charged with administering Ellen's money in trust, and they disagreed almost as much with each other as they did with Ellen.

She wanted $5,000 immediately in a lump sum, so that she could do some long-deferred traveling and buy a small house in the country. But Commissioner Cook, in particular, was understandably concerned that the vulnerable, aged Hunt might be taken advantage of, should she come into such sudden and unaccustomed wealth. Back and forth the commissioners and Addams negotiated, until they finally compromised at a figure that satisfied everyone but the aggrieved Ellen: $1,000 up front and the rest doled out in payments of $150 per month. And, in the event of her death, any remaining funds in the trust would revert to the county commissioners.

It may have seemed like the end to Ellen's sympathizers, but the "victory" was for her only the beginning of another relentless campaign. Until the day she died, Ellen continued her ferocious fight to gain complete control of her money. She tried her best to keep up her old routines: badgering reporters at the three daily newspapers for publicity supporting her claims, the round of her petitioning at Cleveland City Hall, probate court, and common pleas court. Her gait slowing and her skin like yellowed parchment, she lived out her last years at the Catholic Young Women's Hall at 1736 Superior Avenue, drinking endless cups of coffee subsidized by one of her admirers, Helen Driscoll. Age had not withered, nor custom staled Ellen's quenchless indignation: when told that Ohio legisla-

Ellen Hunt.

tors remained deaf to her incessant pleas, she vehemently spluttered: "They're a bunch of no goods!"

Ellen Hunt's anguished crusade finally ended in a hospital bed at
St. Vincent Charity Hospital, where she died on June 19, 1935. She
was buried out of St. John's Cathedral and sleeps, her struggle forever finished, in a Calvary Cemetery plot. Fittingly, the question of
what was due her lingered on even after her death: probate judge
Nelson Brewer refused her request that she be buried in a $5,000
mausoleum and ruled that her funeral and interment expenses not
exceed $1,500. Perhaps the priest at her funeral had the best epi-
taph for this indomitable, inexorable woman:

> Society made her life a modern tragedy. She was up against what
> we call the law, and sometimes laws are hard to interpret. Some-
> times a person is persecuted by the law. Ellen Hunt, who spent

the wearisome hard years seeking justice, today has received it
to her heart's fullest.

The sad story of Ellen Hunt is a quaint tale of a long bygone
Cleveland. But lest you think that the legal perils that victimized
poor Ellen Hunt died with her, consider two cases from the 1960s.
Mrs. Frances Goda of 1963 West 105th Street spent an unpleasant
night in late July of 1963 at Cleveland State Hospital after she was
denounced as "insane" by feuding neighbors. Embarrassed probate
court officials released her after determining that she was perfectly
sane. Two weeks later, the farce was repeated, when Robert J. Vale
was committed to Cleveland State on the say-so of his irate wife.
He soon got out, but whether, like Elizabeth Packard, he reconciled
with his spouse is unknown.

Chapter 25

BLACK MONDAY AT GARFIELD

The Beverly Jarosz Tragedy (1964)

Stealthily, a cat creeps by.
She snags her paw.
And the spider is no more.
— *from a poem by Beverly Jarosz, 1964*

Such a crime must not go unsolved. The crime itself was terrible enough, the life of a young girl taken in mid-day in her own home. But what makes it even worse is the invasion by a murderer into a neighborhood like this. If it could happen there it could happen anywhere.
— *Louis B. Seltzer, December 30, 1964*

Every generation of Clevelanders has its "own" special murder. Certain Cleveland slayings possess a special character—call it Aristotelian pity and horror, if you will—that burn such terrible events into the collective consciousness of an age-specific peer group. Cleveland citizens of the Victorian age shuddered with particular horror at the murder of Cleveland police detective William Hulligan by arch-criminal "Blinky" Morgan in 1887. Young newspaper readers of the Roaring Twenties devoured press accounts detailing the cold-blooded killings of George "Jiggs" Losteiner, the epitome of the ruthless, kill-crazy gangster. A decade later, young Forest City girls thrilled to the fate of sweet-16 Janet Blood, callously shot down on a West Side street for no reason at all. Eighteen years later, the young parents of the post–World War II era recoiled in protective fear when psychopathic pervert Harold

Beach stabbed eight-year-old Sheila Ann Tuley and left her to die on a stranger's porch.

These horrific stories still have the power to chill, even for those with no firsthand memories of them. But for Cleveland Baby Boomers—that enormous generation born between 1946 and 1964—"the" murder will always be that of Beverly Jarosz in 1964.

A generation's nightmare: Beverly Jarosz.

It is by far the most celebrated—if untold—Cleveland murder of the 1960s, and the crime that this author is most frequently asked about. It is also "the" murder that most shocked him personally, as he was the same age as the victim when it occurred. Now, 40 years on and no nearer to a solution, it is time the story was told.

The crowning irony of Beverly Jarosz's last day was that almost all of it was routinely mundane. A bright, personable, attractive girl, 16-year-old Beverly was still enjoying her Christmas break from Marymount High School as December 28, 1964 dawned. It was a cold but dry day, and Beverly's main concern was to hang out with her classmates Barbara Klonowski and Margie Gorney, both of whom also lived in Garfield Heights. Beverly and Barbara intended to get together with Margie at the latter's home that afternoon, and their plan hinged on Barbara's coming over to Beverly's home at 10921 Thornton Avenue.

It was a typical vacation day for Beverly. Sometime early that morning, Beverly's mother left for her job at the Gellin Co. at 1111 Carnegie Avenue. A short time later, Thaddeus, Beverly's father, left to go to his firm, the Universal Lighting and Manufacturing Co. at 3559 East 83rd Street. Sometime about 10:30 a.m., Beverly and

Beverly's Parents Believe She Knew Her Murderer

Cleveland Press, January 4, 1965.

her 12-year-old sister Carol left the two-story, six-room Jarosz bungalow and walked over to visit their grandmother, Maria Vanek, at her 9535 Dorothy Avenue home. Both girls were seen leaving their home by neighbor Julia Prochaska, 57, of 10908 Thornton Avenue.

Beverly and Carol had lunch at Mrs. Vanek's home and chatted with her. About 12:30 p.m., Beverly left to keep her appointment at home with Barbara Klonowski. She was waiting for a bus on Turney Road when a neighbor saw her and told her 18-year-old son to give her a ride home. He did so, and Beverly got back to her house shortly before 1 p.m. She entered her home by the side door. She climbed two stairs to the kitchen and put her purse and a book on the dinette table. She turned on the radio on the dining room table. As it began to play the soothing classical strains of her favorite station, WCLV-FM, she draped her coat on the banister of the stairway to the second floor. Then, as she went upstairs to change her sweater, the telephone rang.

It was apparently a business call from a Steve Stankowicz, who was trying to get in touch with Thaddeus Jarosz. Beverly took his message and scrawled a note about it by the telephone. Then she called a girlfriend and her mother. A few minutes later, probably about 1:20 p.m., Maria Vanek called. Beverly answered the telephone but told her grandmother she couldn't stay on the telephone because she was expecting Barbara at any minute. Beverly may have even thought she saw Barbara at the side door, waiting to get in the Jarosz home . . .

If there was someone at the side door while Beverly was talking to Mrs. Vanek, it wasn't Barbara Klonowski. As prearranged, Barbara was dropped off by her mother in front of the Jarosz home about 1:25 p.m. She walked up the driveway to the front door. She rang the doorbell. There was no answer, so she went to the side door. The outside storm door was locked but Barbara could see that the inner door was wide open. She could even see into the Jarosz kitchen, but there was no sign of Beverly. She knocked on the door. No answer. She knocked on it again. Still no answer, and what was odder still was that Barbara could hear a radio playing loudly inside. Then, about 1:28 p.m., as she was still standing at the side door, she heard a loud thump coming from inside the house. At the time she seemed to have thought it sounded like a dresser being knocked over. Later, she would come to believe that it was the sound of Beverly Jarosz fighting for her life in the upstairs bedroom.

After several minutes of knocking, Barbara went back to the front door. She stood there for about five minutes, thumbing a magazine she found in the mailbox and becoming more and more irritated. Finally, probably about 1:35 p.m., Barbara decided that she had simply been "stood up" by her friend Beverly. She walked to the corner of Granger and Turney Roads, where an acquaintance spotted her and gave her a ride home.

Later that afternoon, Margie Gorney telephoned Barbara to ask why she and Beverly hadn't shown up. Barbara herself was still upset. "I couldn't figure it out," she recalled later. "Beverly was a very reliable girl and I was worried." As the afternoon wore on, she became concerned enough to call Beverly's house. When there was no answer she telephoned Maria Vanek. Mrs. Vanek called Beverly's mother Eleanor, and Eleanor called Thaddeus Jarosz at work. He left immediately for home.

When Thaddeus got home, about 4:15 p.m., he found the back door, normally locked, unlocked. Going to the side door, he found the storm door closed—but not locked—and the inner door wide open. The door to the kitchen was also open, and the radio was blaring loudly from the dining room. Finding no sign of Beverly, he went upstairs to the bedroom she shared with her sister Carol. It was a small room, with two beds for Beverly and Carol. When Thaddeus entered it, he found Beverly lying face down next to her bed. Her left leg was hooked over her bed, and her right leg was

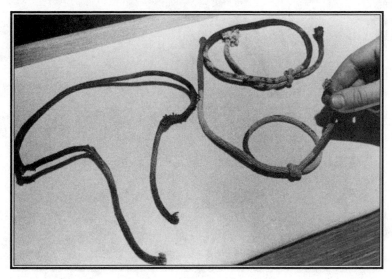

The murder weapon.

stretched out on the floor. A throw rug lay near her body. There was a hole in the low ceiling above the bed, about 9 by 5 inches in diameter. There was blood everywhere, and Beverly Jarosz was very, very dead. Thaddeus called the Garfield Heights police at 4:20 p.m.

It was a killing of almost unparalleled ferocity. Garfield Heights police captain William Horrigan, who led the investigation of Beverly's murder, spoke the blunt truth when he said, "It's the worst killing I've ever seen. It's brutal . . . horrible." Beverly Jarosz had been stabbed between 40 and 42 times with a sharp knife about five inches long. There were slashes on each side of her face, one from ear to chin, one from her Adam's apple to her ear. There were cuts all over her fingers and hands, probably "defensive" wounds suffered as she fought against the repeatedly stabbing blade. And there was a piece of rope lying across her neck.

Actually, there were three pieces of rope, each about 20 inches long. Two of them, knotted with loops, lay under her body. But the one by her neck was the crucial strand, because that was the rope her killer had strangled her with, even as he repeatedly stabbed her with his knife. It was covered with blood and had fray marks on it,

The scene of the crime.

indicating that Beverly's killer had struck it several times with his knife as he pulled it tighter and tighter around her neck.

The investigators of Beverly's death were puzzled from the beginning by several anomalies in her killing. Although the killer had ripped her lower garments off, he had not sexually assaulted her. There were nine wounds in her back, in clusters of threes for no apparent reason. And, although she was found wearing a sweater, there were more wounds in her back than corresponding holes in her sweater. Nor could the police account for the hole in the ceiling above her body. Was it punched out by Beverly's foot or arm during her death struggle? Or was it caused by the leg, arm, foot, or weapon of her killer?

Even more puzzling to investigators, then and now, was how such a terrible crime could have happened to that girl in that house at that time. Beverly Jarosz was notoriously timid about letting strangers in the house. She would not let meter readers in the house when she was alone. Indeed, she had been known to lock her own parents out of the house for fear of answering the door. This circumstance impelled both Beverly's family and homicide investigators to conclude that she had been slain by someone she knew and

Police Ask to Fingerprint Neighbors of Slain Girl

Cleveland Press, December 31, 1964.

had willingly let into her house. As Thaddeus Jarosz put it a week after her murder:

> I'm sort of inclined to believe it was someone she knew—but maybe not too well. Someone who knew her movements from her friends. I think it's somebody who was watching her and planning it all along. It's almost foolish to expect that a stranger would walk in and not know what to expect.

Someone she knew—but who? If it *was* someone she knew, we're certainly no closer to knowing who it was than those who sought the answer in 1964. Beverly Jarosz, by all accounts, was a steady, studious, intelligent, and well-balanced teenager, a daughter any parent would be proud to have. Passionately interested in literature and music, she dreamed of becoming a Latin teacher someday and frequently supplemented her educational opportunities with trips to the Cleveland Museum of Art and by listening to classical music. She liked to write poetry, and she volunteered her time at nearby Marymount Hospital. She was 5 feet, 6 inches, 130 pounds, and had blue eyes and light brown hair. She had boyfriends and she dated some, but she was far from being, as the phrase was in those bygone days, "boy-crazy." So who could she have known that would do something this awful to her?

Beverly Jarosz was as innocent as she seemed, but there were hints of an ominous presence hanging over her before her death. Sometime in July 1964, a mysterious package had appeared in the Jarosz mailbox. It was a gift-wrapped and beribboned Higbee's box, and inside of it was a sterling silver bracelet and ring. On the box were written the words, "To Beverly"—but there was no hint as to the identity of the giver. Eleanor Jarosz would recall that Beverly was understandably frightened by the anonymous gift, and that she immediately shut the door and pulled down all the shades in the house. Nor was she pleased when a second unsolicited gift for her appeared at the Jarosz back door a month later. This time it was a bracelet and pin in a plain box. There were no more gifts after that. But in the weeks preceding her murder, someone began calling the Jarosz home. Whenever a member of the family answered the telephone, the unidentified caller would hang up. The last telephone call had come in early December. It was hardly a leap of logic for lawmen to conclude that the anonymous caller and the phantom jewelry giver might be one and the same as Beverly's killer.

The Beverly Jarosz murder sparked the biggest Cleveland-area manhunt since the disappearance of Beverly Potts in 1951. Aided by the Scientific Investigation Unit of the Cleveland Police Department and Cuyahoga County coroner Samuel Gerber and his staff, Garfield Heights Police Department officers put in thousands of hours of work trying to crack the Jarosz murder. Among them, these law enforcement professionals interviewed over 1,100 persons, took written statements from 531, and fingerprinted 250 persons. Authorities patiently checked out hundreds of tips telephoned into the Garfield Police station, many of them the crank notions of unhinged, credulous, or simply cruel persons. Among the latter was a man who repeatedly called the Cleveland police, daring them to catch him for Beverly's murder. Police sleuths searched every inch of the area around the Jarosz home, not neglecting gutters, drainpipes, rooftops, and shrubs. They repeatedly staked out Thornton Avenue during its busiest traffic hours, asking motorists if they had seen anything there on December 28. On the next garbage pickup day after the murder, Garfield Heights detectives rode the garbage trucks in the murder neighborhood, examining the collected trash for murder clues. The Cleveland city carpentry shop even replicated samples of the damaged bedroom ceiling, so that tests could determine exactly what had punched a hole in it.

Police investigators initially put their highest hopes in the physical evidence of the case. The murder rope, containing distinctive red and blue strands in its core, was believed to be the strongest clue. It was eventually identified by Ted Moss of the Southeastern Cordage Co. as window sash cord that had seen some service as clothesline. Its manufacture was eventually traced to the Schuford Mills Co. in Hickory, North Carolina. But no further link to the rope's purchaser or user was ever found.

There were some equally tantalizing clues furnished by supposed eyewitnesses in the case. The most intriguing was James Krawczyk, 50, a neighbor whose living room window at 5160 Turney Road faced the Jarosz house, 250 feet away. He had been out on strike against the White Motor Co., and he told police he was sitting by that window about 1:45 p.m. on the murder day. Glancing up from writing some checks, he had seen a young man walking down the Jarosz driveway toward the street. The man crossed the street, got into a 1958 or 1960 Buick parked between two other cars, and drove east in the direction of East 112th Street. Krawczyk described the young man as about 20 to 25 years old, between 5 feet, 8 inches and 6 feet in height, wearing a light-colored jacket and tight-fitting trousers. The story was an interesting one, but police could find no one else in the neighborhood who had seen the young man. And Barbara Klonowski could not remember any cars being parked on Thornton Avenue when she left the Jarosz home.

There were other clues in the case providing intense but transitory excitement. On January 11, 1965, exactly two weeks after Beverly's murder, 17-year-old Michael Lindley Bane shot himself to death in the basement of his home in Garfield Heights. In the aroused atmosphere triggered by Beverly's murder, some were quick to conclude that the suicide might be linked to Beverly's slaying. It was not, nor was the report that a fortyish man with a wounded hand had shown up at the Garfield Heights Medical Center at 2 p.m. on December 28. He had left without getting aid, but police were determined to find him. They did—and he turned out to be a 51-year-old rubbish collector who had cut his hand on December 20 while trying to trim a Christmas tree with a hatchet.

A more interesting but far murkier tale was told by a West Side woman to Jarosz investigators. She said that she had been in a laundromat on Turney Road at 1 a.m. on December 29. She noticed some blood spots around the front door, and then, about 10 minutes later, a suspicious-looking young man came in through the back door. He said he was the night watchman—but she later discovered that the laundromat did not employ one. Another suggestive incident was a report about a stolen 1964 Chevrolet. Someone had taken it from in front of 10800 Langton Avenue on the morning of Beverly's murder. That afternoon, perhaps two hours after the slaying, someone blew up the car and left it to burn in a field off East 177th Street. Was it the car used by Beverly's murderer, and subsequently destroyed as potentially incriminating evidence? Of such vague and unsturdy stuff were the Beverly Jarosz murder clues composed.

There were also a few more exotic suspects for police to deal with. One was a 15-year-old delinquent youth arrested in Athens, Ohio, on January 21. When apprehended, he was carrying a dufflebag containing knives, a pistol, lots of ammunition—and a bloodstained T-shirt! He turned out to be an aggressive runaway from Bridgewater, Pennsylvania, and the spots on his T-shirt proved to be varnish. High hopes also were entertained for a suspect held in Detroit on a local strangling, but he, too, was able to prove an alibi.

Not that there weren't plenty of suspects left for interrogation. Everyone who had ever known Beverly was interrogated by police, and quite a number of Jarosz friends and neighbors underwent polygraph examinations. Some of the most important witnesses, like Barbara Klonowski, underwent repeated interrogations, as weary police forced them to go over and over the same material again, in hopes that some random clue might surface.

The Garfield Heights police, aided by virtually all of the police forces in Cuyahoga County, left nothing undone in their relentless, painstaking investigation. Nor did Cleveland's newspapers, especially Louis Seltzer's *Cleveland Press*. Seltzer was then in the twilight of his journalism career, his reputation somewhat tarnished by his editorial handling of the Marilyn Sheppard murder. But Seltzer threw himself into the manhunt for Beverly's killer with the same gusto he had brought to previous dragnets for the killers of Sheila Ann Tuley and Beverly Potts. On December 30, sensing that the murder investigation was already stalled, he committed his newspaper to a $5,000 reward for Beverly in a front-page editorial. Police frustrations with the case had surfaced that morning in comments by an unidentified lawman: "We're no nearer a solution than we were when the body was found. Maybe, for all I know, we're farther away from one." Cognizant of such feelings, and shocked by the horror of the crime, Seltzer argued that Beverly's murder had to be solved, lest similar atrocities be perpetrated:

> If it could happen there it could happen anywhere. Only by tracking down the slayer, obtaining the evidence, and presenting it to a court can a repetition elsewhere be prevented. So long as the murderer of Beverly Jarosz is roaming about free, he constitutes a menace to every other girl or woman in any other neighborhood.

Seltzer's passionate plea and reward offer produced no tangible results. Two weeks later on January 14, he doubled the reward to $10,000. He might as well have offered a million—the Beverly Jarosz case remained exactly where it had been since the afternoon of December 28. New suspects were hauled in, and almost as quickly cleared and released. Additional persons were questioned, then questioned again and again. Garfield Heights police sergeant Vincent Raymond well expressed the frustration of his fellow officers with the perplexing case the police called "Black Monday":

> Here you have a well-bred girl from a good family. Unblemished background. No jilted suitor. No problems. It gets to be an obsession when you live with a thing like this. If I were younger, I'd give 20 years of my life to get this guy.

Inevitably, life eventually resumed its even tenor in the weeks after Beverly's murder. Wearing a party dress and holding a crystal rosary in her hands, Beverly was viewed by mourners at the Golubski funeral home at 9811 Garfield Boulevard on December 30. Three days later, her funeral was held at St. Therese Church in Garfield Heights before her interment in Calvary Cemetery. One thousand persons attended her last rites, and a spray of carnations

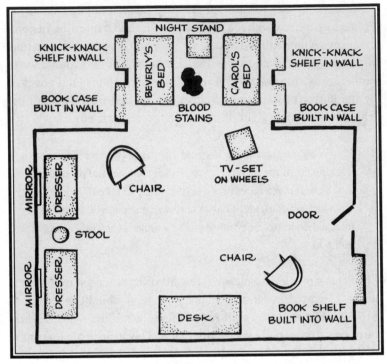

Diagram of the murder scene, Beverly Jarosz bedroom.

was placed on her casket before it was lowered into the earth. On February 4, 1965, the Reverend Patrick Shields of St. Therese Church blessed the Jarosz home as Thaddeus, Eleanor, and Carol returned to the scene of their family tragedy. The locks on the doors were changed, and their telephone number was changed. A scholarship fund in Beverly's memory was established at Marymount High School.

Virtually everything ever known or intelligently surmised about Beverly's murder was stated by Coroner Samuel Gerber at a "murder clinic" for lawmen and reporters on January 14, two weeks after the murder. Reconstructing Beverly's movements from the moment her grandmother telephoned at 1:20 p.m., Gerber guessed that the call was cut short by Beverly espying someone at the door. She thought it was Barbara Klonowski. It was not, but it turned out to be someone Beverly knew, and trusted enough to let him—or possibly her—in through the side door. That explained the lack of any signs of forcible entry at the house. After chatting for several minutes with the visitor, Beverly went upstairs to change her sweater. While she was doing so, her visitor turned up the radio in the dining room. He stealthily crept up the stairs to her room with the three strands of rope and a knife in his hands. He came up behind her with the unlooped rope and . . .

Although her 40-odd stab wounds were potentially lethal, it was the strangulation that killed Beverly. She must have fought like a tiger against whoever held the rope, which is why her assailant stabbed her repeatedly at the same time he pulled both ends of the rope around her neck. Both he and Beverly must have been covered with blood by the time the struggle was over. He then stood up on Beverly's bed, punching a hole in the low ceiling out of sheer frustration. Aware that Barbara Klonowski was still at the door below, the killer must have waited several minutes until he was certain she had departed. He then walked down the driveway, perhaps observed by neighbor James Krawczyk, and disappeared forever.

When showing the graphic murder photos and evidence to his audience of reporters and police, Gerber said, "I hope that these pictures will be shown to a jury someday. This was as vicious a crime as I have seen in my 29 years as coroner." Gerber never got his chance with a jury. The days after Beverly's murder passed by, then the months, then the years, then the decades. It's been almost 40 years since Beverly Jarosz opened the door to a killer, and there has been no progress in the case during that time. Captain William Horrigan, who conducted the original investigation, eventually retired from police work in 1977. In 1989, he commented on the case to a *Plain Dealer* reporter. He claimed in that interview to have had a pretty good idea of who committed the murder even before Beverly was buried:

> I had who I was convinced was the killer the second day after the murder. But I couldn't get enough evidence to prosecute him. He passed several interrogations. But I have kept track of him through the years. You couldn't use his name anyway. But I hope one day he'll blow his top and talk. And, if he has a bad accident, and is on his death bed, I'll be there to hear his confession.

It's worth pointing out that Horrigan's comments have a familiar ring. Virtually every retired policeman has a story to tell about how he knew the "real" killer of some unsolved crime. And how the criminal couldn't be prosecuted because: 1) he was dead or in an insane asylum; 2) he was related to someone important, preferably a mayor or police chief; or 3) there was not enough hard evidence to convince a jury of his guilt. Such things were said after the unsolved Potter murder in 1931 and the unsolved disappearance of Beverly Potts in 1951, and they will no doubt be said about unsolved crimes of the present and future. That doesn't make them true—which is why our system of justice demands that evidence be placed before a jury.

It also needs to be said that the Jarosz case remains perhaps the ugliest murder in Cleveland history. Since Beverly's killer was likely known to her, popular opinion has always been ready to cast suspicion at any family member or friend in the years since her death. Just last year, the author received a letter from a woman interested in the case. She thought I should "know" that one of the local priests had never—to her knowledge—been investigated as a suspect in the Jarosz case. To such minds I can only repeat the caution of King Edward III: *Honi soit qui mal y pense* (Evil be to him who evil thinks). And to Beverly Jarosz, may she rest in peace, always the sweet girl she was before becoming the ultimate nightmare for her generation of Clevelanders.

Chapter 26

"STRAIGHTEN THEM OUT"

The Celia Barger Horror (1953)

Over the past decade and a half the author has encountered over a thousand tales of Cleveland woe. Sifted, researched, and indexed, they yet crowd his home with their voluminous and disturbing contents. Somewhat over a hundred of those stories have found their way into four published volumes, an Internet book, and divers magazine and newsletter articles. Many of them, especially those involving crimes against children and defenseless women, have made him—and, he suspects, most of his readers—shudder with horror at the evil that can lurk in the hearts of Clevelanders. Having now come to the end of his Cleveland tale-telling, he bids farewell to both Cleveland and its considerable burden of historical woe. What follows is the worst Cleveland story he knows.

Physicians are required to have licenses. Automobile drivers have licenses. Even dog owners must have licenses. Parents, on the other hand, do not. Given that absurd reality, it's a reasonable notion that Helen and Celia Barger should never have been born. It's a terrible thing to say, or even think—but consider just how unwanted and unlucky those two children were.

Their father, John G. Barger, one of 10 children, grew up in rural Ohio. Enlisting in the Army Air Force in 1941, he served through World War II. Afterwards, he decided to stay with the Air Force, eventually achieving the rank of technical sergeant. Sent to Korea when the war broke out in 1950, he spent 18 months there and endured 144 combat missions before being routed back to the States. He also acquired a wife, Sally, which is where the Barger story really begins.

Many military service marriages don't work out, and the Barger union was no exception. Married to John in 1944, Sally gave birth to their first daughter, Helen, in 1945 and a second daughter, Celia, in 1947. Despite their offspring, though, the marriage didn't thrive, and by 1949—just two years after Celia's birth—conjugal relations had deteriorated to the point where John had to put the girls into St. Peter's Orphanage in Memphis, Tennessee. The details of

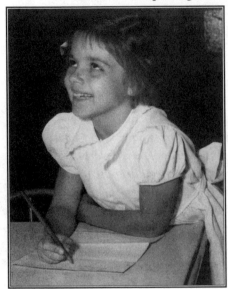

The survivor:
Helen Barger, 8 (1953).

the marital breakup are sketchy, but the formal ground for John's eventual petition of divorce was Sally's "gross neglect of duty." It is likewise suggestive that it was John—not Sally—who got custody of their children, an unusual divorce outcome in the 1950s. The official end of the marriage came on March 16, 1953. As it happened, however, Celia and Helen's problems were just beginning.

With no mother in the picture, John Barger was hard pressed to find care for his two daughters. When they were released from the orphanage in June 1952, he persuaded his sister, Anna Mulato, 53, to take them into her home in Mingo Junction, Ohio. Already coping with chronic high blood pressure, Anna soon found the two sisters too hard to handle. After she told John she couldn't take care of them anymore, he asked his brother Matthew and Matthew's wife Mary, both 31 years old, to take them into their home in Cleveland. It seems to have been a temporary arrangement, for the girls were only with the Bargers for two months at their 1339 West 83rd Street home. In November 1952, Helen went back to live with Anna Mulato, and Celia was taken by John's sister, Susan Urzdich, 36, also living in Mingo Junction. Once again, the girls were too hard to handle: Anna Mulato's blood

One happy family: Celia, David, and Helen
Barger (1953).

pressure wasn't getting any lower, and Susan Urzdich had her
hands more than full with three boys of her own. In February 1953,
the girls went back to the Bargers in Cleveland. John Barger, never
heroic about assuming responsibility for what happened, would
later insist that it was his ex-wife's idea that the girls live with them
again.

The terms on which they returned were bitterly disputed—after
the tragedy later that year. For the most part, Matthew and Mary
insisted they had only taken the girls because John Barger pled so
piteously to have them taken off his hands. John, on the other hand,
would later recall that they begged for the children, especially as
Mary Barger, owing to the consequences of several medical operations, could not conceive offspring of her own. Indeed, in a statement to Parma police—later repudiated at her trial—Mary admitted that she had only taken the girls on a second time after
receiving written assurances from John G. Barger that she could
keep them until they reached their majority because, as tender-
hearted Mary put it, "I didn't want to become attached to them and

have him take them from me." In all of her statements after the fact, however, Mary tended to downplay the material fact that John G. Barger also agreed to pay the Bargers $200 a month—most of his Air Force salary—to take care of his girls.

Whatever the motivation, the girls moved into the Bargers' West Side home in February 1953. We'll never really know what they were like before the awfulness began. Today, a half-century later, their pictures stare out at us, appealing girls with melting smiles, seemingly pleading to please and to be loved. It's clear, however, even discounting the lying Bargers, that there was more than sugar and spice in Helen and Celia's makeup. Chronically unwanted children, they had spent three years in an orphanage and then been shuttled from one reluctant relative to another before coming again to the Bargers. A number of witnesses could testify that their personalities were badly damaged by such experiences. Dr. Evelyn Stein, the girls' family doctor who treated them several times in 1953, thought they were "emotionally disturbed." Mrs. Dorothy Sullivan, the owner of the Barger flat on West 83rd, would testify that the girls were "afraid to talk." Anna Mulato said that they were "problem children," especially Celia, who was given to screaming and head-beating temper tantrums. As Mulato put it at Mary and Matthew's trial, Celia would "scream out of clear sky and throw her head against a pillow. I couldn't do anything for her." Susan Urzdich echoed Mulato's experience, stating that Helen and Celia were "too difficult to handle." She, too, also found Celia the greater burden, complaining, "[Celia] needed extra special care and demanded more attention than my three boys."

Whatever their merits or defects, Helen and Celia entered a special kind of hell the day they returned to the Bargers in February 1953. Mary Barger, already stressed out by the recent adoption of a two-year-old son, David, was in no mood to tolerate any misbehavior on the part of Helen and Celia. Matthew, a bricklayer who worked extended shifts at the Jones & Laughlin steel plant, was often absent from the home and, in any case, completely dominated by Mary. So almost all the discipline given the girls was devised and administered by Mary Barger. And what discipline it was . . . meted out by the homely, heavyset, 200-pound Mary.

The wicked stepparents: Mary and Matthew Barger (1953).

The early 1950s were a different world from ours. Child abuse, as with wife-beating, was not acknowledged and dealt with as openly and effectively as it is nowadays. One could still hear the expression "spare the rod and spoil the child" uttered without apology, and children were often subject to levels of corporal punishment that went well beyond what would be legally or even socially acceptable today. It is clear, however, that Mary Barger transgressed even the lax punitive norms of her era from the day Helen and Celia entered her home.

We don't know the truth of Mary's assertions about the girls' behavior. According to Mary, Helen and Celia could—and frequently would—vomit and defecate just to spite her. Often refusing to go to sleep, they would scream uncontrollably and thrash to the point of hurting themselves by falling down and running into things. The screaming seems probable, but the more extreme and self-destructive behavior seems improbable at best. Landlady Dorothy Sullivan testified that the girls were forced to eat meals, so the vomiting may have been a natural reaction to their feeding. What isn't debatable is the fact that Mary Barger punished the girls with hideous, persistent, and remarkable ferocity. Both girls were

'Ice Torture' Of Dead Girl Laid to Pair

A 16-year-old niece of Matthew and Mary Barger today described to police an ice water "torture" treatment she said they inflicted on six-year-old Celia Barger, whose death now is under investigation.

The story of Shelva Peterson was given to Parma Police Chief Lester Roeper and Detective Virgil Costley as they re-questioned her about punishment meted to Celia, daughter of Barger's brother, T-Sgt. John Barger.

Shelva came here late in May from Bergholz to live with her aunt and uncle and to serve as a baby-sitter. She previously had told of beatings given Celia and her sister, Helen Barger, 8, and of watching her aunt apply a hot iron to the sisters' bodies.

Tells of Icy Bath

"Shelva tells us that late in June, when the family lived at 1389 W. 83d St., she was present when both little girls were put into a bathtub full of ice water," Chief Roeper said.

"She said her aunt and uncle chipped 25 pounds of ice into the water before putting the girls in the tub. She also said that Mrs. Barger pushed both of the children's heads under water and held them there for a short time."

Heart Muscles Injured

Chief Roeper conferred with Richard de Nobel, Parma city solicitor, to determine what charge to place against the Barger couple after Coroner Samuel R. Gerber ruled Celia's death "was one of violence due to multiple contusions all over her body."

Dr. Gerber said the "contusions

Continued on Page 5, Column 1

Cleveland News, August 20, 1953.

beaten frequently during the six months they lived with the Bargers. The beatings began in the basement at 1339 West 83rd, where Mary, or sometimes Matthew, would take them so Mrs. Sullivan wouldn't hear their mistreatment. Matthew was a traditionalist, usually spanking them with his hands or using his belt. Mary, on the other hand, was a creative and sadistic abuser, slapping, kicking, pounding, and pummeling the girls over every part of their bodies. Sometimes she used a shoe, sometimes a board, sometimes a two-foot stick. By the time Mary got caught, Helen and Celia would be bruised and scarred on virtually every part of their small bodies.

But that wasn't even the worst of it. Mary Barger was a truly demented sadist, and it is clear that something had snapped in her angry, frustrated head. As the summer of 1953 came on, she began to devise new, ingenious punishments for the two girls. In these tortures, she was often aided by her niece, Shelva Jean Peterson, 16, who had come for the summer from Amsterdam, Ohio, to "help

Aunt Mary" with the children. And how did Shelva Jean help? Well, one of the things she did was to assist Mary in bathing the girls. Acting on what she claimed was the advice of Dr. Evelyn Stein, Mary Barger had her husband procure 25-pound blocks of ice. Chopping it into chunks, she used it to concoct "ice baths," in which she forcibly immersed the girls when they had "tantrums" or could not go to sleep. "Watch Celia fight the water!" she would cackle, as she plunged the terrified girl under the water for interminable seconds. Sometimes, as an alternative chastisement, she would simply lock the girls in small, dark closets. Every night they were forced to sleep on the floor of a second-floor bedroom, without a mattress or pillow, just a sheet and blanket.

Things just got worse when the Bargers moved to 5588 West 24th Street in Parma on July 23, 1953. More frequent ice baths and beatings quickly ensued. But the Parma house had a bigger basement, and Mary knew just what to do with it. First, she sent Shelva to the nearby John Muir Elementary School playground at West 24th Street and Fortune Avenue. There, acting on Mary's instructions, Shelva collected stones of various sizes and brought them back to the basement. Taking the stones, Mary Barger mixed them with nutshells and spread them on the basement floor. What followed were repeated punishment sessions in which Mary would make the girls kneel on the stones until she was satisfied with their repentance.

One can imagine the mental condition of Helen and Celia Barger as August 1953 arrived. Constantly beaten and tortured by their inventive aunt, they must have been in a traumatized psychological state like that of extermination camp victims. And they had no recourse or means of escape. Although somewhat reluctant, their cousin Shelva was a cowed accomplice to Mary's irrepressible sadism. As Shelva explained her complicity later, "I thought of calling the police but I didn't know, being in a strange city." And Matthew Barger left everything to his wife, punctuating her creative torments with beatings of his own. John Barger, the girls' father, was a distant presence who, in any case, had no inkling of their harsh treatment. Indeed, he visited the Barger home several times that year, and the girls were too traumatized to utter a word about the terror of their daily lives. Mary Barger would later claim—with no proof or corroborating evidence—that she wrote to John Barger "about 35 times," begging him to take his children back during the spring and summer of 1953. Whatever the truth, he did not, and the situation lurched toward its inevitable tragic climax.

That climax came on an early August afternoon in the Parma basement. Matthew was not home, and Shelva and Mary took Celia down to the basement for a punishment session. At some point during that session, Mary went berserk. Picking up a stone the size of a baseball, she began beating the kneeling Celia with it. She probably hit her 10 or a 12 times with great force. Mary may have blacked out then: 45 minutes later, she would later recall, she had no memory of the beating when a shocked Shelva told her what she had done. Even tolerant Matthew Barger thought this incident was a bit on the extreme side. When a frightened Mary Barger had him look at Celia's bruises, he ordered Mary to get her stone-and-shell "mess" out of the basement. But he did not call a doctor for the obviously badly injured Celia. He would later excuse this lapse by explaining that his job made a doctor visit inconvenient. And so the punishments continued for another two weeks. On at least one occasion Helen and Celia were burned on their legs with a hot iron, and Mary Barger burned both of the girls with lighted matches.

The end came on Tuesday, August 18. It's difficult to reconstruct exactly what happened that day. The Bargers lied about everything at their trial, particularly about the events of that day and the next. The only living witnesses, Helen Barger and Shelva Peterson, were both young, severely traumatized, and sometimes unreliable witnesses. But what follows is likely what must have happened . . .

One of the Bargers, perhaps both of them, beat Celia Barger that evening, either for vomiting up some chili or soiling her pants. When she and Helen would not—or could not—go to sleep, Mary Barger had a bright idea about how to make the girls tired enough to sleep. After Shelva got the girls dressed, about 10 p.m., the entire family went to the John Muir playground, already wreathed in darkness. Mary, standing at one end, commanded the girls to run to Matthew, standing at the other end. Then they had to run back to

Says Tortured Girl Died in Forced Run

Sister Tells of Hours of Racing Until Victim Collapsed

By TOM BRADY

Possibility that six-year-old Celia Barger ran herself to death under command of the aunt and uncle held in County Jail on manslaughter charges today sent Parma police into a new phase of their investigation.

The aunt and uncle, Mary and Matthew Barger, have admitted mistreatment and torture of the dead girl and her sister, Helen, 8. The aunt is charged with manslaughter, the uncle with aiding and abetting a manslaughter.

The Bargers will receive a preliminary hearing on the manslaughter charge before Parma Municipal Judge George P. Allen at 9:30 a.m. on Aug. 31. They will be represented by Attorney H. C. Western.

The new lead came through this reporter who interviewed Helen in Juvenile Detention Home.

In repeating her earlier stories of how the aunt and uncle forced the two children to run at John Muir Elementary School Playground Tuesday night to make them tired so they'd sleep, Helen said.

Cleveland Press, August 22, 1953.

Mary, back to Matthew, back to Mary . . . and on and on in their run to death.

The 1950s *were* different. If you don't believe it, consider what happened next. About 11:45 p.m., at least an hour into the playground run, the Bargers' odd family tableau attracted the attention of Albert Mabin and Steve Kornajcik, two Parma police patrolmen cruising by in their police car. When the officers asked the Bargers why their children were running back and forth in a playground at 15 minutes to midnight, they explained that they were trying to make them sleepy. "Well, that's a good way to tire them out," said one of the patrolmen, and they got back into their patrol car and left. Painting an even more bizarre scene, one of the policemen would later state that the entire family was still dressed in their pajamas.

It isn't clear what happened after that. The children ran for some time—Cleveland newspaper headlines would later proclaim that Celia was "run to death." She may have been conscious when the Bargers left the playground; she may have collapsed there. Helen, the most trustworthy witness, told two different versions of the early morning events. But we do know that the same two Parma policemen, officers Mabin and Kornajcik, were driving on Broadview Road about 5 a.m. when they suddenly spotted the Bargers in their car. Mary and Matthew had Celia with them, and they were speeding north toward Pearl. The two policemen pursued them to their destination: Deaconess Hospital on Pearl Road.

Matthew brought Celia into the hospital at 5:15 a.m. Her hair was soaking wet—perhaps another nocturnal ice bath?—and nurse Lydia Fulkerson watched as Matthew casually tossed the limp Celia onto a table. He told Fulkerson that his niece was still breathing and needed a doctor to look at her. Fulkerson took a good look at Celia's body and told Matthew, "There's no use doing that anymore."

Fulkerson had seen enough in her brief examination of Celia's battered body to know what was going on. The corpse was a mass of bruises, abrasions, and suspicious-looking scars, so she asked Mary if she knew how the child had incurred such injuries. Mary replied that her injuries had resulted from a fall off a swing a few days before. When a persistent Fulkerson asked if she hadn't noticed the severity of her injuries while bathing Celia, Mary snapped that she didn't bathe her, she left that to Shelva. Minutes later, Mary and Matthew Barger were taken into custody and turned over to the Parma police. Several hours later, Helen and Shelva were taken into custody by authorities, who discovered more burns, bruises, and scratches on Helen.

Given their initial behavior after arrest, it's unlikely that the Bargers could have beaten the rap. Charged that very day with first-degree manslaughter, Mary only held out for 12 hours before signing a nine-page statement in which she confessed to everything: the beatings, the rocks and shells, the ice baths, the burning with the hot iron, and the assault with the rock. Later, talking to reporters, she nonetheless tried to justify her inhuman behavior, painting herself as the tormented victim:

> Maybe the fact that I couldn't have children of my own had something to do with this. They'd throw temper tantrums, they'd throw themselves down the stairs, beat their heads against the walls. They kicked me, they bit me, they vomited. They lied. They never told the truth. Their father didn't care for the girls. I

wrote the father in the Army, but I never heard from him. I probably would have beaten my own children if they'd done things
like that. After I realized what I did to the girls I was sorry. But
I knew I would do it again. . . . I feel terrible about all of this. I
just completely lost control of my temper. I suppose I do deserve
punishment.

Perhaps unsurprisingly, Mary also mentioned that her father had
beaten her when she misbehaved as a child growing up in Amsterdam, Ohio.

Charged with aiding and abetting manslaughter, Matthew
Barger was initially more contrite and less defiant. "I know I'm
done," he blurted to reporters, "I don't care what happens to me."
Signing a statement in which he admitted spanking and beating the
girls a bit, he blamed most of their rough treatment on his wife,
repeatedly saying, "I don't know what happened. I don't know how
it happened." At the same time he justified the ice baths, claiming
they were done on the advice of a doctor. As for Mary's behavior,
well, as he said, "She's a very good housekeeper, keeps a house
spotless. Ask anyone. . . . I never interfered with my wife. She said
she was just straightening the kids out. The kids didn't seem to
mind." In a more rueful moment he remarked, "I guess my mother
was right when she told me on her deathbed not to marry my wife."

Even if the Bargers had denied their crimes, they could not
escape the damning statements of Helen Barger and Shelva Jean
Peterson. Speaking from the safety of the Cuyahoga County
Detention Home, Helen detailed the months of torture that had cli-
maxed in her sister's death. Her memory of the last scene at John
Muir playground was chilling:

Aunt Mary and Uncle Matthew took us to the schoolyard and
made us run to tire us out. We ran and ran and would try to stop,
but they would make us run again. they wouldn't let us stop. We
ran and ran all night. At 12 o'clock, 1 o'clock, 2 o'clock,
3 o'clock and I don't know how long until Celie fell down in the
grass. She couldn't get up . . . I knew she was dead. I said,
"What's wrong with Celie, Mommy," but she wouldn't answer

me. Celie was dead but she was still mad at us. She said, "Don't call me Mommy. I'm not your mother." Aunt Mary and Uncle Matthew were scared then. I knew they were scared because Celie was dead.

Still showing signs of her profound disorientation, Helen expressed her love for "Aunt Mary and Uncle Matthew" and plaintively asked, "They won't be in jail a long time, will they?"

Shelva Jean Peterson supported virtually all of Helen's story, telling of the ice baths and how she had held the girls while Mary burned them with matches or a hot iron in the basement. "What else could I do?" she told reporters. "I was brought up to do what I'm told."

Matthew Barger was put in the Parma jail, while Mary was initially incarcerated in the Cleveland Central Police Station jail, as Parma had no facilities for female prisoners. Within a couple of days they found themselves in the Cuyahoga County Jail, with Mary on the seventh floor and Matthew on the sixth. Meanwhile, Air Force Sgt. John Barger had been notified of his daughter's death. Given compassionate leave from Stewart Air Force Base in Smyrna, Tennessee, he was on a plane to Cleveland the day after his daughter's death. Arriving at Cleveland Hopkins Airport, he was stunned to discover, after seeing a newspaper, that his daughter Celia had not died in an automobile accident, as he had thought. Reunited with Helen that evening, he insisted that he did not hold a grudge against Matthew or Mary but that he wanted them to get the full penalty of the law. Dumbfounded at his children's fate, he recalled his recent visits, insisting, "I visited my daughters four or five times since I placed them with my brother and sister-in-law. They seemed happy and well fed. I can't figure it out. My brother was always kind to even animals."

After a careful autopsy by assistant Cuyahoga County coroner Lester Adelson, Celia was laid out for view at the F. H. Cranium Funeral Home, 6204 Detroit Avenue, on Friday evening, August 21. About a thousand persons, both friends and strangers, showed up to pay their last respects to the little girl in the big headlines. She was dressed in white with a white veil, her reddish hair was visible, and she clutched a rosary in her hands. There were many floral tributes, many from sympathizers who wanted to remain anonymous. Sometime late that night, after the public had departed, Celia's mother, Sally, slipped in to see her daughter and to murmur, it was said, something about "my share of the blame." The next morning a solemn Mass of the Angels was offered over the body of Celia at Our Lady of Mount Carmel Church at West 70th Street and Detroit Avenue. Later, she was buried in Holy Cross Cemetery.

Bound over to the grand jury on August 31, 1953, in separate hearings before Parma municipal judge George P. Allen, the Bargers were soon out on bail, $10,000 for Mary and $5,000 for Matthew. As expected, Mary was charged with first-degree manslaughter and Matthew with aiding and abetting it. Hardly concealing his contempt for Mary, Judge Allen publicly complained that "the facts in this case indicate that Mrs. Barger should face a charge of second-degree murder, rather than manslaughter."

Four months later, in January 1954, the Bargers went on trial before a three-judge panel composed of Judges Joseph Arti, B. D. Nicola, and Edward Blythin (later to become infamous as the partisan judge at the first Sam Sheppard trial). Represented by attorneys Phillip Barragate and Hyman C. Wedren, the Bargers were determined to contest every shred of evidence and testimony in the case, and courtroom spectators were not disappointed by the trial's theatrics.

The state's case was blunt and simple. Assistant Cuyahoga County prosecutor Dennis McGuire carefully described the injuries suffered by Celia Barger over a period of months, which, he argued, caused her death. Assistant Cuyahoga County coroner Lester Adelson had found no fewer than 25 significant internal and external injuries to Celia's body, and McGuire read out Adelson's numbing catalog in court: many scrapes and bruises, a crushed kidney, a damaged heart, and hemorrhages in the areas of the chest, heart, throat, and thymus gland. Some terrible things had happened to this defenseless child, McGuire asserted, and the state was going to prove that Mary and Matthew had done them.

Not so, responded Phillip Barragate for the defense. Echoing the Bargers' claims that Celia had been a willful, explosive, and self-destructive child, Barragate told the jury that Celia's death had been her own fault:

Shortly before her death she threw herself against an iron glider. The day before her death she threw herself down the basement steps from a landing and she landed on a tricycle. She died as a result of self-inflicted injuries.

Barragate also insisted, as per Mary Barger, that both children were in the habit of vomiting at will and throwing themselves against things to injure themselves. Summarizing his portrait of Mary and Matthew as loving foster parents, Barragate praised their charity in taking Helen and Celia into their home:

> The Bargers took them in and treated them with kindness. But because of a lack of parental love the girls were rebellious and uncontrollable.

It was one thing to say such things; it was another to prove them. Barragate failed utterly at his thankless task. He could not shake Adelson's confident belief that Celia's injuries could not have been self-inflicted. He couldn't shake Adelson's assertion that Celia's death had resulted from being beaten with a rock in early August. Adelson was adamant in his conviction that Celia's death was caused by the crushed kidney and heart failure.

Barragate had little better luck with Shelva Peterson, who testified for the state. Although she recalled one instance of Celia's throwing herself to the basement floor, she flatly denied that she had witnessed Celia throwing herself against a glider or down the Barger basement stairs onto a tricycle. Nor did Barragate win any points for Mary in his questions about the rock-beating incident in the basement:

> Barragate: How high did Mary Barger raise her hand?
> Peterson: Over her head.
> Barragate: Isn't that about four feet?
> Peterson: I don't know. I can't measure in feet.

Worse yet, Shelva brought a plenitude of specific detail to add verisimilitude to her memory of the crucial events. She recalled how Celia was half-naked at the time Mary beat her with a rock.

She remembered the color of the shoe Mary beat Celia with (a red loafer) and how Aunt Mary remarked that she could hit Celia and Helen "as often as she liked because the neighbors wouldn't be able to hear her."

Deaconess Hospital nurse Lydia Fulkerson followed Shelva on the stand, detailing Matthew's callous tossing of Celia's corpse and Mary Barger's evasive lies about the cause of her injuries. Then came Helen Barger, who calmly recalled the details of how she and her sister had been tortured and the macabre scene of their last night at John Muir playground.

Mary Barger got the chance to tell her side of the story on January 14, 1954. She didn't get very far that morning. Shortly after she took the stand, her lawyer interrupted her to tell her that the three presiding judges had just refused Barragate's motions for either a directed acquittal verdict or a reduction of the charge to assault and battery. Suddenly pitching forward, Mary Barger fell to the floor in what was later described as an "hysterical coma." Her sister Wilma rushed to her, slapping her cheeks in an effort to bring her out of it. Taken unconscious from the courtroom, Mary eventually revived and returned that afternoon and the next day to continue her version of the events. Characterizing the Barger children as willful demons, she reiterated her fiction that Celia had thrown herself into a glider "six or eight times." She repeated the tale that Celia had deliberately thrown herself down the basement stairs onto a tricycle, this time transposing the event to the last day of Celia's life. When asked why she didn't call a doctor after that incident, she replied that she didn't consider it an unusual occurrence. Crying almost constantly, Mary repeatedly denied that she had ever mistreated, must less tortured, her nieces. No, she had never burned the girls, although she admitted once lighting a match to frighten Helen. No, she had never made Shelva Jean hold the girls while she burned them. No, she had never hit them with anything but her hand or a loafer. Yes, she had once used an iron on the girls—but it was an unheated one. And yes, she had signed a nine-page statement on August 19, admitting virtually everything of which she was accused. But she had been abused by the Parma police, denied food for 12 hours after her arrest, and was never allowed to read the statement she had signed.

Mary's version of Celia's last night differed sharply from the versions offered by Helen and Shelva. No, Celia had not been beaten that evening. Mary's memory was that after Celia vomited, the girls were put to bed. They awoke about 11 p.m., so they were taken to the playground to run themselves sleepy. They returned home shortly after they were spotted by the police. Then, at 3 a.m., Celia awoke crying in pain. Mary could see that her stomach was bloated, so she had Shelva help give her an enema. When that didn't help, they gave her another, and when she lapsed into unconsciousness, Matthew drove them to the hospital.

Matthew Barger didn't fare any better on the stand than his wife. Crying so hard at one point that the trial had to be recessed, he repudiated the more damning parts of his signed confession and complained of his "third-degree" treatment by Parma police. He also accused them of trying to force him to put all of the blame on his wife. Initially denying he had ever laid a hand on either girl, McGuire's relentless cross-examination forced him to admit using a belt on them several times. But he insisted that he had only been following Dr. Stein's orders about the ice baths:

> Barger: She told us to throw them in ice water.
> McGuire: Did you throw them in ice water?
> Barger: No, I dunked them in ice water.
> McGuire: Did you put their heads under water?
> Barger: I don't remember.

The witnesses for the defense were hardly helpful to Matthew and Mary Barger. True, psychiatrist J. B. Cohn of Shaker Heights testified that he thought it was possible for Celia to have deliberately hurled herself down the Barger basement stairs. But he probably didn't burnish his professional credentials with his reply to McGuire's questions about the likely effects of the Bargers' disciplinary regime:

> McGuire: Do you think a child who is put in a dark closet or dunked in ice-water, or who might have been beaten with a shoe could have temper tantrums?

Cohn: That would be difficult to answer because two of the three punishments you mentioned are ancient methods for dealing with temper tantrums.

Although he allowed that such punitive methods were "ancient" and "archaic," Dr. Cohn insisted that the ice water treatment could be interpreted as a form of "hydrotherapy." Mary Barger's sister, Wilma Eastman, followed Cohn on the stand. She testified that after Celia Barger died, Shelva had told her that she had cooperated with the Parma police only because they had threatened her with 10 years in prison if she didn't incriminate the Bargers.

The trial now recessed for several days. Testimony was needed from Matthew and Mary's relatives in downstate Ohio, and they were too ill to travel to Cleveland. So prosecutor McGuire and defense attorney Wedren journeyed southward to take depositions from Anna Mulato, Susan Urzdich in Mingo Junction, and Mary's parents, Mr. and Mrs. Sherman Dillon, in nearby Amsterdam. As expected, Mulato and Urzdich testified that the girls were behaviorally disturbed—but not given to intentionally injuring themselves, as claimed by the Bargers. Both aunts recalled Celia as needy, an "unruly child, so starved for affection that we fear we may have spoiled her." The Dillons, for their part, echoed the testimony of Wilma Eastman. Testifying about conversations they'd had with their granddaughter Shelva after Celia's death, they swore that she had told them she was "all mixed up" when questioned by the Parma police and that they had threatened her with imprisonment or a perjury charge if she did not play ball.

That was the end of the defense witnesses, as Hyman Wedren informed the court upon his return, complaining that three Cleveland doctors had reneged on their promise to testify for the defense. Then came several state rebuttal witnesses to demolish charges made by the Bargers during their lachrymose testimony. Dr. Evelyn Stein flatly denied that she had prescribed ice baths for Helen and Celia. Perhaps smarting from the refusal of his doctors to testify in court, Barragate insinuated she had changed her testimony to mollify wrathful public opinion:

Barragate: Could it be, doctor, that the unfavorable publicity in
this case has caused you to change your mind that you told the
Bargers to give ice baths?
Stein: Absolutely not.

Genevieve Ball, the secretary to the Parma police chief who had
typed up Mary's August 19 confession, refuted her claim that she
had been under duress or unaware of what she was doing. Parma
police detective Virgil Costley, who had done much of the initial
investigative work, likewise denied coercing either of the Bargers
during their prolonged interrogations. Shelva Peterson also reappeared, to contradict assertions that she had been threatened or
manipulated by the police.

Closing arguments in the trial began the morning of January 25.
McGuire portrayed the Bargers as "medieval torturers . . . whose
minds were steeped with blind and brutal cruelty." Barragate's
closing rhetoric portrayed the Bargers as benevolent foster parents
and charged the state had failed to prove that Celia's presumed fatal
chest injury was caused by Mary hitting her with a rock. The arguments last 140 minutes, and the judges retired to deliberate.

They returned after 2 hours and 40 minutes at 7 p.m. . . . with a
unanimous verdict of guilty for both Bargers. Speaking for the
court, Judge Arti stated that the evidence and testimony compelled
them to conclude that the Bargers had been responsible for a "combination of events that had caused the death of Celia Barger."

It was not one incident that took this child's life but rather a
series of incidents, all of which contributed to her death. That they
extended over a period of time there is no doubt.

Addressing the assertion that Celia's injuries had been self-
inflicted, Arti cited Adelson's long list of grievous wounds and dismissed the Bargers' claims as "wholly incredible." Noting the
defense lawyers' repeated claims that Helen and Celia had been
"problem children," Judge Arti riposted, "However, gentlemen,
even problem children are entitled to the protection of society from
wrongful acts." He then revoked bond for both Mary and Matthew
Barger and sentenced them to 1 to 20 years in Marysville Reformatory and the Ohio Penitentiary, respectively.

Predictably, Mary and Matthew didn't take the news with meek resignation. They heard the verdicts without flinching, and Mary was relatively subdued when asked if she had anything to say before sentence was pronounced: "I still say I am not guilty of hitting Celia with a stone, your honors, and I thank the Lord God, my supreme judge. He will take care of me from here on in." But to the press outside the courtroom she spluttered:

> We'll take this to the highest court we can go. We'll manage to get the money some way to fight it. I did not get a fair trial. One reason, the judges were prejudiced because of all the publicity since last August. As God is my judge I didn't do it.

Accusing the state witnesses of lying, she denounced Dr. Stein with particular venom:

> Dr. Stein lied all the way through. I've known her about 12 years. She operated on me five times. I will say she shook my hand and cried when she wished me the best of luck.

And, once again, Mary concluded by painting herself as the victim:

> I was never angry enough not to know what I was doing. I never lost my head with the children. If anyone was tortured it was Matthew and I during the past two weeks.

Matthew, as usual, played a relatively subdued second to his wife's starring role. Blaming the newspapers, he sourly whined:

> You guys built it up. I don't know what to say. You saw how the judges were. All I know is that I'm not guilty. I'm all mixed up. I didn't get much sleep.

Considering their crimes, the Bargers didn't pay a very heavy penalty for their bestial cruelties. Finally transferred to their respective prisons at the end of March 1954, they immediately began working for their release. Unsuccessful in their attempts to appeal their convictions, they soon focused their efforts on getting paroled. Mary's first parole bid was turned down only a year later, in February of 1955. Three months later they lost the legal right to their adopted child, David, who had been put in the Parmadale orphanage after their conviction. Permanent custody of the boy—who, curiously, had never been harmed by either Mary or Matthew Barger—was given back to Catholic Charities in October of 1955.

Matthew Barger won parole the day after Christmas in 1956, after serving less than two years of his 1 to 20 term. He was finally released on January 31, 1957. Mary, the guiltier of the two, remained in prison until she was paroled on March 31, 1960. If the Bargers are alive, they would be in their early 80s. Helen Barger, if alive, would be almost 60. And Celia Barger sleeps in Holy Cross Cemetery, forever five years old and forever knowing a peace she never knew in her life on earth.

PHOTO CREDITS

Chapter 1   p. 4 *PD*; p. 5 *Press*; p. 6 *News*; p. 9 *Press*; p. 7 *Press*; p. 8 *News*; p. 10 *CSU*: Photo by Glenn Zahn

Chapter 2   p. 14 *Press*; p. 15 *Press*

Chapter 3   p. 19 *Press*; p. 18 *Press*

Chapter 4   p. 22 *Leader*; p. 29 *Leader*; p. 30 *Leader*

Chapter 5   p. 36 CPL; p. 37 CPL/Corbis; p. 39 CPL; p. 38   *Press*; p. 42 *Press*

Chapter 6   p. 47 CSU; p. 46 CSU; p. 44 *News*

Chapter 7   p. 50 CSU; p. 52 CSU; p. 51 *Press*

Chapter 8   p. 56 CPHS; p. 59 CPHS; p. 57 *Press*; p. 62 *Press*; p. 60 *Leader*; p. 78 *World*; p. 80 *Press*

Chapter 9   p. 82 CSU; p. 83 *News*; p. 84 *Press*; p. 86 *Press*

Chapter 10   p. 90 *Leader*; p. 91 *Leader*

Chapter 11   p. 94 CSU; p. 95 *Press*; p. 95 *Press*

Chapter 12   p. 105 CSU; p. 99 *News*; p. 101 CSU; p. 103 CSU; p. 108 CSU; p. 98 *News*; p. 110 *Press*

Chapter 13   p. 112 *News*; p. 114 *News*; p. 113 *Press*

Chapter 14   p. 116 Auth

Chapter 15   p. 118 *Press*; p. 123 *Press*; p. 121 *Press*; p. 127 *Press*; p. 128 *Press*

Chapter 16   p. 134 CSU

Chapter 17   p. 136 *Leader*; p. 143 *Leader*

Chapter 18   p. 147 *PD*; p. 158 *PD*

Chapter 19   p. 160 *Press*; p. 163 *Press*

Chapter 20   p. 175 D.L. Lake, An Atlas of Cuyahoga County; p. 167 *Leader*

Chapter 21   p. 183 *Press*; p.178 CPL; p. 179 CPL; p. 190 *News*; p.194 *News*

Chapter 22   p. 198 *PD*; p. 201 *World*; p.200 *PD*; p.199 *PD*: p.208 *World*

Chapter 23   p. 212 CSU; p.214 *Press*; p. 213 CSU; p. 221 CPL; Photo by Tony Tomsic

Chapter 24   p. 227 Auth; p. 225 *Press*; p. 229 CPL; p.224 *Press*; 228 *News*

Chapter 25   p. 235 CSU; p.242 CSU; p.236 CSU; p.232 CSU; p.237 *Press*; p.233 *Press*

Chapter 26   p. 246 CSU; p. 247 CSU; p.249 CSU; p.250 *News*; p.253 *Press*